Danny Goodman

with

Fougère Robertson

# Fear Excel for the Mac No More

Danny Goodman

with

Fougère Robertson

Brady

New York London Toronto Sydney Tokyo Singapore

**Brady Publishing**

A Division of Prentice Hall Computer Publishing
15 Columbus Circle
New York, NY 10023

ISBN: 1-56686-083-0
**Library of Congress Catalog No.:** 93-25265

**Printing Code:** The rightmost double-digit number is the year of the book's printing; the rightmost single-digit number is the number of the book's printing. For example, 93-1 shows that the first printing of the book occurred in 1993.

96 95 94 93 4 3 2 1

Manufactured in the United States of America.

# Dedication

To Harry, who gave me my enthusiasm and persistance; to Juliet, who gave me my intelligence; and to both of you for my love of books.

# About the Author

Fougère Robertson has a Macintosh training and consulting company, MacAcademy of the Bay Area, which is part of the national MacAcademy network. She has taught thousands of people from all over the U.S. and from Scotland to Indonesia how to achieve mastery over their computers. A student once said of her, "For a geek, she is remarkably non-nerdish."

Fougère lives with her husband, a graphic designer and Macintosh consultant, in Marin County. When not working on their computers, they are probably hiking, gardening, at the local cinema, or reading cyberpunk science fiction.

# Acknowledgments

Thanks to Greg Harvey for getting me started; to Danny Goodman for keeping me on track; to Jono Hardjowirogo for being so friendly and supportive; to Roberta Dolson and Richard Sobol for their valiant efforts to keep the text clear and simple; to John Gieg for his talented illustrations; and, most importantly, to Steven Englander, who added much-needed wit and humor.

# Credits

**Publisher**
Michael Violano

**Acquisitions Director**
Jono Hardjowirogo

**Managing Editor**
Kelly D. Dobbs

**Editorial Assistant**
Lisa Rose

**Novice Reviewer**
Stacey Beheler

**Illustrator**
John Leonard Gieg

**Book Designers**
Michele Laseau, Kevin Spear

**Cover Designer**
Jay Corpus

**Indexers**
Jeanne Clark, Craig Small

**Production Team**
Diana Bigham, Katy Bodenmiller, Scott Cook, Tim Cox, Mark Enochs, Linda Koopman, Tom Loveman, Beth Rago, Carrie Roth, Greg Simsic

**Marketing Director**
Lonny Stein

**Marketing Coordinator**
Laura Cadorette

# Contents

# Introduction

## Welcome to *Fear Excel No More*

- If you failed high school algebra
- If you failed your math mid-term in your first year of college, passed at year's end with a C, and never took another math class
- If your friends never let you divide the check at a restaurant
- If you've avoided using a computer as much as is humanly possible
- If you have anxiety attacks whenever you try something new

This is the book for you.

## Are You Ready for This Book?

Before starting this book, you should understand basic computer operations. If you can't answer the following questions, you will have an easier time with this book if you first read *Fear Macs No More.*

1. What does a double-click do?
2. You're looking at a list of your files. You want to see the files sorted by the date they were last saved. What command do you use and which menu offers that command?
3. You can't remember where you saved a file. What command do you give?
4. You want to activate (open) Microsoft Excel. What steps do you take?

1st Encounter

# What Is Microsoft Excel?

## Goal

Understand what a spreadsheet program is and when it is useful.

## What You Will Need

Your computer turned off and a relaxed, positive attitude.

## Terms of Enfearment

| | |
|---|---|
| Program | Charts |
| Application | Formulas |
| Spreadsheet | Cash-flow projections |
| Worksheet | Budgets |

# Briefing

Welcome to the world of number crunching, financial analysis, chart and graph making! This book is devoted, body and soul, to teaching you the basics of using an electronic worksheet.

In this first encounter, or strange encounter of the first kind, you're going to get a general sense of what Microsoft Excel is all about and how it works.

Microsoft Excel is software, as opposed to hardware, which is the actual machinery of the computer. Software is a set of instructions to the computer, telling it what to do. For our purposes, *program* and *application* mean the same thing as software.

# What the Heck Does It Do?

Microsoft Excel lets us use the computer to create *worksheets* and *charts.*

A *spreadsheet* (or *worksheet* as it is often called) is a combination of lettered columns and numbered rows forming a grid made of cells. Cells hold text and numbers. Cells also hold *formulas* that look at the numbers and perform calculations.

The worksheet replaces your calculator, paper and pencil, and ledger sheets, just as word processing software replaces the typewriter. Take a moment to throw your calculator, paper, and pencil out the window. You have now achieved the famous "paperless" office. (Keep one pencil as a memento.)

You perform mathematical operations with formulas. When you add up a bill in a restaurant and then multiply the cost of the dinner by 20 percent for the tip, you are using a formula that looks something like this: (Item 1 + Item 2 + Item 3) × 20%.

Microsoft Excel lets you analyze and understand numbers. You type numbers representing your (never high enough) income and (always too many) expenses. You then create some formulas that add up those numbers and other formulas that show the difference between them. Starting in the sixth encounter, you will spend a lot of time creating formulas.

# Playing the What-If Game

Perhaps you need to set up a budget. Using Microsoft Excel lets you ask, "What if I spend this much on partying or that much on life insurance?" You can type different numbers and let your formulas show you the changing outcome (often called the bottom line).

Formulas are what make spreadsheet programs so great. On a spreadsheet, a formula might add up the numbers in a column of numbers that represent estimated expenses. You then could change one or more numbers in the column, and the number at the bottom of the column would change.

In figure 1.1, note how all the numbers in the two columns are the same except for the top number. The total in both columns is actually a formula that tells Microsoft Excel to add up the numbers. No matter what numbers are entered into the column, the formula will always show the correct sum. With a calculator, you have to run the tape again and again—and have a regular supply of tape stored up.

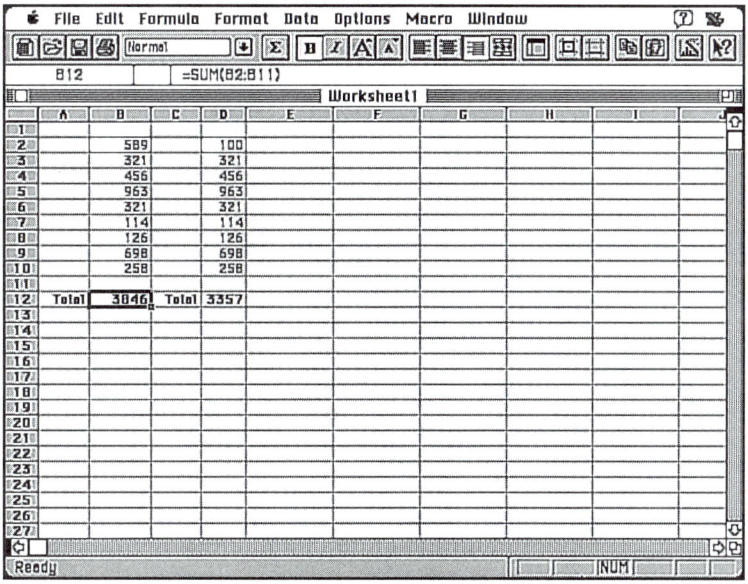


**Figure 1.1**
*Two columns of numbers, all the same except for the top one and the total.*

# Hope and Prayer

Many people use Microsoft Excel to project their *cash flow* over time. In a typical scenario, you would type an initial amount in one cell. This is the amount that you hope and pray to earn in the first period—the example in figure 1.2 shows $1,000 in cell B2.

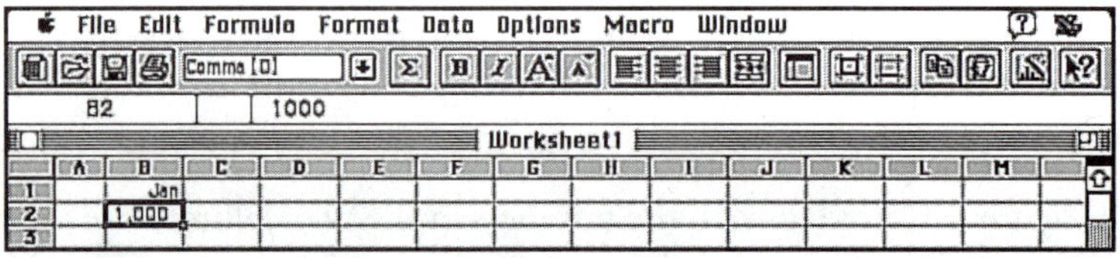


Figure 1.2
*Cell B2 selected.*

The time can be a week, a month, a year, or a quarter. Ideally, $1,000 per day sounds fair. You can work with any interval that makes sense or fits your needs. In the example, we have typed a percentage, 10%, in cell A2. This percentage reflects the growth we hope and pray to see in each time period.

Next, you could ask Microsoft Excel, by putting together a formula in another cell, to figure out the growth (see fig. 1.3).

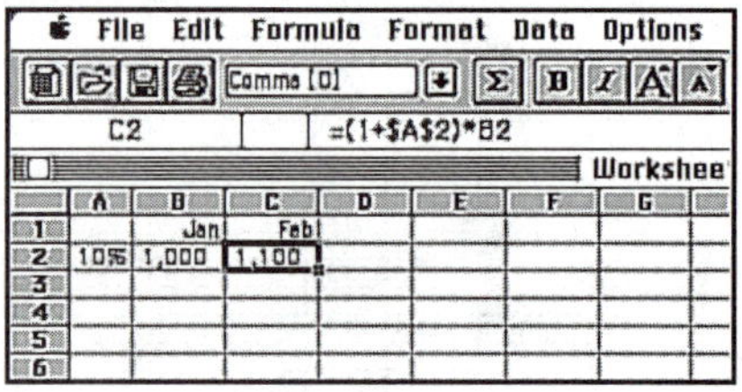


Figure 1.3
*Creating a formula to track growth.*

You also could copy this formula so that you could see the effect of the 10% growth on any number of time periods (see fig. 1.4).

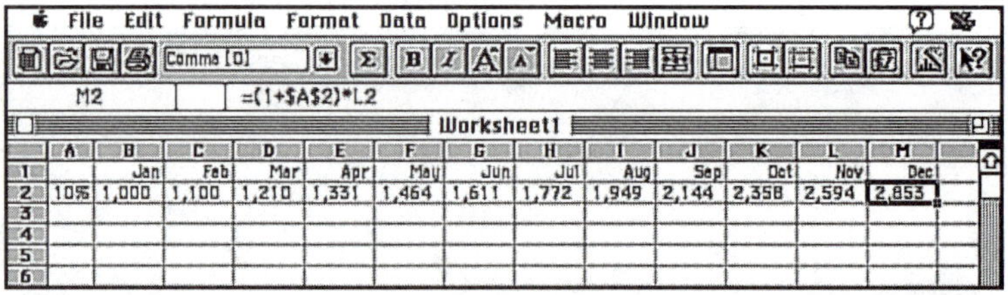


Figure 1.4
*Copying the formula.*

# The Ripple Effect

After you set up the worksheet, you can change the initial amount or the percentage of growth and then see the impact of the changes ripple across all the months or years.

You can use Microsoft Excel to keep track of your sales or the sales of different departments (or salespeople, divisions, or companies) and have other summary worksheets that keep track of what's going on in the departmental worksheets (see fig. 1.5).

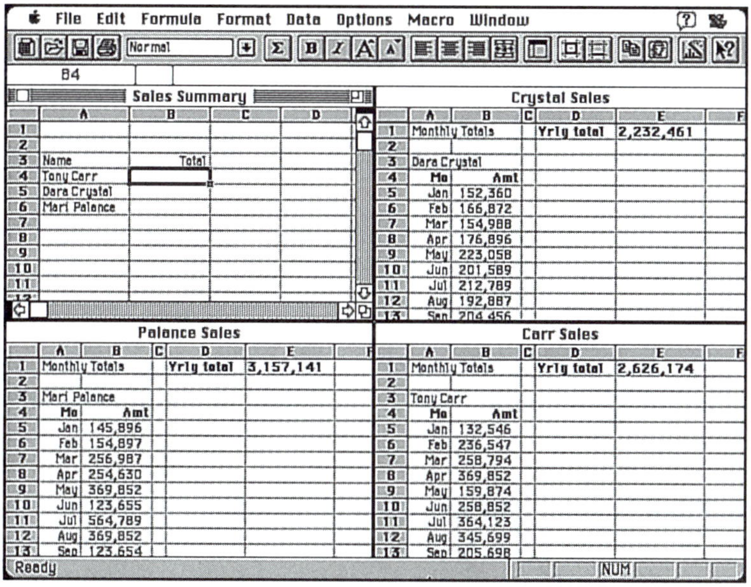


**Figure 1.5**
*Worksheets that are linked together.*

You can enter mortgage information like the current interest rate, a loan amount, and the length of the loan and have Microsoft Excel calculate the monthly payment and print out a schedule that shows how much principal and interest you pay each month (see fig. 1.6).

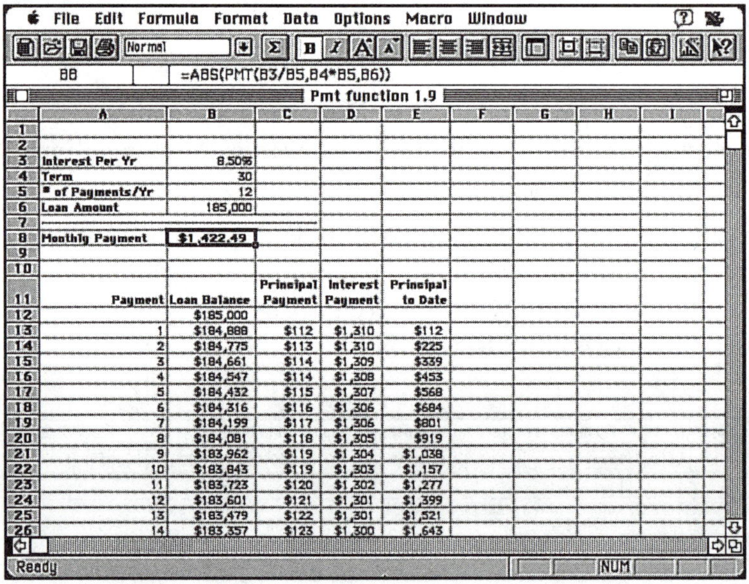


| | A | B | C | D | E |
|---|---|---|---|---|---|
| 1 | | | | | |
| 2 | | | | | |
| 3 | Interest Per Yr | 8.50% | | | |
| 4 | Term | 30 | | | |
| 5 | # of Payments/Yr | 12 | | | |
| 6 | Loan Amount | 185,000 | | | |
| 7 | | | | | |
| 8 | Monthly Payment | $1,422.49 | | | |
| 9 | | | | | |
| 10 | | | | | |
| 11 | Payment | Loan Balance | Principal Payment | Interest Payment | Principal to Date |
| 12 | | $185,000 | | | |
| 13 | 1 | $184,888 | $112 | $1,310 | $112 |
| 14 | 2 | $184,775 | $113 | $1,310 | $225 |
| 15 | 3 | $184,661 | $114 | $1,309 | $339 |
| 16 | 4 | $184,547 | $114 | $1,308 | $453 |
| 17 | 5 | $184,432 | $115 | $1,307 | $568 |
| 18 | 6 | $184,316 | $116 | $1,306 | $684 |
| 19 | 7 | $184,199 | $117 | $1,306 | $801 |
| 20 | 8 | $184,081 | $118 | $1,305 | $919 |
| 21 | 9 | $183,962 | $119 | $1,304 | $1,038 |
| 22 | 10 | $183,843 | $119 | $1,303 | $1,157 |
| 23 | 11 | $183,723 | $120 | $1,302 | $1,277 |
| 24 | 12 | $183,601 | $121 | $1,301 | $1,399 |
| 25 | 13 | $183,479 | $122 | $1,301 | $1,521 |
| 26 | 14 | $183,357 | $123 | $1,300 | $1,643 |

**Figure 1.6** *Microsoft Excel figures out your monthly payment and the Amortization schedule.*

Examples are infinite. You can crunch our numbers any way you need or want. Pulverize. Squeeze. Tweak.

After you prepare a worksheet, you can ask Microsoft Excel to produce charts that quickly and graphically show the relationships between the numbers. Microsoft Excel has the capacity to create all kinds of charts, from simple pie charts to 3-D bar charts and beyond.

## They're Out To Get Us

Many of us haven't had anything to do with math since high school, and we're afraid of it. However, all of us work with numbers every day.

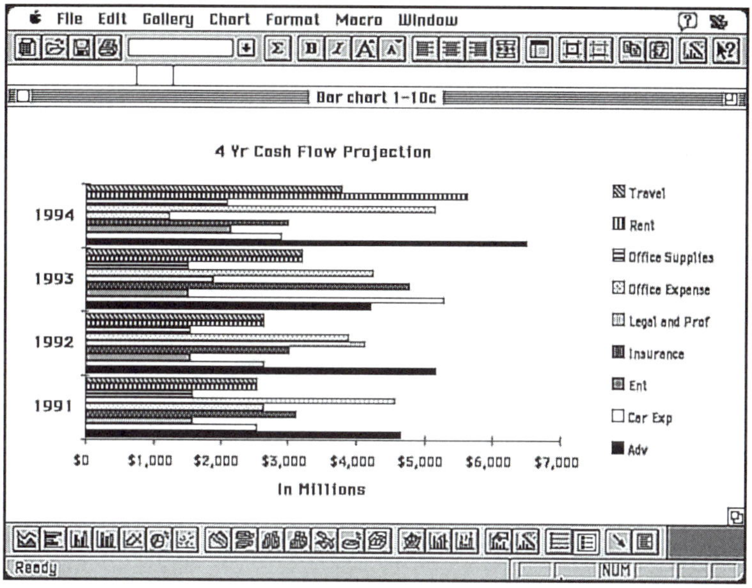


Figure 1.7
*Four charts.*

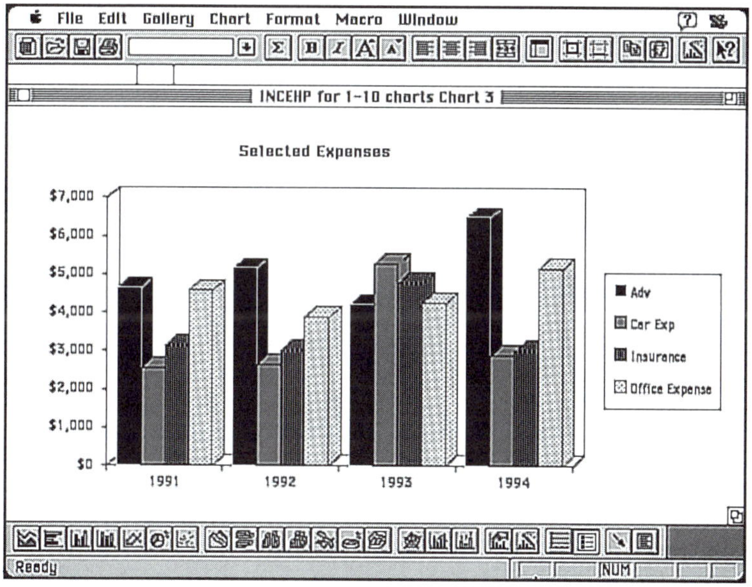

Figure 1.7
*continued*

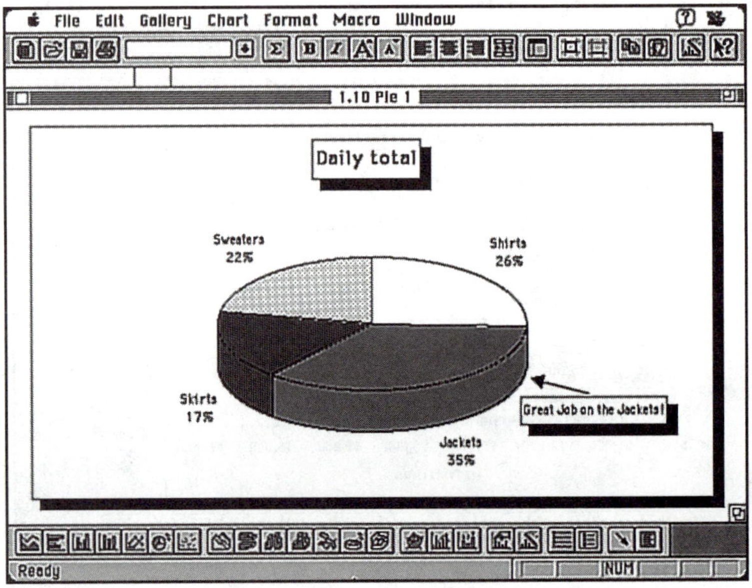


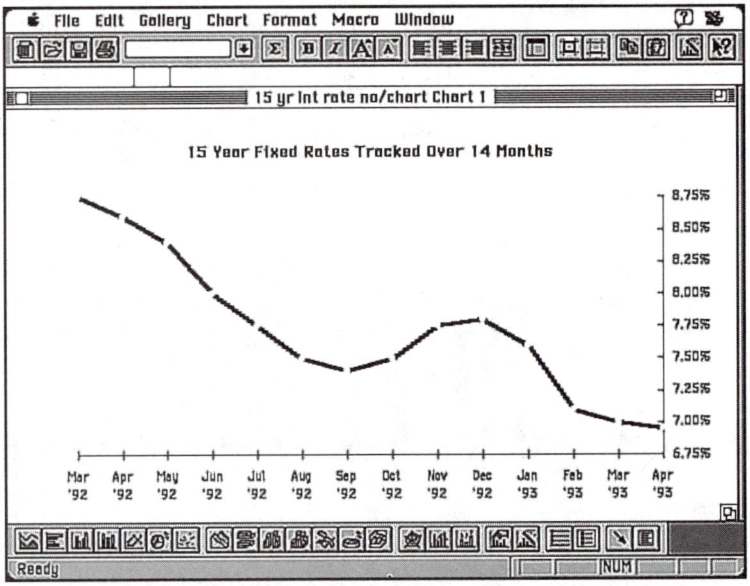

Every time we count our change at the local movie theater, pay our (countless) bills, balance our bank account (we can dream, can't we?), think about whether we should buy a big ticket item, and figure a tip, we are using numbers—making them our servants. We are used to figuring out the formulas (like subtraction and multiplication) in our heads, but we need to readjust to thinking through the logic of a formula step by step, just like we did in high school.

# Practice

## Schwarzenegger and Company

You are going to flex our math muscles a little bit to get ready for learning Excel. Working with math, numbers, and formulas is not SO horrible. To prove that math isn't so horrible, figure the following problems the old-fashioned way, using pencil, paper, and your brain (or calculators). As you formulate the answers, notice the hoops your brain goes through as you come up with the answer.

1. Add up the column in figure 1.8. You get no help on this one.

33
72
98
107.62
89.89

**Figure 1.8**
*Add this column of numbers.*

2. You buy 5 pounds of carrots at 39¢ a pound and 3 of those fancy designer lettuces at 79¢ a pound. How much do you owe?

   $5 \times .39 = ?$
   $3 \times .79 = ?$
   Carrots Subtotal + Lettuces Subtotal = ?

3. You're a college student trying to get more parental support. Draw a pie chart that depicts a *budget* in which 25% goes to rent, 25% to food, and 50% to tuition (see fig. 1.9).

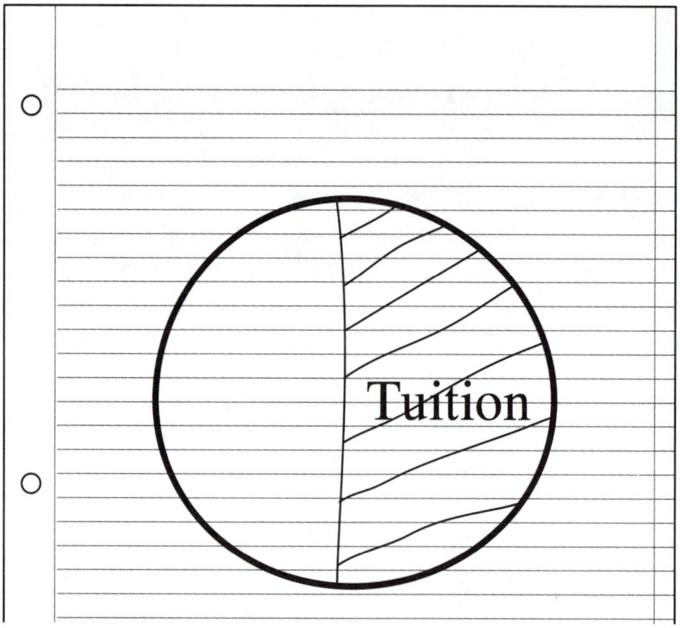


**Figure 1.9**
*Complete the pie chart.*

4. You spend $2000 on Advertising, $1000 on Utilities, and $2000 on Office Expenses. What percentage is the Advertising Expense?

   You start the process with a formula summing the expenses: 2000+1000+2000 = 5000

   Then you divide advertising by that total: 2000 divided by 5000.

   Now you have a fraction. Remember which is the numerator and which is the denominator? No Way!? Remember how to make a fraction into a decimal number? How about turning the decimal number into a percent (see fig. 1.10)?

$$\frac{2000}{5000} = \frac{2}{5} \times \frac{2}{2} = \frac{4}{10} =$$

$$\frac{40}{100} = 100 \overline{)\,40.00} \;\; .40 = 40\%$$

Figure 1.10
*Turning a Fraction into a Percent.*

Notice how all the numbers are the same, from the first fraction to the percent. They just have a different look.

5. If you spend 1000 in one month, how much will you spend in each of the next 6 months if the amount increases by 5% each month?

   Solve this problem by multiplying 1000 by .05. Then add 50 to 1000 to get 1050 for your second month. Repeat the process for each new month: 1050 × .05 = 52.50. 1050+52.50=1102.50 for your third month, and so on.

Why not multiply 1000 by 1.05? This gives you the second month's amount in one operation rather than two (see fig. 1.11).

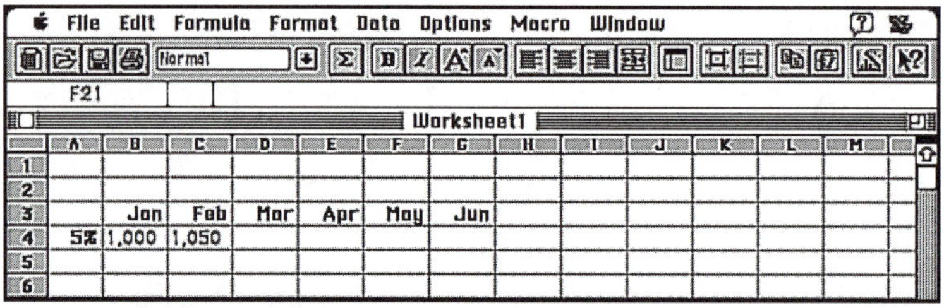


**Figure 1.11**
*Solving the problem.*

# Summary

Microsoft Excel crunches numbers in an infinite variety of ways. Thousands of people—yes, normal, regular people—use it to project their cash flow, prepare budgets, and generate charts.

# Exorcises

1. What does software mean?
2. Give an example of a "what if?" scenario.
3. What do you plan to use Microsoft Excel for?
4. If you were creating a budget worksheet, what time period would make the most sense for you—daily, weekly, monthly, quarterly, or yearly?
5. What's the bottom line of the worksheet in figure 1.12?

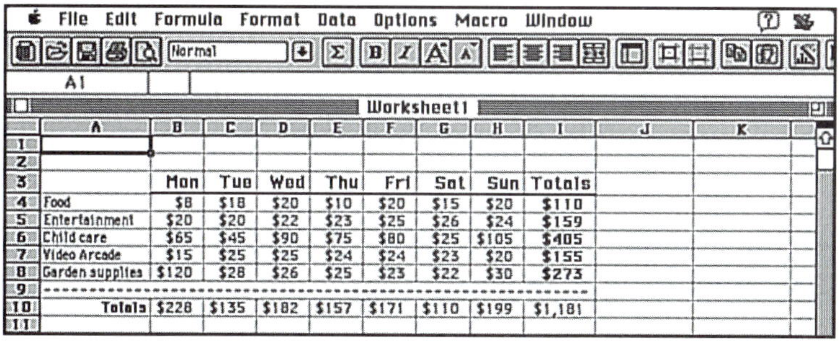


| | Mon | Tue | Wed | Thu | Fri | Sat | Sun | Totals |
|---|---|---|---|---|---|---|---|---|
| Food | $8 | $18 | $20 | $10 | $20 | $15 | $20 | $110 |
| Entertainment | $20 | $20 | $22 | $23 | $25 | $26 | $24 | $159 |
| Child care | $65 | $45 | $90 | $75 | $80 | $25 | $105 | $405 |
| Video Arcade | $15 | $25 | $25 | $24 | $24 | $23 | $20 | $155 |
| Garden supplies | $120 | $28 | $26 | $25 | $23 | $22 | $30 | $273 |
| Totals | $228 | $135 | $182 | $157 | $171 | $110 | $199 | $1,181 |

**Figure 1.12**
*Weekly budget.*

2nd Encounter

# Installing Microsoft Excel

## Goal

To discover whether Microsoft Excel 4.0 is alive and kicking on your computer; and if it isn't, to survive the installation procedure.

## What You Will Need

Start with your computer turned on. You need to own the program and have all the disks available.

## Terms of Enfearment

| | |
|---|---|
| Installation | Extensions |
| Registration | Upgrade |
| File menu | Find dialog box |

# Briefing

If you share your computer with other people in the office, someone may have already installed Microsoft Excel on the hard drive. If so, consider yourself lucky and move on to the next encounter.

If you think that Microsoft Excel is on your computer, but you don't know how to find it, this encounter will show you the way to find or install your soon-to-be-favorite program.

The program and all its supporting files take up a great deal of room. You need nearly 9 megabytes of empty space on the hard drive for a complete *installation.*

## Automatic Transmission

Microsoft Excel has an automatic installation procedure that begins with putting the disk named *Disk 1-Setup* into the floppy disk drive.

After we start the procedure by putting the first disk in the disk drive and double-clicking on a file called Microsoft Excel Setup, the software takes over and copies the Excel program and seven disks full of supporting files onto the computer's hard drive. The software makes all the decisions about where to put the files, ejects the disks one at a time, and requests the next one. All you have to do is remove one disk and put in the next.

## The Little Guys

Before installing Microsoft Excel, turn off all the little programs that run in the background—the *extensions.* These include programs that check floppy disks for viruses and other problems. These extensions can interfere with the installation. The easiest way to turn them off is to restart the computer and then hold down the Shift key.

## Tell Bill Gates

After the installation, you are going to immediately fill out the *registration* form and mail it back to Microsoft. Why should you fill out and mail the registration form? It's the only way that Microsoft knows you are the legal owner of the software. Also, registering puts you in their database so that you receive *upgrade* offers on time.

## Going Upscale

Periodically, a new version of a software program comes out. Normally, the upgrade has new and changed features that make life a little easier for the end users of the program. Usually, the upgrades are sold to registered users for a fraction of the cost to a new user.

## They're Out To Get Us

If you find Microsoft Excel but do not find all the other supporting files, it is possible that the person who installed the program did a custom, rather than a complete installation.

In a custom installation, the person doing the installation selects the files to be copied onto the hard drive. Usually, people do a custom installation because there's not enough room on the hard drive for all the files.

It's also possible that everything has been installed but is organized differently, with differently named folders.

In either case, it makes sense to find the person who did the installation and beg, plead, or cajole him or her to explain where the other files are.

# Practice

## You Can Run, But You Can't Hide

If you have been using another program, return to the Finder (see fig. 2.1).

**Figure 2.1**
*Application menu with Microsoft Word and the Finder.*

1. Choose Find from the *File menu* and type Microsoft Excel in the *Find* dialog box that appears (see fig. 2.2).

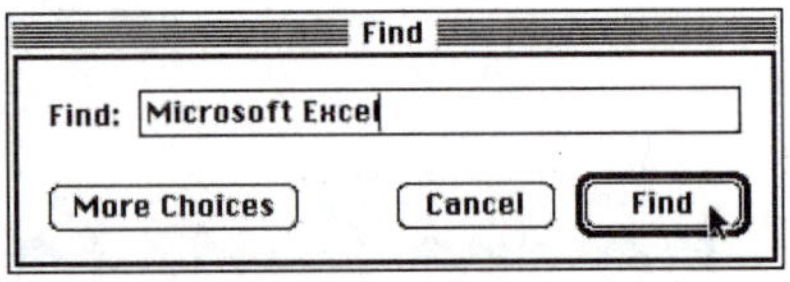


**Figure 2.2**
*Find dialog box.*

2. If the program has been installed on the hard drive, a folder will be selected, or a window will open and the program will be selected. You might see the icons in a folder holding the Microsoft Excel program.
3. If you are looking at the icons, go up to the View menu and choose View by Name. A folder holding a complete installation of the program should look like figure 2.3.

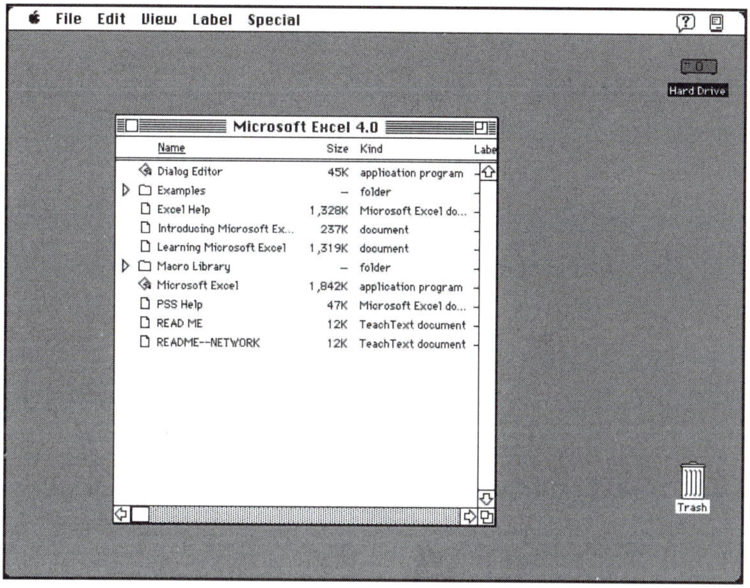


Figure 2.3
*View by Name.*

# Biting the Bullet

If you have found the program and see all the items in this list, you can skip the rest of this Encounter, and go on to the 3rd Encounter. If you do not find Microsoft Excel, you need to install the program.

# Off with Your Shrink Wrap!

1. Pull the shrink wrap off the software manuals (this is the hardest part of the chapter), take the seven disks out of the disk envelope, and put the registration form aside until you complete the installation.
2. Lock all seven disks to protect them from harm. Hold the disk with the label facing you. Push up the little black tab on the top right so that you see daylight through the disk. Now it's locked and cannot be altered or erased during the installation process.

Figure 2.4
*Lock the disks to protect them.*

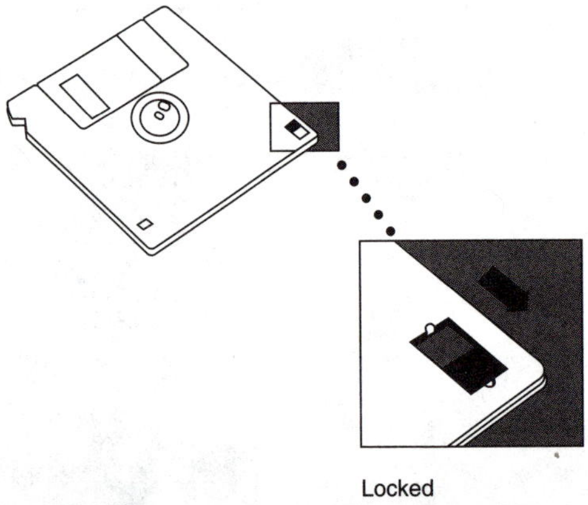


## Space—the Final Frontier

You need almost 9M of space on the hard drive. To find out how much room remains on the hard drive, choose By Icon from the View menu at the Finder level. Look along the top of any open window (see fig. 2.5).

Figure 2.5
*Amount of available space.*

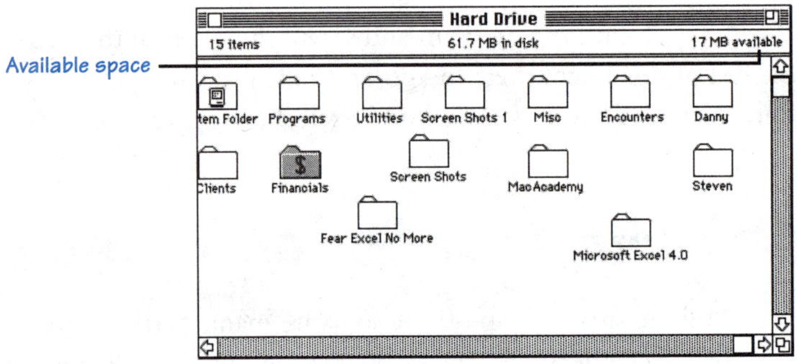


## Smooth Sailing

1. Make certain that no programs are running by pulling down the Application menu. You want to see just the Finder running. If any programs are still running, select them and choose Quit from the File menu.

2. Now turn off the extensions. Choose Restart from the Special menu. As soon as you see the smiling computer, smile back politely and hold down the Shift key. When you see the message `Extensions off`, you can release the Shift key.

   If you do not see the message telling you that Extensions are off, it's probably because you didn't hold the Shift key down at the right time. Just do it again. This time be sure to hold the Shift key down as soon as you see the smiling computer.

   The Desktop will probably show up more quickly than usual, because no extensions are loading. When the Desktop appears, you're ready to begin.

## An Organized Desk Is a Happy Desk

Make sure that your Hard drive window is open and active. During the installation, Microsoft Excel will ask you where to put the program. So, create a folder for it now.

1. Choose New Folder from the File Menu. Type *Microsoft Excel 4.0.*
2. You also need a place to store all the beautiful worksheets you are going to create in the course of this book. So choose New Folder again and call this one, *Fear Excel No More.*

## The Heart of the Matter

1. Put the disk titled *Disk 1-Setup* in the floppy disk drive. An open window labeled *Disk 1-Setup* should appear (see fig. 2.6). If it doesn't, double-click the floppy disk icon.

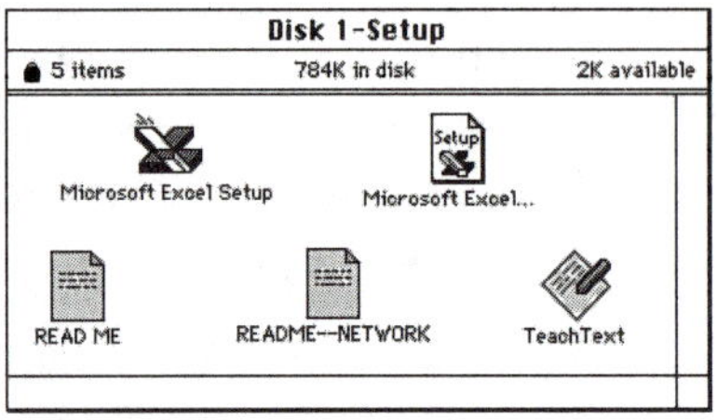


**Figure 2.6**
*Disk 1-Setup window.*

2. Double-click on the icon labeled Microsoft Excel Setup. Enter your name, organization, and the serial number that is on the registration card. Click OK.

3. Click the Complete button in the next window that appears (see fig. 2.7).

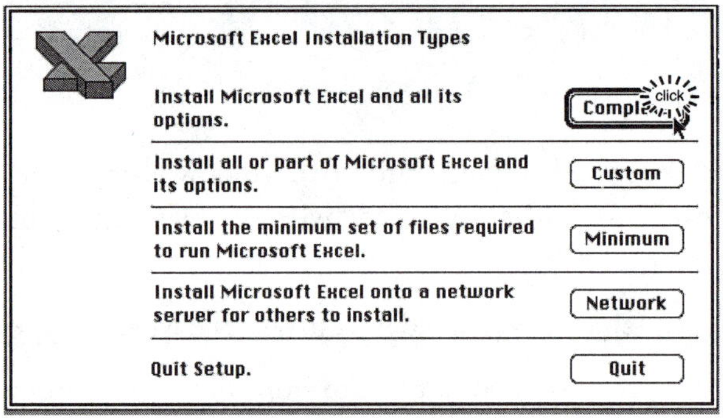


**Figure 2.7**
*Click the Complete button.*

4. Make sure that your hard drive is selected and double-click the folder you created earlier (see fig. 2.8).

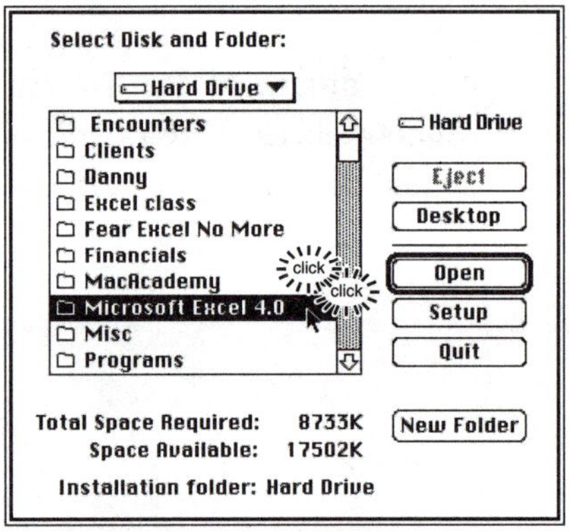


**Figure 2.8**
*Open the Microsoft Excel folder.*

5. Notice that Microsoft Excel tells you the name of the Installation folder on the lower left. Click the Setup button. From here on out, all you have to do is remove one disk and put the next one in when Microsoft Excel asks for it.

## Summary

In the Finder, you can use the Find command from the File menu to find out if Microsoft Excel is currently installed on your hard drive. If Excel is not installed, you may need to buy the program, if you haven't done so already.

## Exorcises

1. What key do you hold down in order to start the computer without loading extensions?
2. Why is it useful to register your software?
3. How do you lock a disk?
4. How much free space is needed for a complete installation of Microsoft Excel?
5. What is one method for finding out how much space is available on a hard drive?

3rd Encounter

# Starting Up

## Goal

To feel comfortable with starting up the program and understanding the screen.

## What You Will Need

Start with the computer turned on, showing the Desktop. Excel has been installed.

## Terms of Enfearment

| | |
|---|---|
| Formula bar | Cell reference |
| Cell | Active cell |
| Column | Current cell address |
| Row | Cell pointer |
| Load | |

# Briefing

To begin working with the program, you must find Microsoft Excel on the hard drive. If you installed the program using the directions in the last encounter, it's in a folder called Microsoft Excel 4.0 on the hard drive. When you can see the program icon, activate it with a double-click.

Software is a set of instructions to the computer telling it what to do. Double-clicking on the program commands your Macintosh to read the software and load it into Random Access Memory (RAM), which tells the Mac everything it needs to know to make worksheets.

When the program has loaded, an untitled and empty document appears (also called a worksheet or spreadsheet). This is comparable to pulling a ledger from a file cabinet, putting it on your desk, and turning to an empty page.

The document is untitled, even though `Worksheet1` appears in the title bar (see fig. 3.1). It's waiting for you to add the words and numbers and formulas.

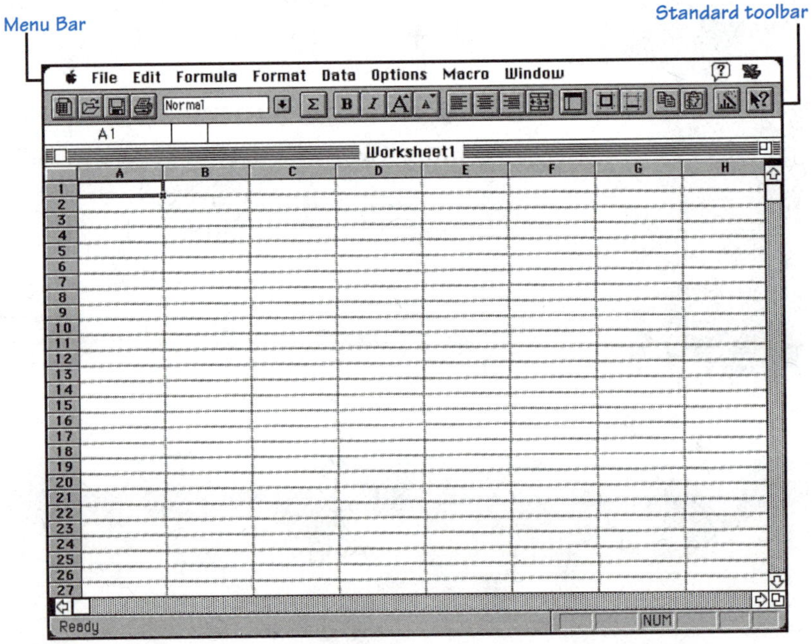


**Figure 3.1**
*An untitled Excel worksheet.*

## Bossing Excel Around

At the top of the screen is the menu bar. Using the commands in the different menus is one way to tell Excel what to do.

Excel has a number of different menu bars, depending on what you're doing.

## Tools of the Trade

Underneath the menu bar at the top of the screen is the Standard toolbar, a wonderful feature that makes common activities, such as adding up columns, opening documents, and boldfacing the contents of cells, easier to do.

A click on a button in the toolbar makes something happen. For example, a click on the first tool tells Excel to create a worksheet. Notice how it is blank (a clean, fresh new worksheet). A whole new world is waiting for your commands.

The second tool tells Excel to bring up the Open dialog box. Notice how it is a folder that is *opening*. The third tool (a disk icon) tells Excel to save your document.

Using a tool is an alternative to using a command on a menu. Because the tool is visible all the time, you don't have to look for it. To find out what a tool does, move the mouse pointer over it, hold down the mouse button, and look at the lower left corner of the window. This area, the Status bar, holds a brief explanation of the tool (see fig. 3.2). If you don't want to actually use the tool, move the mouse pointer away before releasing the mouse button.

The right side of the Status bar lets you know which special keys, like the Caps lock key, are on and off.

The *formula bar* is below the toolbar. It gives you information about where you are on the worksheet and the contents of the worksheet. Below the formula bar is the worksheet itself.

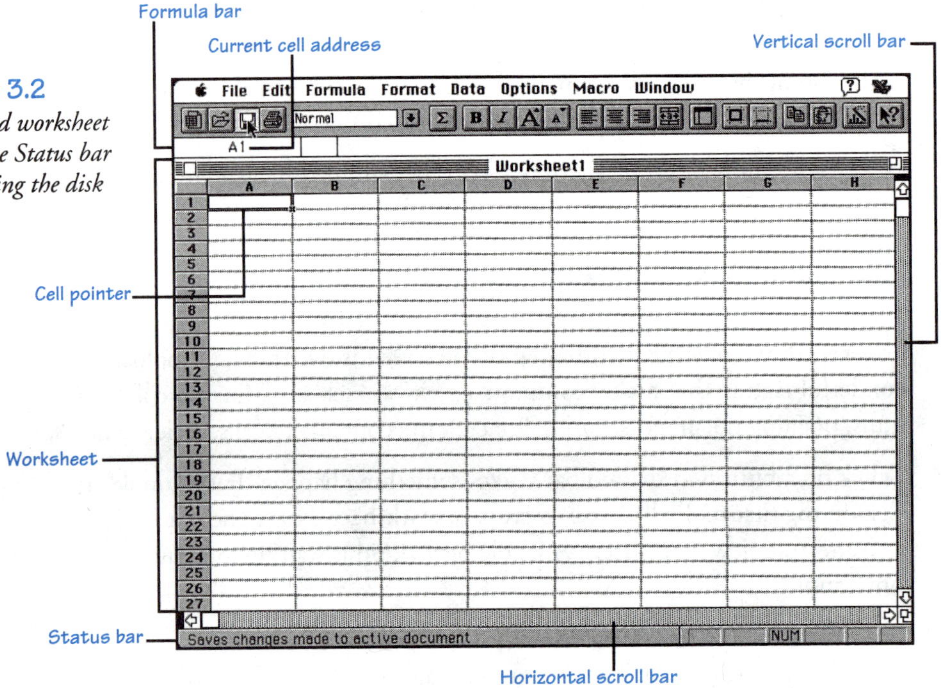


**Figure 3.2**
*Untitled worksheet with the Status bar describing the disk tool.*

At the bottom of the window and on the right side are the scroll bars that allow you to scroll through the document.

## Cell! Cell! Cell!

Cells in the worksheet store the information you type. Each cell is the juncture of a *column* and a *row*. For example, the *cell reference* A1 describes the place on the worksheet where column A and row l meet. The cell reference Z500 identifies the juncture of column Z and row 500. The column letter always comes first, followed by the row number.

The cell you type information into is called the *active cell* or the *current cell address*. The active cell is identified by a darker or colored border, called the *cell pointer* (see fig. 3.2).

It can also be identified by looking at the far left side of the formula bar, which always shows the current cell address.

# Where the Action Is

Most of the important action takes place in and around the active cell, so you always want to know where it is. You can move to and select a cell using a number of different methods:

- Click on the cell, making it the active cell.
- Press one or more of the cursor arrow keys to move the cell pointer up, down, left, or right. Moving the cell pointer to a cell means that you are selecting that cell.
- Press the Return Key to move the cell pointer down and press the Tab key to move the cell pointer to the right.

**Figure 3.3**
*Movement keys.*

Usually, you want to press the key that takes you in the direction you want to go. If you need to move to a cell that's several columns or rows away, clicking with the mouse on that cell to select it might be faster than pressing movement keys on the keyboard.

# They're Out To Get Us

You may not be able to find the program. If you don't know where it is, go back to the last encounter, which has instructions for finding files.

Your toolbar may look different than the one shown. Yours may have fewer tools on it. If it does, you may be working with a smaller monitor. No problem; the tools we use in the practice session for this encounter should still be on your toolbar.

The toolbar could look different if someone has changed it. We will show you how to do this in a later encounter. For now, here are instructions for returning the Standard toolbar to its original state (called the *default*):

1. Choose Toolbars from the Options menu (see fig. 3.4).

2. Click Reset.

That should teach them to mess with your computer!

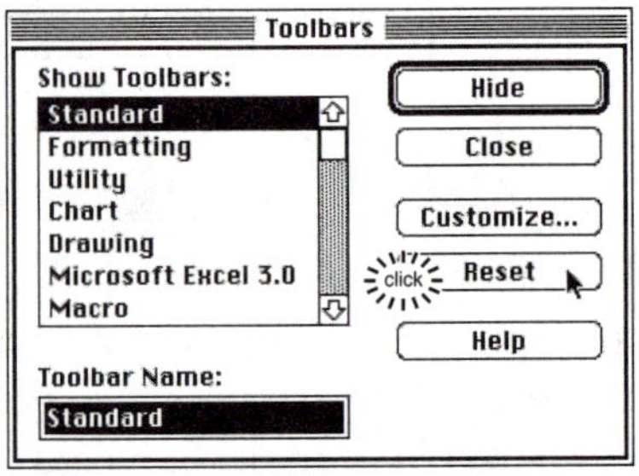


Figure 3.4
*The Toolbars dialog box.*

If you press the Return key and the cell pointer does not move down one cell, someone has changed this. To make the Return key move the cell pointer down, choose Workspace from the Options menu and click the Move Selection After Return check box.

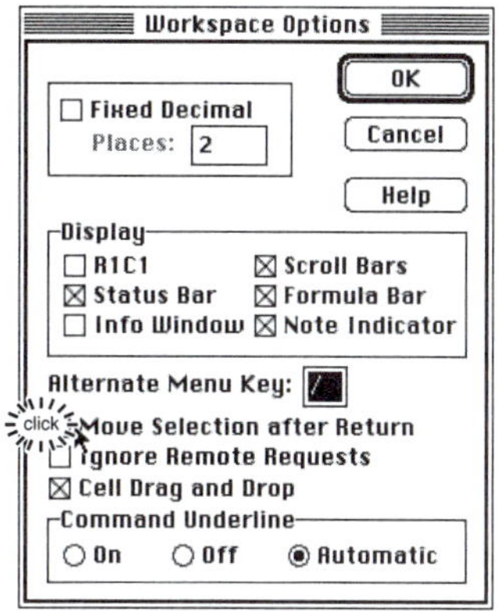


**Figure 3.5**
*The Workspace Options dialog box.*

# Practice

Create a storage place for your practice files.

If you didn't make a folder earlier to store your documents, do it now:

1. Make your hard drive window active.
2. Choose New Folder from the File menu.
3. Type *Fear Excel No More.*

# Open Sesame

Find Microsoft Excel on your hard drive and double-click the icon to open. When the program has loaded (activate and open are synonyms for *load*), `Worksheet1` appears on the screen.

Note that `A1` is displayed in the left section of the formula bar. Also note the cell pointer surrounding A1. This tells you that A1 is the currently active cell.

## Mousing Around

1. Move the mouse around until you see a shaded thick cross pointer like the one shown in figure 3.6.
2. Click somewhere in the center of the screen and look at the formula bar. Note the new cell address.
3. Move the mouse two or three inches in any direction and click the mouse button again.

   As you move the mouse, the crosshair sometimes changes to an arrow pointer. Don't worry about that for now, we'll explain why later on.
4. Look at the formula bar—it should be showing a different cell address. This is now the active cell which you selected with a click.

## Is This Your Current Address?

1. Move the mouse so that the cross pointer is under the A at the top of the first column and move it down three rows until it's positioned just to the right of the number 3. Now that it's positioned below the A and to the right of the 3, click the mouse button.

   You've just selected cell A3, which makes it your current cell address. Confirm this by looking at the formula bar. Select each of these cells and check out the formula bar.
2. Select D10 by clicking on it.
3. Select E4 by using the right-and the up-arrow keys.
4. Select C7 by using the down-and the left-arrow keys.
5. Select F7 using the Tab key.
6. Select G7 using the Tab key.
7. Select G8 using the Return key.

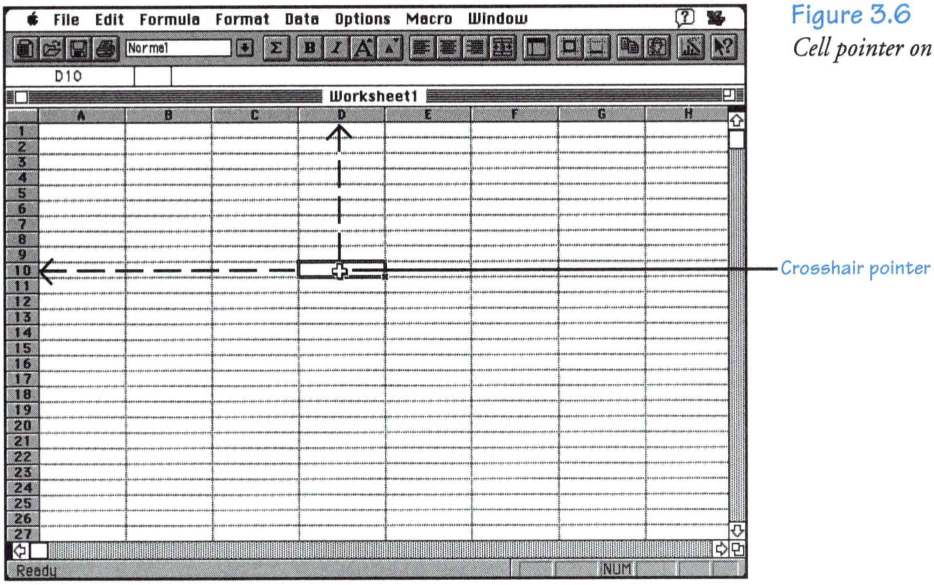


Figure 3.6
*Cell pointer on D10.*

8. Select G9 using the Return key.
9. Select B2 by clicking on it.
10. Select A1 any way you want.
11. Type your name and press the Return key.

# The Golden Rule of Saving—Thou Shalt Save Frequently and Often

1. Click the Save tool (the disk icon that is the third tool from the left) to bring up the Save dialog box.
2. Note that the text box is selected (highlighted). This means that you can type a name for the file and that your name replaces the selected text. Save *Practice* in the *Fear Excel No More* folder.

If Fear Excel No More is not the name of the current folder, move to it by following these steps:

1. Click the Desktop button.
2. Double-click the name of your hard drive.
3. Look for the Fear Excel No More folder in the alphabetized list.
4. Double-click Fear Excel No More (see fig. 3.7).
5. Click the Save button.

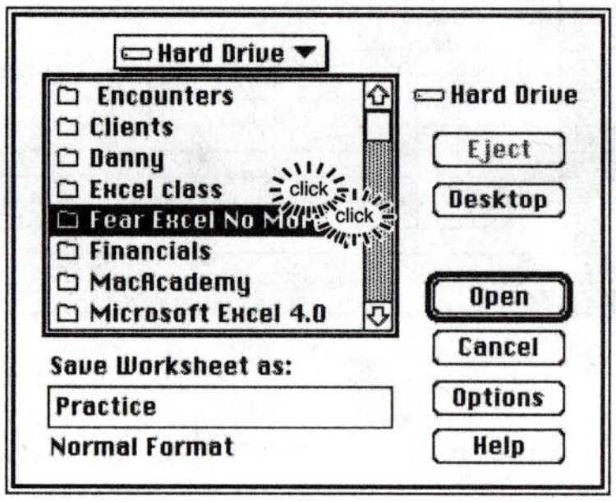


**Figure 3.7**
*Double-click on the Fear Excel No More folder to select it.*

## It's a Closed Issue

1. Close the worksheet that you just saved with the name Practice by clicking the close box (see fig. 3.8).
2. Notice that the menu bar shrinks to only three menus (see fig. 3.9). It always does this when no worksheets are open. You can see that Excel is still running because its icon is at the upper right corner of the screen.

The short menu bar can be confusing, but all you have to do is load another worksheet.

## Starting Over Again

1. Start another new worksheet by clicking the New Worksheet tool pointed out in figure 3.9.

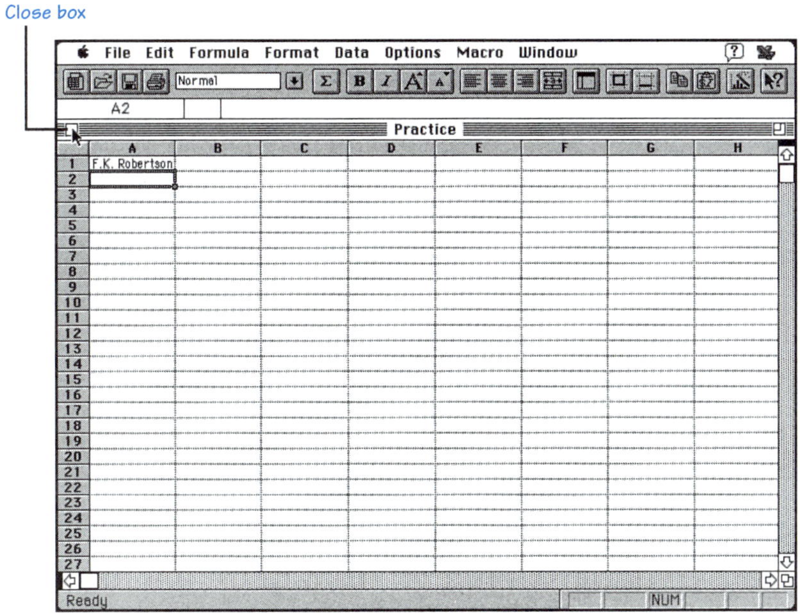


**Figure 3.8**
*Closing a document.*

**Figure 3.9**
*Shortest Excel menu bar.*

2. Close the new worksheet by clicking the close box. Again, you have the shrunken menu bar.

# Opening a Document Closed Earlier

1. Open the file called Practice that you saved recently, by clicking the Open Worksheet tool (second from the left).
2. Double-click the file name in the list (see fig. 3.10).

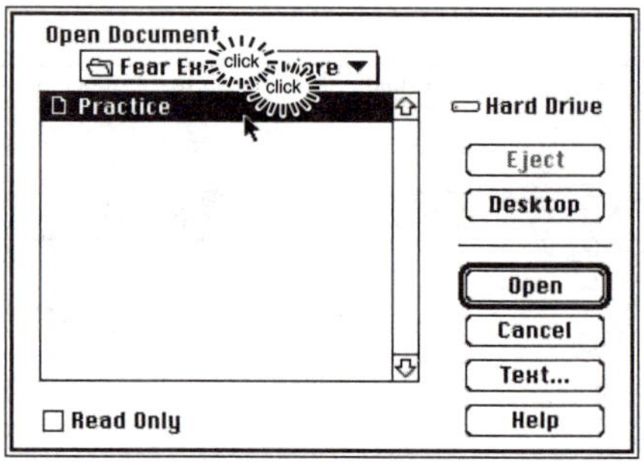


Figure 3.10
*The file Practice in the file list.*

# You're at the Helm

You just gave Excel a series of commands by clicking on tools and the close box. All of these commands are also in the File menu.

1. Look at the File menu by placing the mouse pointer on File and holding down the mouse button (see fig. 3.11).
2. Note that you can also tell Excel to start a New worksheet, Open a worksheet, Close a worksheet, and Save a worksheet using the commands in the File menu (but the tools are faster and more fun).
3. End the work session by choosing Quit from the File menu.

Figure 3.11
*Commands in the File menu.*

# Summary

Excel is activated with a double-click. A worksheet is made up of columns and rows. The cell, which is the juncture of a column and a row, holds what you type. The active cell is identified by the cell pointer and in the formula bar. To move to a cell, click it or use the movement keys. To move to a cell is to select it. You can use the toolbar to give many useful commands that are also available in the menus.

# Exorcises

1. What does a click on a tool signify?
2. Which tool allows you to save a worksheet?
3. Which tool gives the command to open a worksheet?
4. Where is the status bar?
5. What is the cell pointer?
6. Which is the proper way to refer to a cell— X34 or 34X?

## 4th Encounter

# Entering Text and Numbers

## Goal

To understand how to type words and numbers into the cells of the worksheet.

## What You Will Need

Excel running with a new worksheet visible on the screen.

## Terms of Enfearment

Insertion point
Cursor
Alignment
Autofill
Fill handle

# Briefing

## Action, Lights . . .

You're now ready to begin production of your first worksheet. When completed, this worksheet will look like figure 4.1.

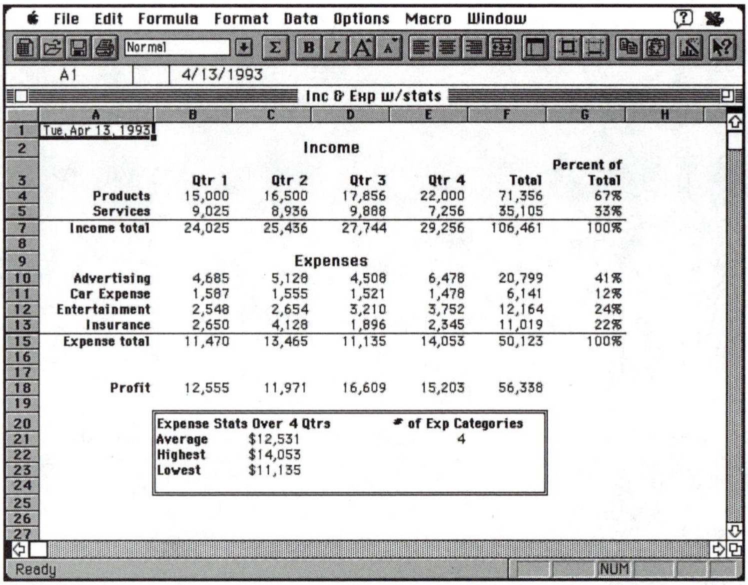


| | A | B | C | D | E | F | G |
|---|---|---|---|---|---|---|---|
| 1 | Tue, Apr 13, 1993 | | | | | | |
| 2 | | | | Income | | | |
| 3 | | Qtr 1 | Qtr 2 | Qtr 3 | Qtr 4 | Total | Percent of Total |
| 4 | Products | 15,000 | 16,500 | 17,856 | 22,000 | 71,356 | 67% |
| 5 | Services | 9,025 | 8,936 | 9,888 | 7,256 | 35,105 | 33% |
| 7 | Income total | 24,025 | 25,436 | 27,744 | 29,256 | 106,461 | 100% |
| 8 | | | | | | | |
| 9 | | | | Expenses | | | |
| 10 | Advertising | 4,685 | 5,128 | 4,508 | 6,478 | 20,799 | 41% |
| 11 | Car Expense | 1,587 | 1,555 | 1,521 | 1,478 | 6,141 | 12% |
| 12 | Entertainment | 2,548 | 2,654 | 3,210 | 3,752 | 12,164 | 24% |
| 13 | Insurance | 2,650 | 4,128 | 1,896 | 2,345 | 11,019 | 22% |
| 15 | Expense total | 11,470 | 13,465 | 11,135 | 14,053 | 50,123 | 100% |
| 18 | Profit | 12,555 | 11,971 | 16,609 | 15,203 | 56,338 | |
| 20 | | Expense Stats Over 4 Qtrs | | | # of Exp Categories | | |
| 21 | | Average | $12,531 | | 4 | | |
| 22 | | Highest | $14,053 | | | | |
| 23 | | Lowest | $11,135 | | | | |

**Figure 4.1**
*Income and Expenses worksheet.*

Look at how much is going on in this worksheet. In comparing the different Income and Expense categories, you can see totals for each quarter of the year, a profit amount, percentages of the total in every category, and statistical comparisons.

# Begin at the Beginning

It will take several encounters to complete this worksheet. In this encounter, you're going to explore what happens when you type text and numbers. And, we are going to begin at the beginning.

# Get the (Insertion) Point?

As you start to type, the characters appear in the middle of the formula bar, followed by a blinking vertical line called the *insertion point* or *cursor.*

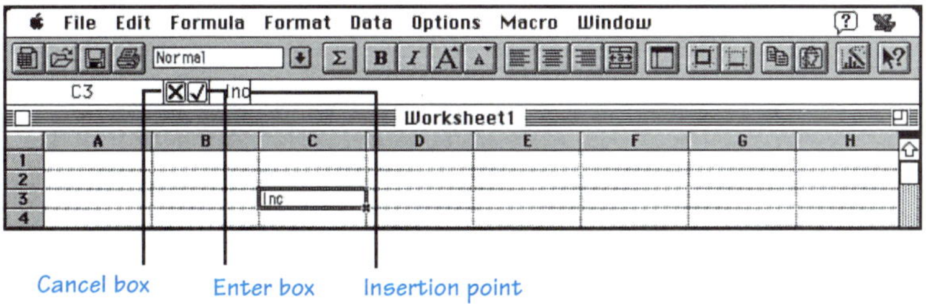


**Figure 4.2**
*The insertion point in the formula bar.*

# X Marks the Spot

The insertion point tells you two things:

- The text you just typed is not actually entered into the cell yet.
- As you type, characters appear where the cursor is blinking.

To the left of the text, is a box with an X and another with a ✓The X is called the *Cancel box*; the ✓is called the *Enter box* (see fig. 4.2).

A click on the Cancel box is like telling Excel, "I changed my mind." If you click on the Cancel box, the characters disappear.

# Checkmate

Clicking the Enter box (✓) enters the text just typed into the active cell but does not move the cell pointer.

You can also enter what you've typed without moving the cell pointer by pressing the Enter key. The Enter key is different from the Return key which moves the cell pointer down. Look for your Enter key on the numeric keypad (see fig. 4.3). Powerbook keyboards have the Enter key next to the spacebar.

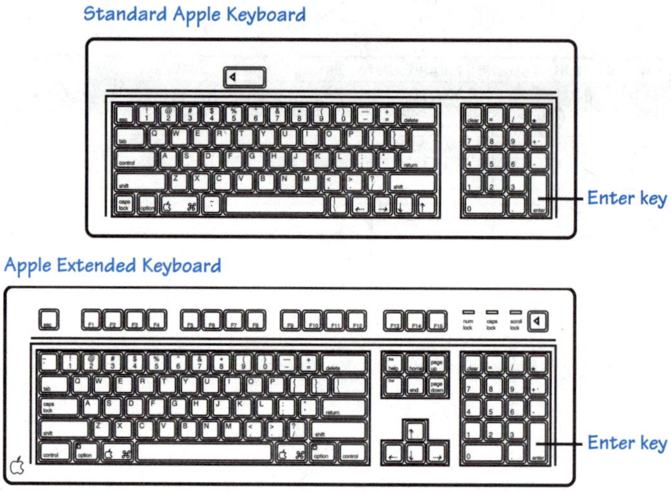


**Figure 4.3**
*Two keyboards.*

# Twice Is Nice

If you type something and press any of the keys that *move* the cell pointer—cursor keys, Return key, or Tab key— two things happen at the same time:

- Whatever you just typed is entered into the active cell.
- The cell pointer moves to the next cell, ready for more typing.

After your data is entered, the blinking insertion point, the Enter box, and the Cancel box disappear from the Formula bar.

# Line Up

Words, after they are entered, line up on the left side of the cell, and numbers line up on the right side of the cell. That is the default *alignment*—the way that Excel does it, until we change it.

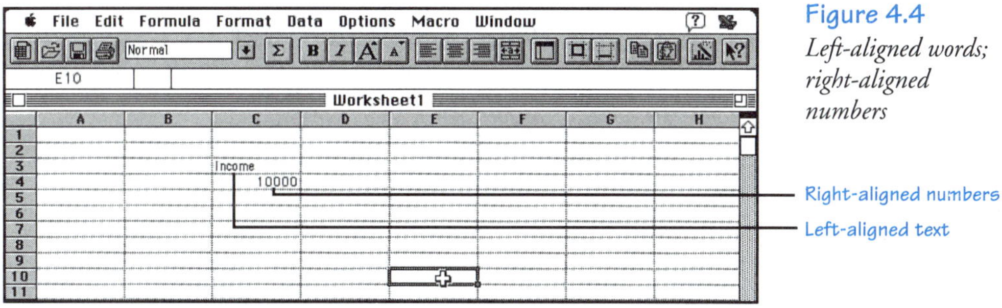


Figure 4.4
*Left-aligned words; right-aligned numbers*

# Fill 'er Up

Often we need headings that are related, such as Quarter 1, Quarter 2, Quarter 3, and Quarter 4. Equally as often, we need a series of numbers, such as 1, 2, and 3. We can ask Excel to type many of these series for us.

This wonderful feature is called *Autofill*. To use this method, type the first item, *Qtr 1*, in cell B2 and enter it by clicking the Enter box so that the cell pointer doesn't move.

# Getting a Handle on It

Next, position the mouse pointer on the bottom right corner of the cell that has the little box on it. This little box is called the *fill handle* (see fig. 4.5). We haven't mentioned it before, but it is always there, on the cell pointer. When the pointer is positioned over the fill handle, it becomes a bold cross hair (see fig. 4.6). You are going to become very familiar with this little fellow. To make the Autofill happen, click on the fill handle and drag to the right (see fig. 4.7).

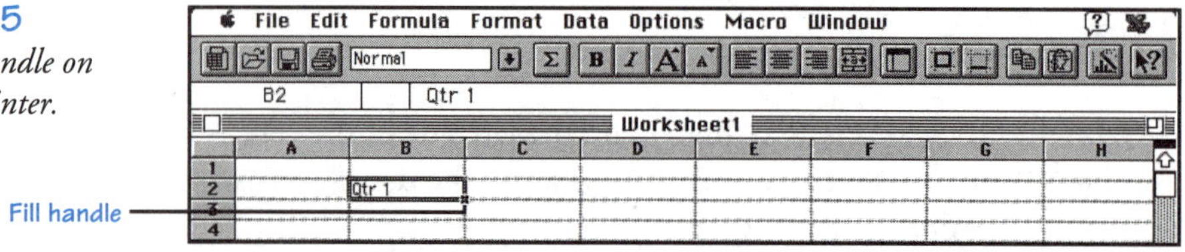


Figure 4.5
*The fill handle on the cell pointer.*

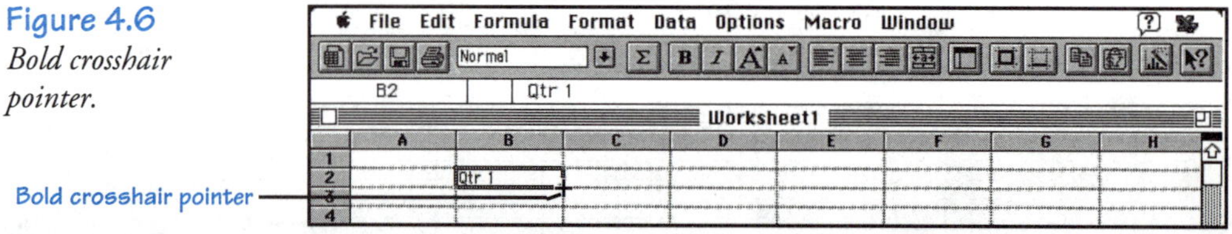


Figure 4.6
*Bold crosshair pointer.*

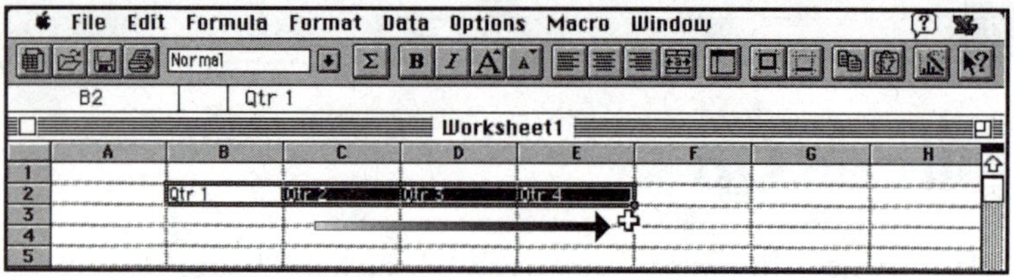


Figure 4.7
*The series created.*

Autofill works with all kinds of series. You can use it to produce the days of the week, months, years; almost any series that has a logical progression.

# I Knows What I Knows

Producing a series of numbers is a little different than producing a series of months or quarters. You have to type the first two numbers in the series rather than just the first one, before click-dragging with the Autofill pointer. The reason for this difference makes sense. Excel needs to know how you want the series to grow. If you type 1 and 2 and then use the Autofill command, Excel knows that you want the series to continue with 3, 4, and so on.

If you type 5 and 7, Excel knows that you want a series that begins with 3 and then jumps one digit.

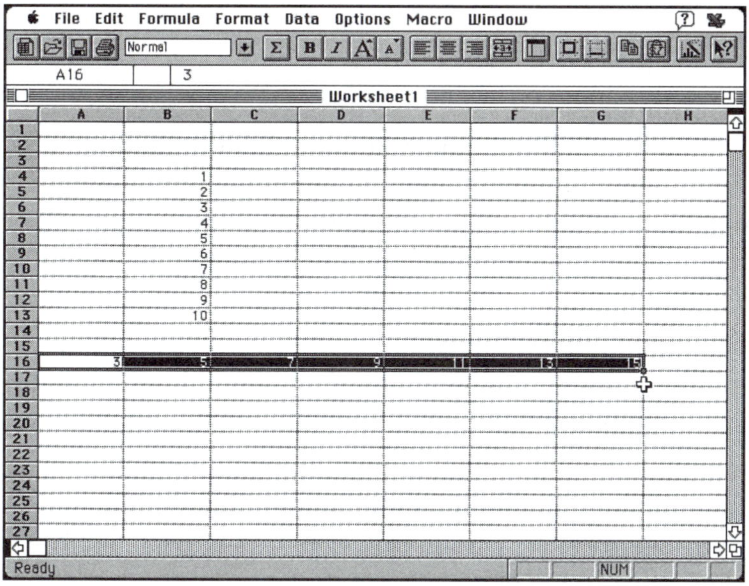


Figure 4.8
*The series after Autofill.*

# They're Out To Get Us

As you type and move from cell to cell, you may make mistakes and have to fix them. Just like in real life!

# The Big Fix

There are five different ways to fix mistakes.

- **Delete/BackSpace.** If you realize that you're making a mistake as you type, press the Delete key (also called the BackSpace key), erase the mistake, and continue typing the item correctly.
- **Undo Unto Others.** If you realize that you made a mistake, as soon as you enter it and before doing something else use the Undo command, which tells Excel to undo the last action. It's the first command in the Edit menu. This command doesn't work 100 percent of the time but is usually available.
- **Don't Reface, Replace.** When you see a cell that holds a mistake made earlier, click on the cell that holds the problem text and type something else. Whatever you type replaces the earlier item.
- **Clearance Sale.** If you have to clear out the contents of a cell completely, select the cell, press the Delete key (also called the BackSpace key), and press any of the keys that will move the cell pointer or click the Enter box. This empties out the active cell.
- **Life Is Change.** You can change the contents of the cell by editing in the formula bar.

Maybe you typed the word "Expense" in a cell and realize "Expenses" would be better. You can click on the cell holding "Expense" and click in the formula bar after the final letter. The insertion point will appear and start blinking (see fig. 4.9). You can then type the letter "s" and enter the changed word.

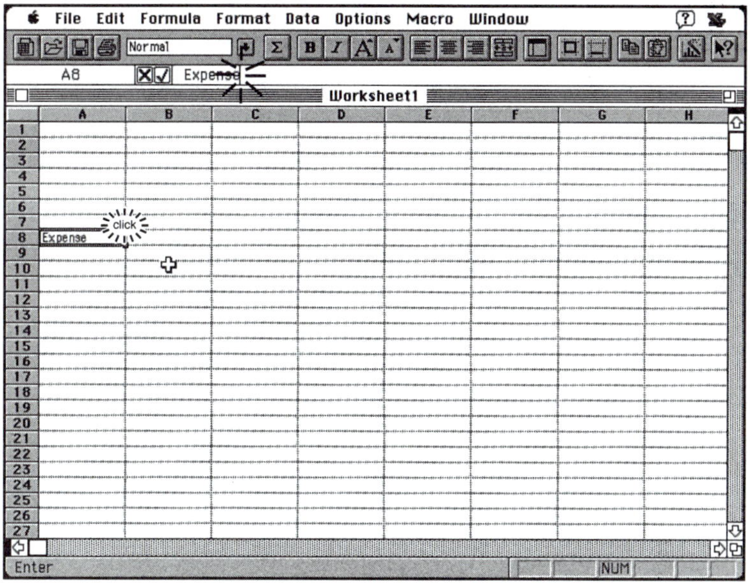


Figure 4.9
*Insertion point blinking after "Expense."*

You can also delete mistakes by selecting the cell holding the mistake, clicking in the formula bar after the mistake, and pressing the Delete key to remove characters one by one. Then type the correct version. You can also click-drag across the mistake and type text to replace the selected text (see fig. 4.10).

When you click in the formula bar, it is as though you had never entered the contents of this cell. You can do what you want to the stuff in the formula bar and enter it again.

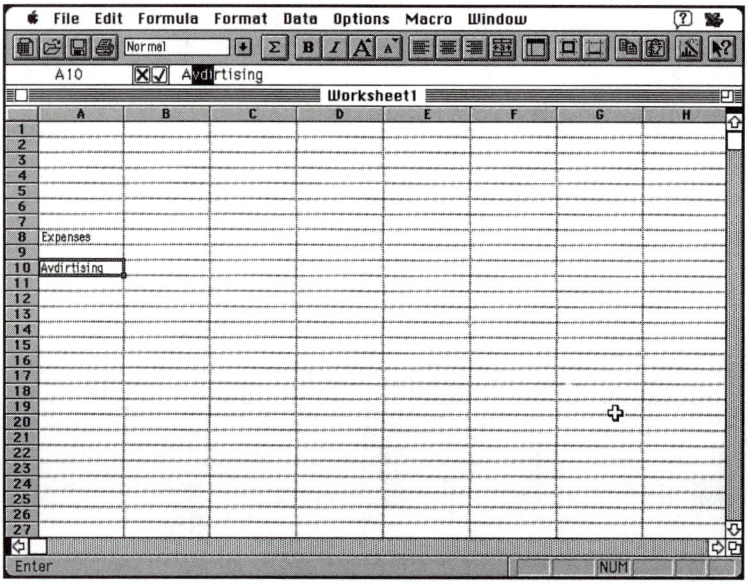


Figure 4.10
*Text selected with click-drag.*

# Practice

## Typecasting

1. Select A3. Start to type the word *Income* in this cell. After typing the first three letters, look at the formula bar (see fig. 4.11).

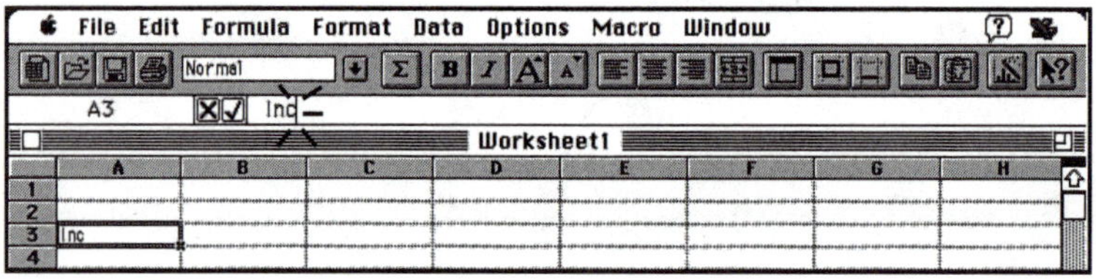


Figure 4.11
*"Inc" in the formula bar.*

2. You can see the three letters followed by the blinking insertion point. Click the Cancel box. Note that `Inc` no longer shows up in the formula bar. It's history.

# Erasing

1. Now type *Inv.* Whoops, that's a mistake, you actually need a "c" not a "v."
2. Use the Delete key to erase the "v" and then type the correct letter.
3. Type the whole word now and enter it by clicking the Enter box (✓).

Look at the formula bar. The cursor is no longer blinking, and the Enter and Cancel boxes have disappeared.

The text is now officially entered in the cell. Note that the cell pointer hasn't moved.

# Getting a Move On

1. Press the Return key to move down to cell A4.
2. Type the word "Sales." Glance at the formula bar, and you see the text waiting to be entered with the cursor still blinking.
3. This time, press the Return key rather than clicking the Enter box (✓).

Look at the formula bar. Note that the Cancel and Enter boxes are gone. Also, note that you don't see the word "Sales" because pressing the Return key moved the cell pointer away from that cell.

# Tabbing Around (Don't Forget Those Arrow Keys)

1. Now press the Tab key. Notice how the cell pointer has moved one cell to the right.
2. Type *500* and press the Tab key again. 500 has been entered, and the cell pointer has moved.

3. Press the up-arrow key and type *Expense*. Press the right-arrow key and type 1000.
4. This time, press the Enter key. Note how the cell pointer does not move.

## Back to the Mouse

Now click on an empty cell a few cells down. Glance at the formula bar. Remember how the far left section always tells you your location?. Type *-678* and press the down-arrow key.

## Editing a Cell

1. Click on the cell containing the word `Expense`.
2. Click in the formula bar at the end of the word.
3. Type an *s*.
4. Press Return.

## Spring Clearing

Practice clearing the contents of one or more cells:

1. Click any cell that has data.
2. Press the BackSpace key.
3. Press the Return key.
4. Do the same with another cell.

# We've Got You in the Crosshair—Using Autofill

1. Type *Qtr 1* in any cell.
2. Enter it by clicking the Enter box, making sure that the cell remains your active cell.
3. Move the mouse pointer to the bottom right corner of the cell until it is positioned on the fill handle. Wait until the pointer turns into the bold crosshair (see fig. 4.6).
4. Click and drag three cells to the right. As you drag, glance at the formula bar.
5. Release the mouse button when you reach Qtr 4 (see fig. 4.12).

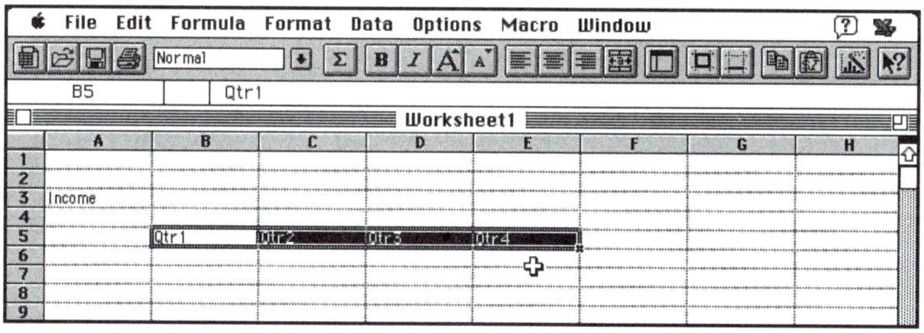


Figure 4.12
*Four Quarters entered with Autofill.*

# Time Flies When You're Having Fun

1. Type *January* in another cell.
2. Make sure that cell remains active by clicking the Enter box.
3. Move the pointer to the fill handle. Wait for the bold crosshair.
4. Click and drag down, while watching the formula bar (see fig. 4.13).

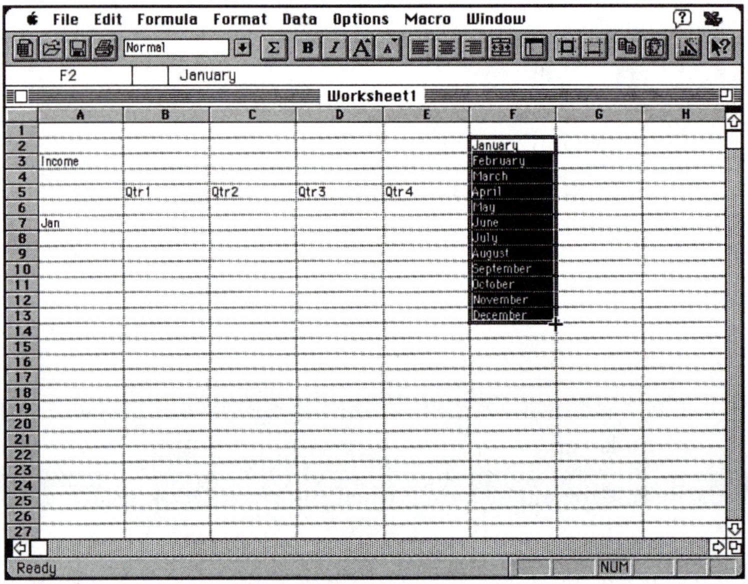


**Figure 4.13** *Series of months entered with Autofill.*

# Please Take a Number—Creating a Series of Numbers

1. Move to an empty cell and type the number 1.
2. Press the Return key and type the number 2.
3. Select both of these cells by clicking on the cell holding the 1 and drag down to the cell holding the 2.
4. Move the mouse pointer to the fill handle of the cell holding the number 2.
5. Click and drag down while watching the formula bar. Stop when the formula bar shows 10 (see fig. 4.14).

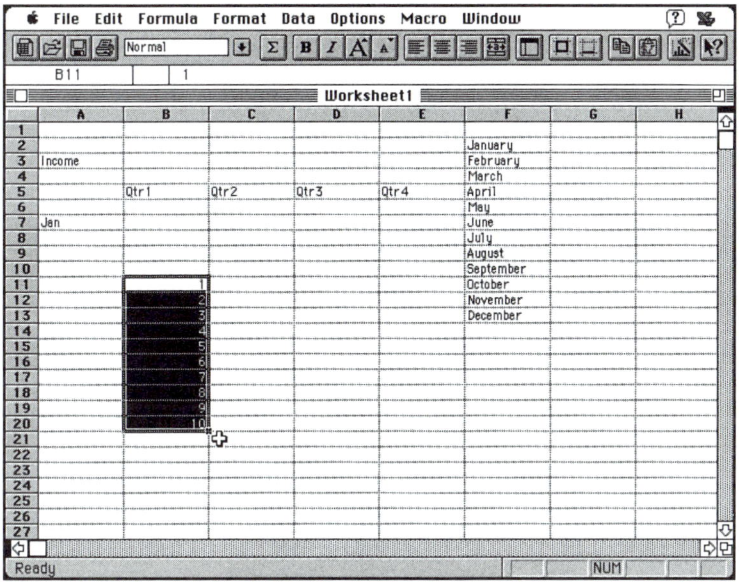


**Figure 4.14**
*Series completed.*

# Closing Up Shop

Close the worksheet by clicking on the close box in the top left corner of the document.

You don't want to save this worksheet, so send it to Data Heaven. When Excel asks, `Save changes in Worksheet?`, click the No button. The worksheet is no more.

# A Truly Momentous Occasion

1. Click the New Worksheet tool. We are about to rock and roll!
2. Type *Income* in A1.

3. Start your column headings in B2. The headings you need to use to follow the examples and exorcises in this book are shown in figure 4.15.

4. Start your row headings in A3 and go down to A16 for the Profit heading.

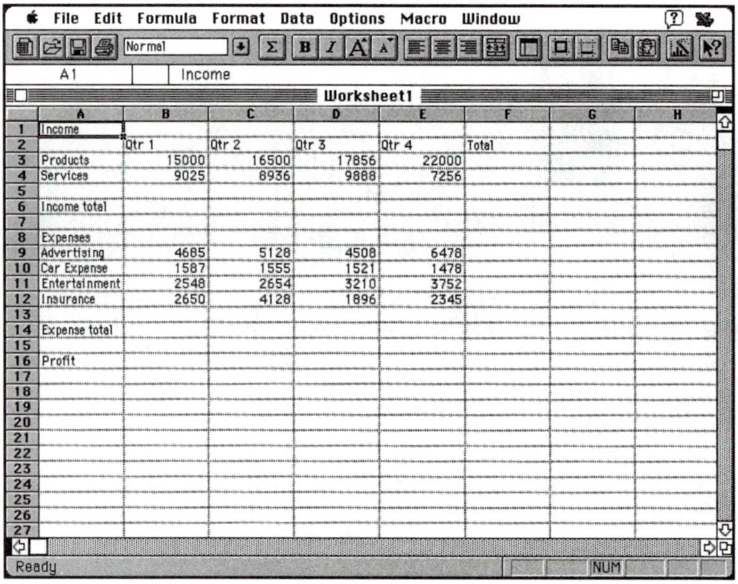


**Figure 4.15**
*The Income and Expense worksheet.*

# Save, Save, Save, Save

1. After you've been typing for a while, save the worksheet by clicking the Save tool (third from left) in the toolbar.

2. Call it Income and Expense and put it in the Fear Excel No More folder.

3. When your worksheet matches the illustration and you've had enough, click the Save tool again.

4. Choose Quit from the File menu.

You deserve a hot fudge sundae, or maybe a banana and a hike, depending on your current cholesterol level.

# Summary

You've seen how you can enter data into your worksheet by selecting a cell, typing, and then moving to another cell. When you type something incorrectly, you can fix it by typing over the mistake or by clearing out the cell.

The Autofill feature lets you create series of words and numbers with very little typing.

# Exorcises

1. What is it that surrounds the active cell with a darker border?
2. What is the name of the bar that will always tell you the active cell?
3. Pressing the Return key will move the cell pointer in which direction?
4. Name two keys that will move the cell pointer to the right.
5. The active cell can also be called your current cell ________.
6. What is the name of the little box in the bottom right corner of the cell pointer?

5th Encounter

# Moving Around the Worksheet

## Goal

Learn common techniques for getting to where you need to go as quickly and efficiently as possible.

## What You Will Need

Start with Excel running, with the Income and Expense worksheet visible.

## Terms of Enfearment

Return and Tab keys
Scroll bar
Formula menu
Command key
End key
Home key

# Briefing

After using Excel for a while, you will discover something interesting: typing the data is simple. However, getting the formulas right and making the printout look perfect takes time. You may end up moving through your documents over and over: up to the top, down to the bottom, to the beginning of each section, back to the active cell, etc.

Your life with Excel becomes easier when you know how to move through a document quickly and efficiently. It's like knowing which backroads to take during rush hour.

In the last encounter, we covered the basics, including clicking on a cell to select it and using the cursor arrow keys and the *Return and Tab keys* to move the cell pointer from cell to cell. In this encounter, we are going to learn more ways to move around the worksheet.

# Moving Distances in a Single Bound

The two *scroll bars* offer a number of useful techniques (see fig. 5.1).

Each click on the down arrow moves you down one row. Each click on the right arrow moves you one column to the right. The actions are reversed when you click on the up arrow and the left arrow.

Clicking in the vertical scroll bar above or below the scroll box jumps you up one screen or down one screen. Clicking to the left or the right of the scroll box in the horizontal scroll bar jumps you one screen to the right or the left.

You can also drag the scroll boxes along the scroll bars. Dragging the scroll boxes to their farthest limits will take you to the end of the active area. Usually, the active area is the part of the worksheet whose cells contain text, numbers, and formulas. On a blank, new worksheet, the active area is two screens down and two screens across.

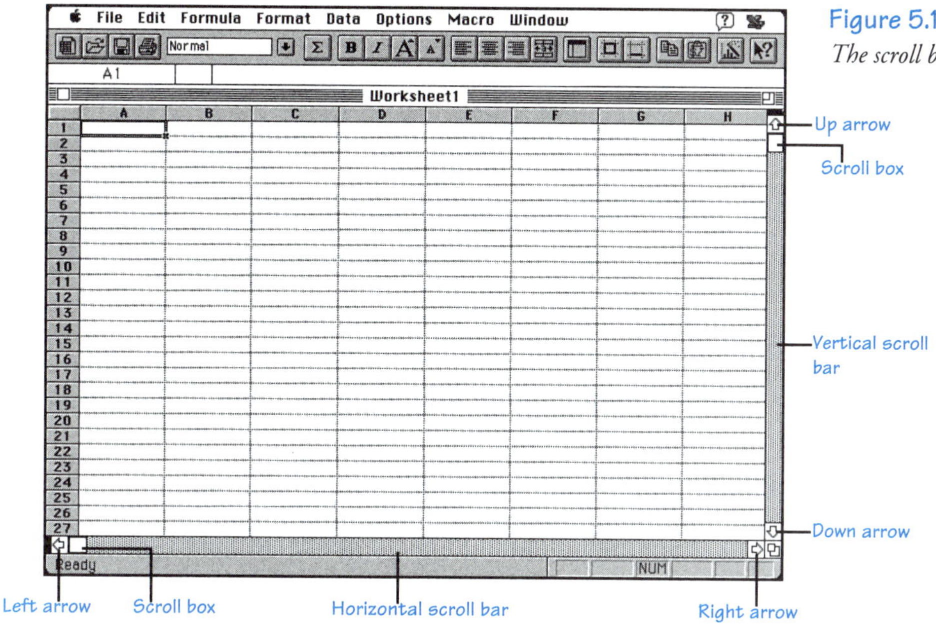


Figure 5.1
*The scroll bars.*

To move beyond the active area, hold down the Shift key while dragging the scroll boxes. The worksheet has 16,384 rows and 256 columns. The first 26 columns go from A to Z; the next 26 columns start with AA and go to AZ; then they go from BA to BZ and so on, until IV, which is the name of the final column.

Clicking the scroll arrows, dragging the boxes, and clicking on the scroll bars allow you to look at different parts of the worksheet. *None of these methods move the cell pointer.*

To make changes, move the cell pointer and select the cells you need to change. You can move the cell pointer using the Return, Tab, and cursor arrow keys. Additionally, you can press Shift-Return to move the cell pointer up and Shift-Tab to move the cell pointer to the left.

With an extended keyboard, there are even more ways to move the cell pointer (see fig. 5.2 and table 5.1).

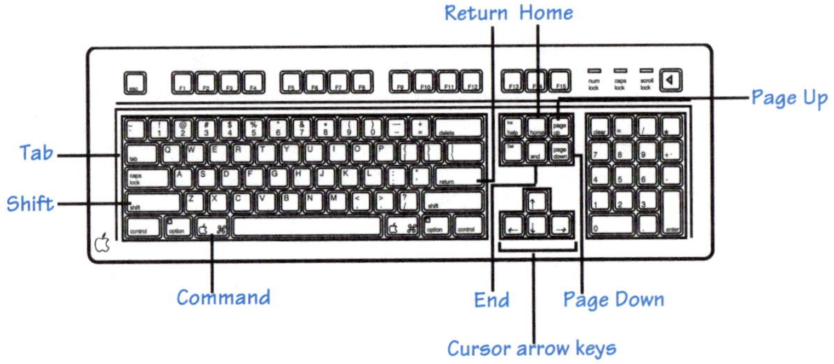


**Figure 5.2**
*The extended keyboard.*

**Table 5.1. Extended Keyboard Keys**

| *Key* | *Description* |
|---|---|
| Return | Moves cell pointer down one cell |
| Shift-Return | Moves cell pointer up one cell |
| Tab | Moves cell pointer right one cell |
| Shift-Tab | Moves cell pointer left one cell |
| Cursor arrow keys | Move cell pointer one cell up, down, left, and right |
| Command + Cursor keys | Moves cell pointer one block of data |
| Page Up, Page Down | Move cell pointer up and down one screen |
| Home | Moves cell pointer to first column in same row |
| End | Moves cell pointer to last column with data in same row |
| Command-Home | Moves cell pointer to A1 |

The Goto (Go to. . .) command in the Formula menu also lets you jump to any cell on the worksheet. After giving the Goto command, a dialog box appears in which you can type a cell reference, like C555 (see fig. 5.3). As soon as you confirm the command by clicking the OK button, the cell pointer appears in its new location.

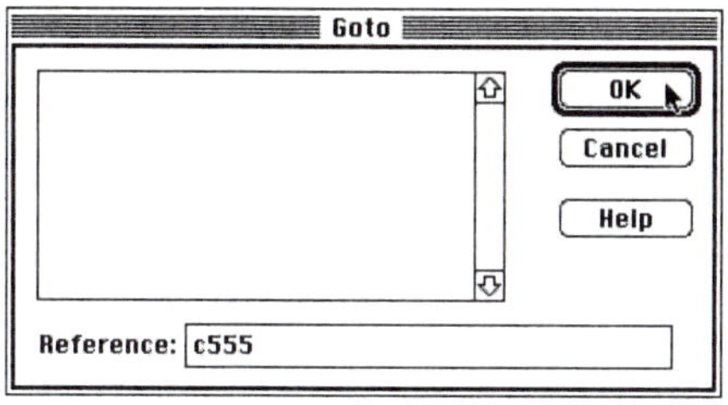


Figure 5.3
*Goto window.*

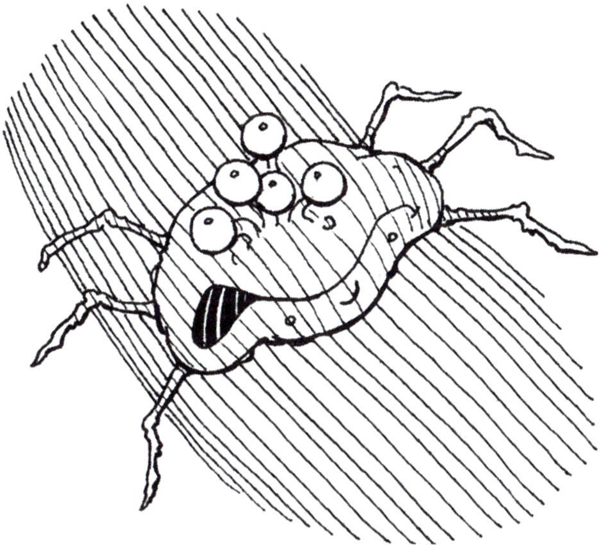

# They're Out To Get Us

## Far and Away

Sometimes, you can end up far away from the active cell, especially if you have been using the scroll bars to see different parts of the worksheet.

To get back easily, choose Show Active Cell from the Formula menu. Remember, if you're not sure where the active cell is, just glance up at the *formula bar.*

Sometimes, you can move the cell pointer without meaning to. Frequently, this happens if you hold down the *Command key* while pressing one of the cursor keys. To fix this, hold down the Command key and press the opposite cursor key. In other words, if you just pressed Command + the down-arrow key, and you end up in Never Never Land, pressing Command + the up-arrow key sends you back to familiar territory.

## Home, Sweet Home

If you get disoriented, return Home (to cell A1) using the Goto command. If you have an extended keyboard with a *Home key*, press Command-Home.

If you press the Page Up key or click the up arrow in the vertical scroll bar and nothing happens, it's probably because your cell pointer is in row 1, and it can't go up any further. If you click the left arrow in the horizontal scroll bar and nothing happens, it's probably because your cell pointer is in column A.

# Practice

## Homebody

Let's move around the Income and Expense worksheet. Go back to A1 (called "Home" by worksheet veterans). Choose Goto from the Formula menu, type *A1*, and click the OK button. Don't worry if another cell reference is in the Goto window. When you type A1, it will be replaced. What, me worry?

## Scrolling Up and Down, Left and Right

1. Click and quickly release the right scroll arrow; a new column appears on the right side of the window. Continue to click and release until you can no longer see columns A through E on the screen (see fig. 5.4).

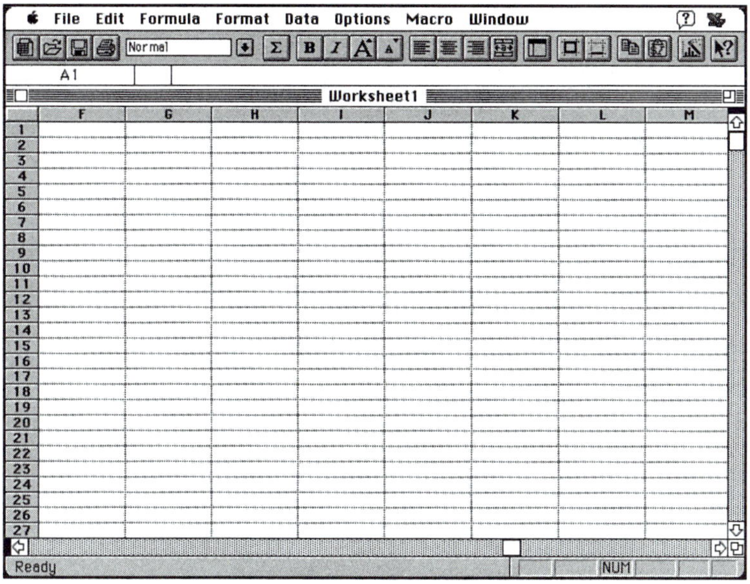


Figure 5.4
*Scrolled to column F.*

2. Click and release the down scroll arrow. A new row appears at the bottom of the window. Do this until you can no longer see rows 1 through 5 at the top of the window.

   Glance up at the formula bar and note that A1 is still the active cell. Ah hah! Clicking the scroll arrows does **not** move the cell pointer.

3. Click on the up scroll arrow and hold the mouse button down until you go all the way back to the top.
4. Do the same with the left scroll arrow until the scroll box returns all the way to the left side of the window. That makes sense—holding down the mouse button causes the scrolling to shift into high gear.

## Going Down

1. Click and drag the scroll box in the vertical scroll bar down to the middle of the bar; then release the mouse button.

Look at the row numbers on the left side of the window. You've moved down just about a full screen's worth of rows. Drag the scroll box back up to the top and get reoriented.

2. Drag the scroll box to the bottom of the scroll bar. You should be down about two full screens (see fig. 5.5).

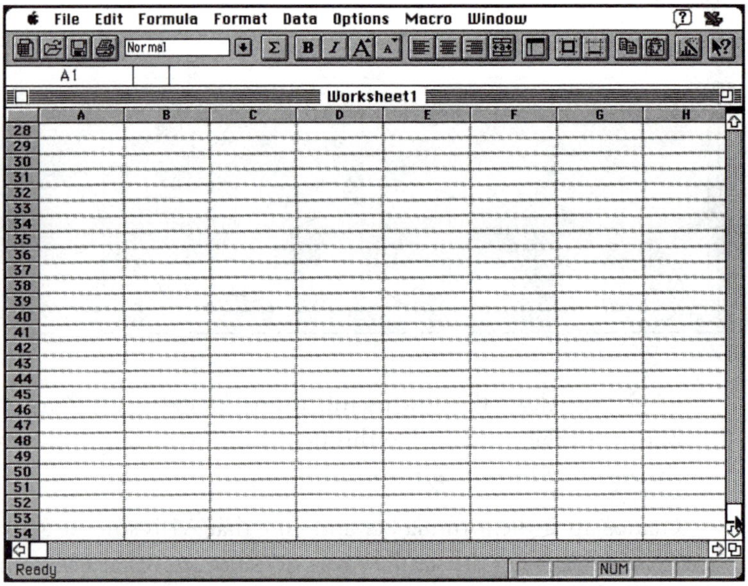


**Figure 5.5**
*Two screens down.*

# Using the Horizontal Scroll Bar

Do the same thing with the scroll box at the bottom of the window in the horizontal scroll bar.

First click and drag it to the middle of the screen and look at the range of columns at the top of the window. Now, drag the scroll box all the way to the right. You should be two screens over, and your worksheet should display column H through O. (This arrangement, of course, depends on the size of your monitor.)

Drag both scroll boxes back to their homes first, just to get reoriented.

## Going All the Way Down

1. Hold down the Shift key and drag the scroll box down the vertical scroll bar.
2. As you drag, glance up at the left side of the formula bar. Note the rows that are passing by, like taking an elevator from the Penthouse down to the basement of a skyscraper.
3. Drag the vertical elevator all the way down to the bottom of the scroll bar, until you get to row 16, 384. Release the mouse button and then the Shift key.

## Going Up

After being suitably impressed, click and drag the scroll box all the way to the top. When going up, you don't need to hold down the Shift key.

## Eyes Right

Hold down the Shift key and drag the horizontal elevator slowly to the right. Watch the formula bar to see how the column lettering works. Drag the elevator all the way to the end until you see column IV (see fig. 5.6).

Rest assured that you will never work on a worksheet this big. It's just nice to go out to the end at least once. Drag the elevator back home all the way to the left.

## Keyboard Kapers

Practice using the keyboard to move the cell pointer.

1. Choose Goto from the Formula menu and then type *C555* and click the OK button.

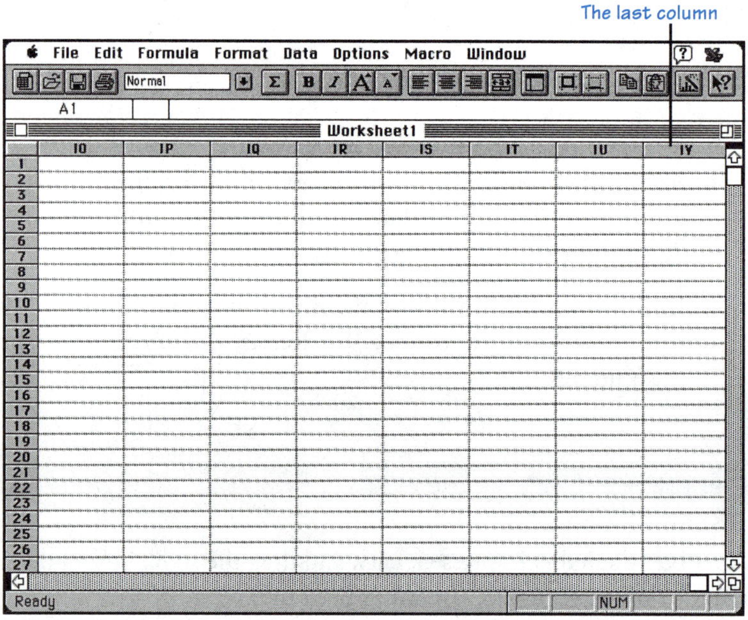


Figure 5.6
*At the last column.*

2. For an even faster method, use the keyboard shortcut for the Goto command: Command-G. Press Command-G, type *A1*, and press the Return key.

## Moving the Cell Pointer through Blocks of Data

1. Hold down the Command key and press the down-arrow key once.
2. Keep doing this until you reach the cell that holds the heading `Profit`. Then press Command + the down-arrow key one more time to go all the way to the very bottom of the worksheet.
3. Hold down the Command key and press the up-arrow key once, then twice, then three times. Note how this key combination moves the cell pointer from one section of filled cells to the next.

# Summary

Many methods enable us to move easily around the worksheet. These methods include the movement keys on the keyboard, the scroll bars, and the Goto command.

Becoming comfortable with these methods requires practice but is certainly worth the effort when you can get where you want to go quickly and easily.

# Exorcises

1. Where are the cursor arrow keys?
2. Where do you click to see the columns and rows that are one screen over to the right?
3. What command allows you to move instantly to a specific cell reference?
4. What keys can you press to move the cell pointer to the right or left?
5. What is the active area?
6. What key must you hold down to move past the active area when dragging a scroll box?

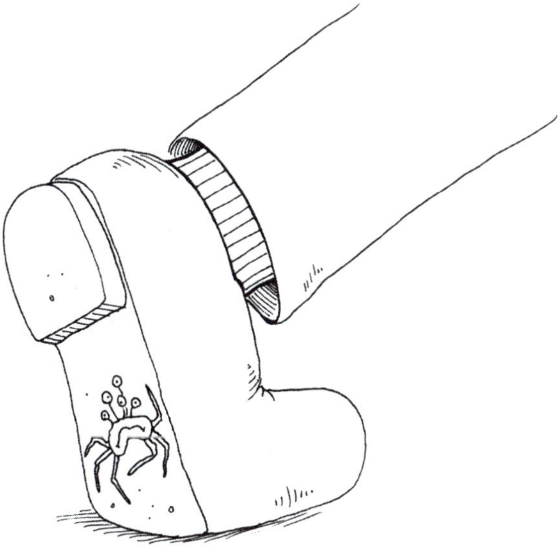

6th Encounter

# Creating Formulas

## Goal

Understand how to create formulas that add, subtract, multiply, and divide numbers.

## What You Will Need

Start with Excel running, with the Income and Expense worksheet visible.

## Terms of Enfearment

- Mathematical operators
- Pointing
- Autosum
- SUM function
- Relative Reference

# Briefing

Formulas are the heart and soul of a worksheet. They are like recipes, except that you end up with the bottom line rather than with a carrot cake. This is where you get creative, where you can get the answers to many questions that begin with "What if."

Whenever you create a formula, you begin with an equal sign (=). This sign alerts Excel that the active cell holds a formula it must calculate.

Almost always, when creating formulas, you want Excel to look at the contents of cells rather than the numbers in the cells. Suppose that you've typed the number 24,897 in cell B3 and the number 11,270 in cell B4. To add the contents of those two cells, you would create the formula =B3+B4, not the formula =24,897+11,270.

The reason you use cell references like B3 in formulas, rather than references to specific numbers, is crucial to understanding how to use Excel.

You want Excel to look at those two cells and add their contents together regardless of what numbers happen to be in them. This way, you can change the numbers referred to in the formula, and the cell holding the formula immediately shows a new result (see fig. 6.1).

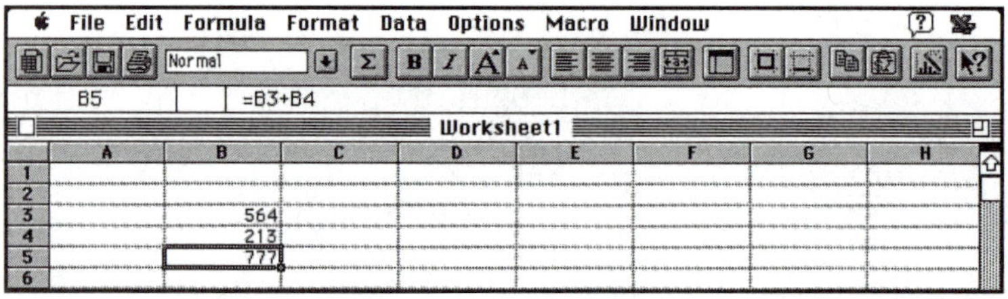


**Figure 6.1**
*New numbers in B3 and B4.*

# Smooth Operator

Many formulas can be created by combining an equal sign with cell references and the appropriate *mathematical operators* (see fig. 6.2):

| | | |
|---|---|---|
| Plus sign | + | Adds |
| Minus sign | – | Subtracts |
| Asterisk | * | Multiplies |
| Forward Slash | / | Divides |

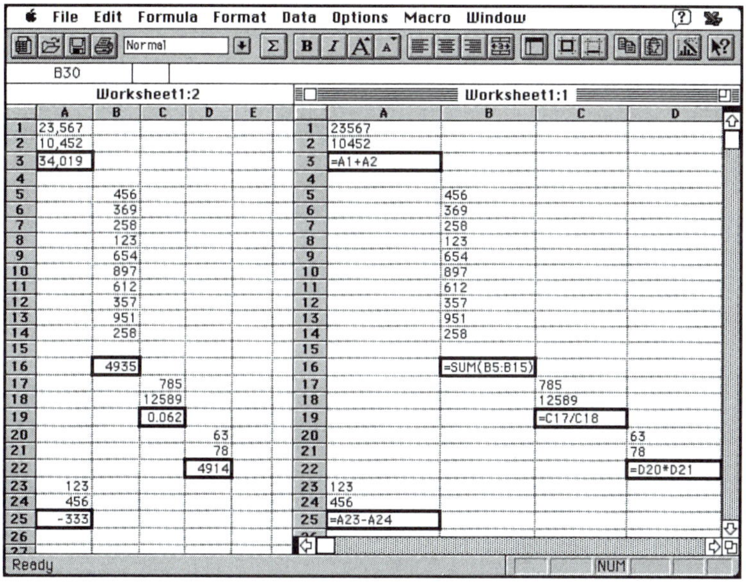

Figure 6.2
*Examples of simple formulas.*

# Go To Your Room

You have to be careful about where you put your formulas. Imagine that you're adding up a column of numbers on a page without a calculator. Normally, you draw a line under the bottom number and put the total below the line. It works the same way on the worksheet. Before actually starting to create a formula by typing an equal sign, you need to tell Excel where to put the formula by selecting the logical place. If you want to add a column of numbers, select the cell at the bottom of that column.

# Your Point Is Well Taken

After beginning a formula with the equal sign, you start to build the rest of it. Instead of typing the whole formula, click on the cells you need in the formula.

If your formula is =B3+B4, type the equal sign, click on B3, type a plus sign, and click on B4. This method of building the formula is called *pointing.* Pointing makes sense because it avoids the problem of typos and reduces the probability of typing an incorrect cell reference. However, you *can* type the cell references (in upper- or lowercase) rather than clicking on them.

After you type an equal sign, Excel expects you to click a cell (or type a cell reference.) When you do, a selection box borders the cell. The selection box, also called marching ants, shows you which cell has just been added to the formula. If you look at the formula bar, you can watch the formula building as you click the cells.

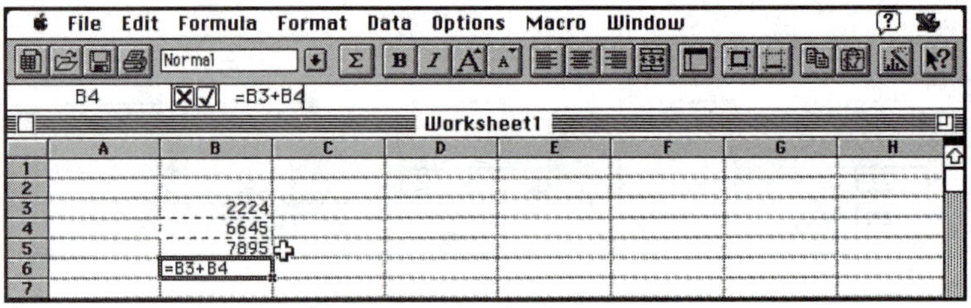


Figure 6.3
*Building a formula.*

When the formula is complete in the formula bar, you must enter it into the cell. Until the formula is entered, you won't see its results calculated.

# Double Your Pleasure, Double Your Fun

The best method for entering the formula is one that allows you to keep the cell pointer on that cell:

- Pressing the Enter key (on the numeric keypad or next to the space bar)
- Clicking the Enter box in the formula bar

Using either method enables you to see the number in the cell that the formula has calculated, while viewing the formula in the formula bar (see fig. 6.4).

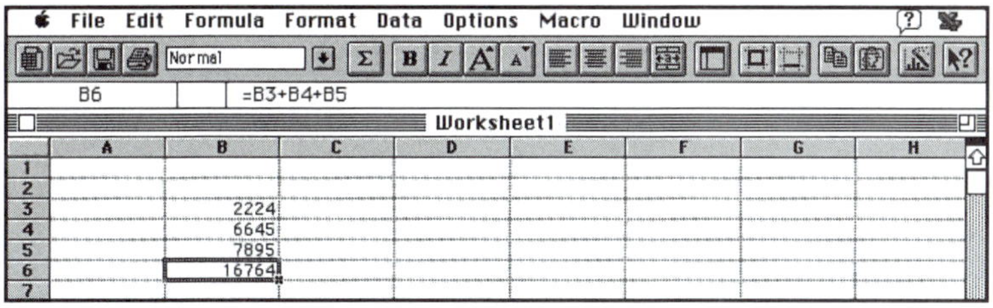


Figure 6.4
*The formula completed and entered.*

## The Big Easy

Excel has made it easy to add up a range of numbers. You start the process by selecting the right cell to hold the formula (often at the bottom of a column of numbers). Next, click the *Autosum* tool.

Figure 6.5
*The Autosum tool.*

## Oh, Those Sumptuous Sums

Amazingly, a formula appears in the formula bar that tells Excel to add up a range of numbers. You don't even have to type an equal sign—Excel does the whole formula for you. The range inside the parentheses includes all the cells you want added together.

As shown in figure 6.6, the colon between the two cell references can be interpreted as "through," as in "Sum up the contents of cells B2 through B13."

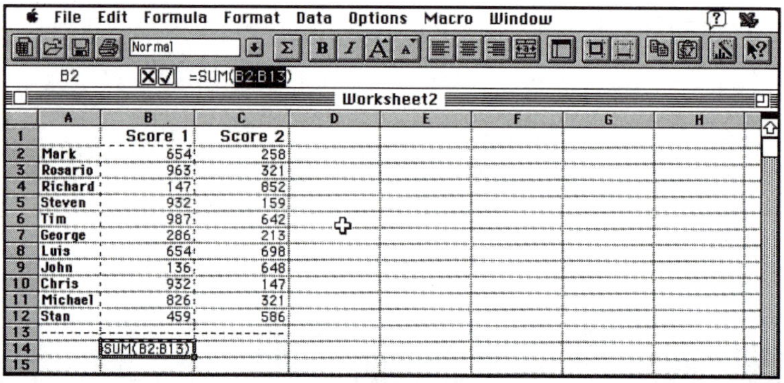


Figure 6.6
*The SUM formula in the formula bar immediately after the Autosum tool is clicked.*

This formula uses a function called *SUM.* It's a built-in method that saves the time and effort involved in building a formula by clicking on each and every cell in a range that could have hundreds of numbers.

## Many Columns, Many Formulas

Usually, you have more than one column of numbers. Fortunately, you don't have to create a different formula at the bottom of every column. You only have to create the first formula, in the first column, because you can use the Autofill command to make copies.

## Fill 'er Up

Remember how to use Autofill? We used it in an earlier encounter to create headings for all four Quarters after typing *Qtr 1.*

Copying formulas uses the same approach. You select the cell holding the formula you want to copy and place the mouse pointer on the fill handle on the bottom right corner of a cell, where it changes to a crosshair. You then click and drag through a range of cells. Excel copies the formula in the first cell to all the cells you drag across (see fig. 6.7).

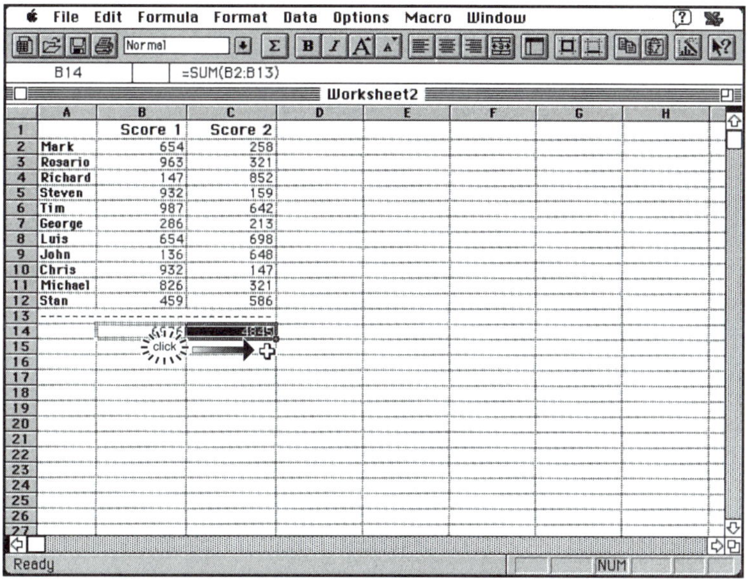


Figure 6.7
*Formula copied.*

# The Theory of Relativity

Excel also automatically adjusts the formula to account for its new location—so that it looks at the numbers in the correct column or row (see fig. 6.8). This is known as *relative referencing.* The formula works because it is looking at a new column of numbers, relative to its new position.

**Figure 6.8**
*Different column, different formula.*

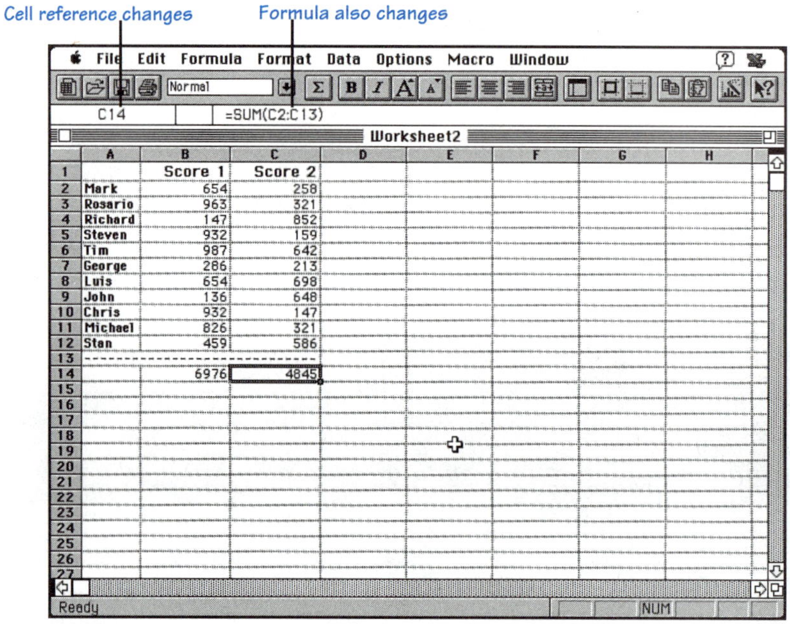

# They're Out To Get Us

## Pay Attention!

When you first start working with formulas, you have to pay a lot of attention to putting them in the right place and pressing the equal sign to start them off.

One common mistake is to put the formula in one of the cells you actually want the formula to look at. To avoid this mistake, always think to yourself, "Here are my numbers, in these cells. Where do I want to see the result of my formula?" That is the cell you want to select before beginning the formula. Click that cell before starting your formula with an equal sign (=).

## Good Formula, Bad Formula

One of the biggest confusions for the beginner is a formula that seems to go bad when you know that you went through the proper steps to produce it. Usually, this happens because you try to enter a formula by clicking on another cell rather than by entering it properly.

The way to enter a formula properly is to press the Enter key, to click the Enter box, or to press one of the keys that moves the cell pointer.

## One Bad Formula Will Spoil the Bunch

The formula will go bad if you click on a cell to enter it—performing this extra click actually places that cell in the formula and messes it up.

The best way to avoid this problem is to be clear that formulas cannot be entered by clicking another cell. However, if a mistake is made, it can be quickly fixed if you get into the habit of looking at the formula bar before moving on. The evidence is right there (see fig. 6.9). It's a bad formula.

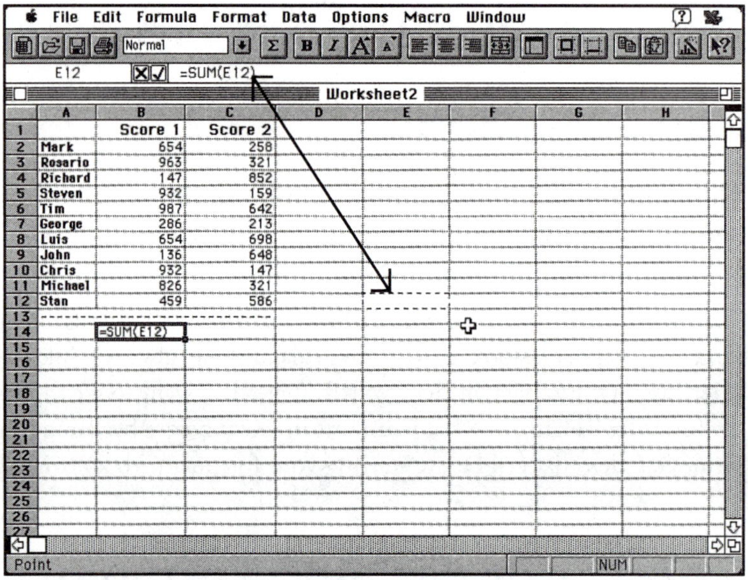


**Figure 6.9**
*This is a bad formula.*

If the Cancel box is still showing, click it and start the formula again. If the bad formula has already been entered, select the cell, recreate the formula, and enter it correctly.

It's rare, but sometimes you may click the Autosum tool, and Excel will guess the wrong range of cells. This is another reason for looking at the formula bar as soon as you click the Autosum tool. When Excel puts the formula in the formula bar, the range of cells within the parenthesis is selected (see fig. 6.10). Because the range is selected, you can click and drag across another range, and Excel will replace the first range with the second.

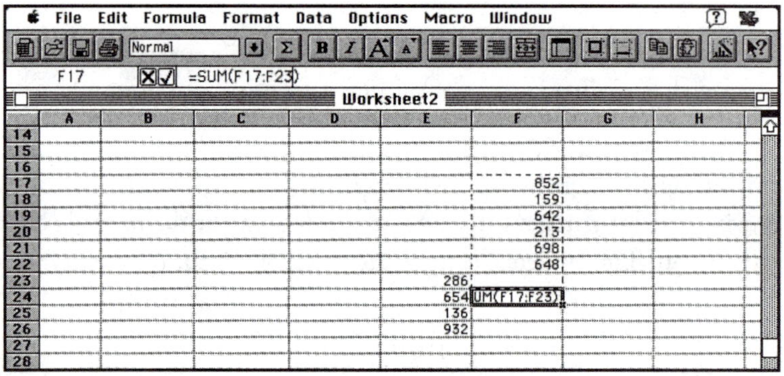


**Figure 6.10**
*Original range is replaced by the selection of a new range.*

# Practice

Your Income and Expense worksheet should look like figure 6.11 if you completed the earlier exorcises. If it doesn't look the same, go ahead and click the New Worksheet tool and type it now.

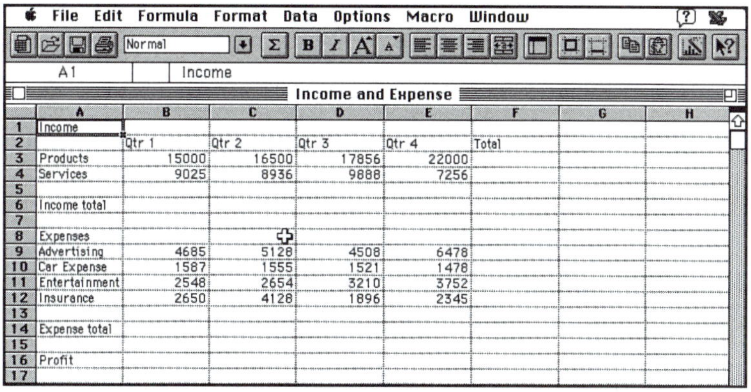


**Figure 6.11**
*The Income and Expense worksheet.*

# Five Fun Formulas

Figure 6.12 shows the locations of the five formulas you will add during this practice session.

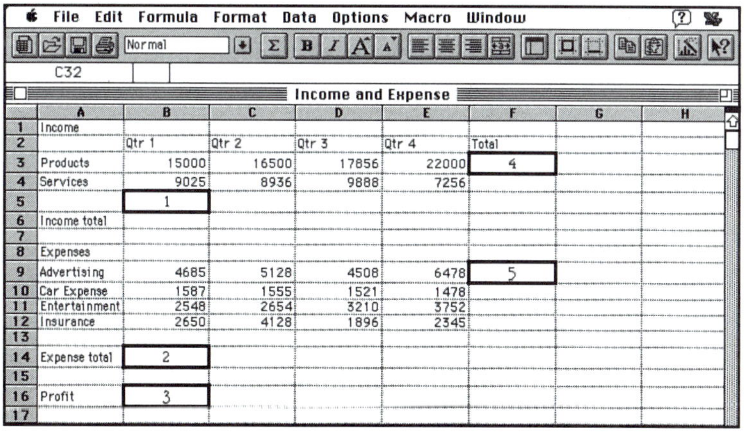


**Figure 6.12**
*Cells waiting to hold your formulas.*

To make up a formula to add the income for Qtr 1, do the following:

1. Click on B6. This cell should be to the right of the heading "Income total" and at the bottom of Qtr 1 Income.

   Make sure that you're in the correct cell by glancing up at the Formula bar. We're going to use the pointing method to create the formula.

2. Start the formula by typing an equal sign (=) as shown in figure 6.13.
3. Click on cell B3.
4. Type a plus sign (+) and click on B4.
5. Look up at the formula bar. You should see =B3+B4. If the formula is not correct, say "never mind" by clicking on the Cancel box. If the formula is correct, enter it by clicking the Enter box.

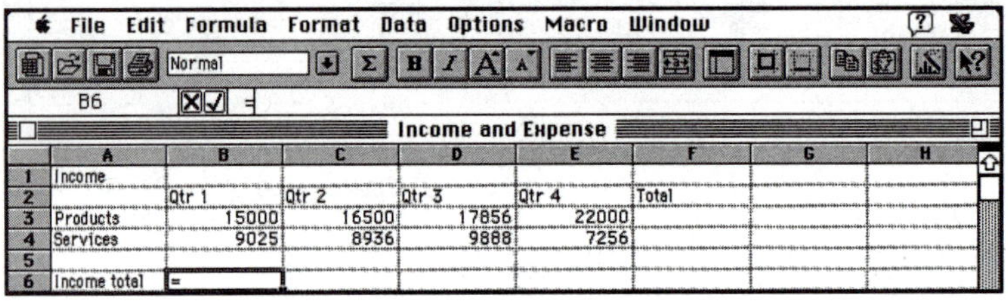


Figure 6.13
*Beginning the formula.*

## Easy Addition

Next, use the Autosum tool.

1. Select the cell to the right of "Expense total" and under the Qtr 1 column in cell B14.
2. Click the Autosum Tool and look at the formula bar. You should see the formula shown in figure 6.14:
3. Enter the formula with a click on the Enter box.

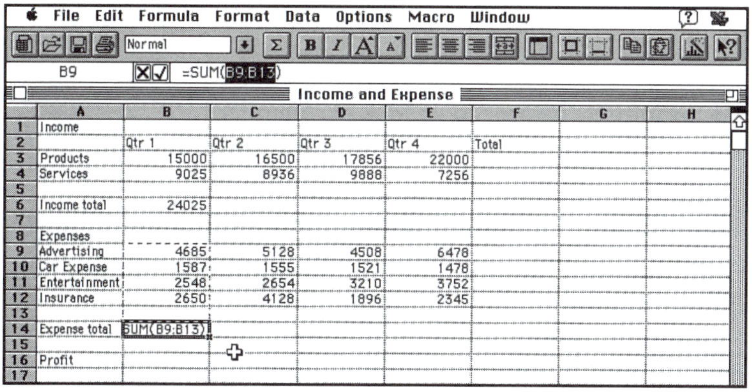


**Figure 6.14**
*Expense total formula.*

# The Bottom Line

To create a formula that will subtract the Expense total from the Income total, complete these steps:

1. Select the cell to the right of the "Profit" heading and under the Qtr 1 column.

2. Type an equal sign (=) and click the cell holding the Qtr 1 Income total (see fig. 6.15).

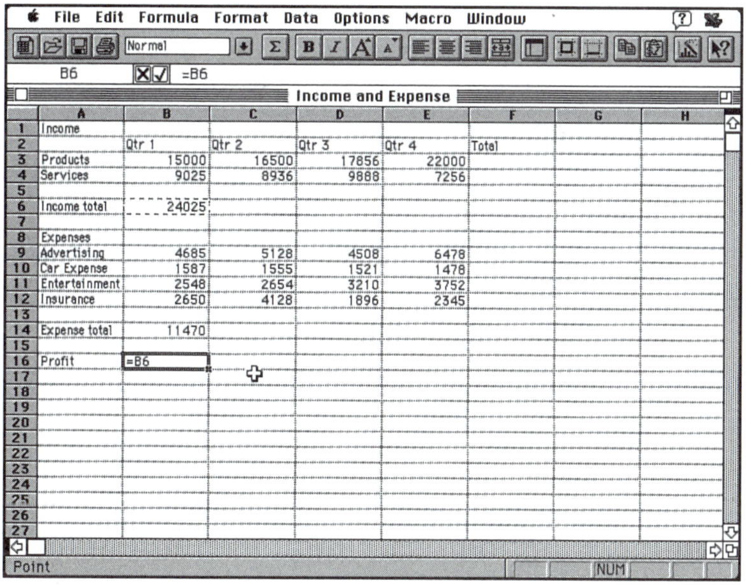


**Figure 6.15**
*Formula started.*

3. Type a minus sign (–) and click the cell holding the Qtr 1 Expense total.

4. Check your formula bar. It should look like figure 6.16.

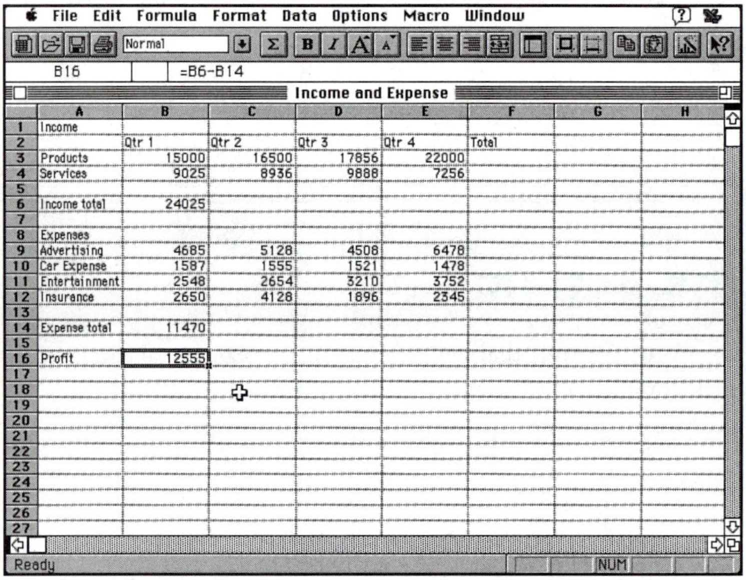


**Figure 6.16**
*The profit formula.*

5. Enter the formula with a click on the Enter box.

To add Products for all four quarters, do the following:

1. Select F3, the cell that should hold the "Products" total for the year at the top of the Total column.

2. Click the Autosum tool and look at the formula bar. It should look like figure 6.17.

3. Enter the formula.

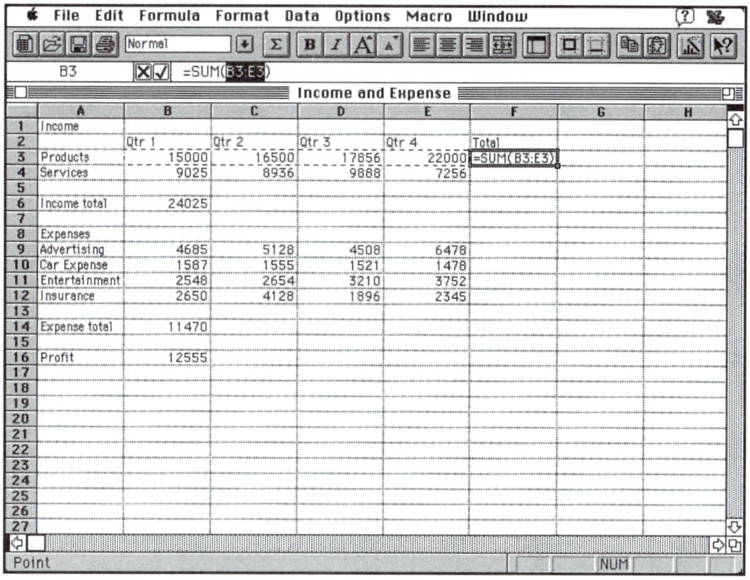


**Figure 6.17**
*Products yearly total.*

# Advertising Expense Total

1. Select F9, the cell that should hold the Advertising total for the year.
2. Click the Autosum tool.
3. Enter the formula.

# Autofill

Go back to the first formula and copy it.

1. Select the Income total formula in B6 with a click.
2. Put your pointer on the fill handle and click and drag over to the Totals column (column F) as shown in figure 6.18.

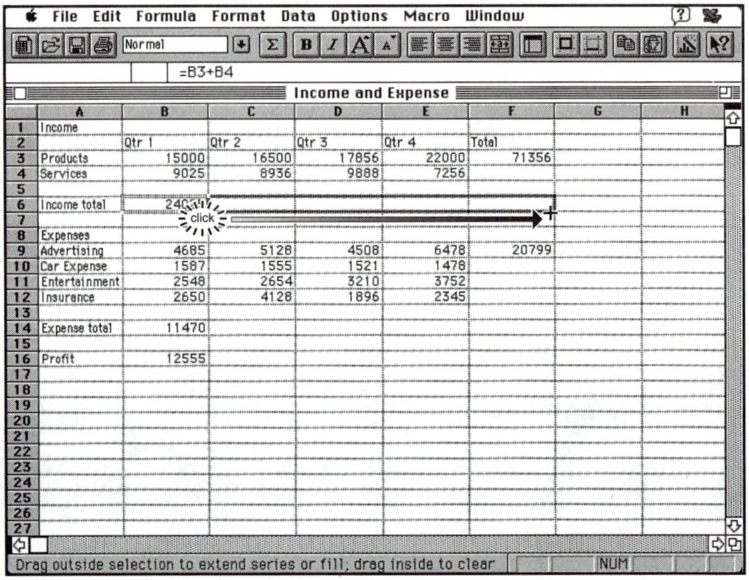


**Figure 6.18**
*Copying the formula.*

# Did the Copy Work?

1. Click the total at the bottom of Qtr 2 and look up at the formula bar.
2. Does this formula make sense? Is it adding up Qtr 2 totals for Products and Services?

   See how Excel has adjusted the formula so that the numbers in column C are added together rather than the numbers in column B? This is relative referencing.
3. Check the other formulas created by the Autofill process by selecting the cells with the totals one at a time and reading the formula bar.

# Copy Expense and Profit Totals to the Right

1. Select the Expense total for Qtr 1; put your pointer on the fill handle; click and drag over to the Total column.

2. Select the Profit total for Qtr 1; put your pointer on the fill handle; click and drag over to the Total column.

## Copy the Products Total Down

1. Select the Product total at the top of the Totals column.
2. Put the pointer on the fill handle.
3. Click and drag down just one cell, where you need the Services total.
4. Double check the accuracy of the copied formula by clicking it and looking at the formula bar. Is this the correct total for Services?

## Copying the Advertising Total

1. Select the Advertising total in the Totals column.
2. Put your pointer on the fill handle.
3. Click-drag down the whole column until reaching the last expense category (see fig. 6.19).

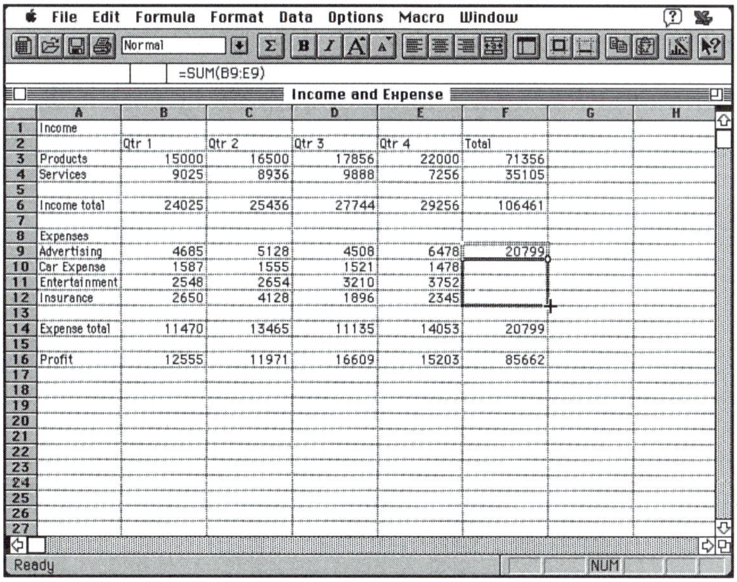


**Figure 6.19**
*Copying the Advertising total from top to bottom.*

4. Select the new total for the second expense category (Car Expense); cast an eye at the formula bar and double check that the new formula is doing its job. The formula bar should read `=SUM(B10:E10)`.
5. Save the worksheet by clicking the Save tool.

# Summary

To get the result you want, where you want it, carefully select the cell that should hold your formula. Start all formulas you create yourself with an equal sign. Use the Autosum tool to add up columns and rows of numbers. Always try to create the first formula in a series and use Autofill to copy the formula. Always make sure that the newly copied formula is correct by selecting the cell with the new formula and looking at the formula bar.

# Exercises

1. With which character do formulas always begin?
2. What is the name of the method that allows you to copy formulas?
3. What happens when you click on a cell to enter a formula?
4. What term describes the way Excel adjusts formulas that are copied?
5. If you have a numeric keypad, which mathematical operators are on it?

7th Encounter

# Selecting and Moving Cells

## Goal

Learn common techniques for selecting and moving cells and cell ranges.

## What You Will Need

Start with Excel running and with the Income and Expense worksheet visible on the screen.

## Terms of Enfearment

Select
Highlight
Autoselect
Discontinuous
Select All
Drag and Drop
Cell Range

# Briefing

## Exact Change

One of the basic rules that most Macintosh programs share is the requirement that you have to *select* or *highlight* your work before making changes. The change can be almost anything: from moving the cells to another location, to copying a formula, to making a heading larger, to deleting the contents of the selected cell or cells.

Learning how to efficiently select cells and groups of cells (called ranges) gets you to the finish line more quickly. Depending on what you need to do, you can select one cell, a group of cells, more than one range of cells at the same time, whole columns and whole rows, and the entire worksheet at the same time.

## . . . As the Driven Snow

In a selected range, the cells are black instead of white, except for the first cell clicked when making the selection, which is white. The white cell is your current cell address. If you start typing after selecting a range, the typed characters are entered into the white cell. You can always tell which cell is currently selected by looking at the formula bar.

To start typing or to change a cell in some way, you often need to select just one cell. The most typical method is to click the mouse button after moving the crosshair pointer over the cell. Another common selecting method is using the cursor arrow keys, the Return, and Tab keys. *To move to a cell is to select it.*

Frequently, it makes sense to select more than one cell at a time. This way, you can change all the selected cells at the same time, rather than one at a time. A group of cells is called a range.

# Range Rover

To select a range, click and drag the mouse pointer. You are highlighting cells as you move. Usually, it is most efficient to drag diagonally, from the top left cell to the bottom right cell.

You can also select a range of cells by clicking on one end of the range and then holding down the Shift key while clicking on the other end. Another selection technique is called *Autoselect*. Autoselect is a method that tells Excel to select a whole block, or section of cells, at the same time.

To select a block of columns containing data, click and drag down the first column from the first row to the last row. Move the mouse pointer to the right edge of the selected range, hold down the Shift key, and double-click (see fig. 7.1).

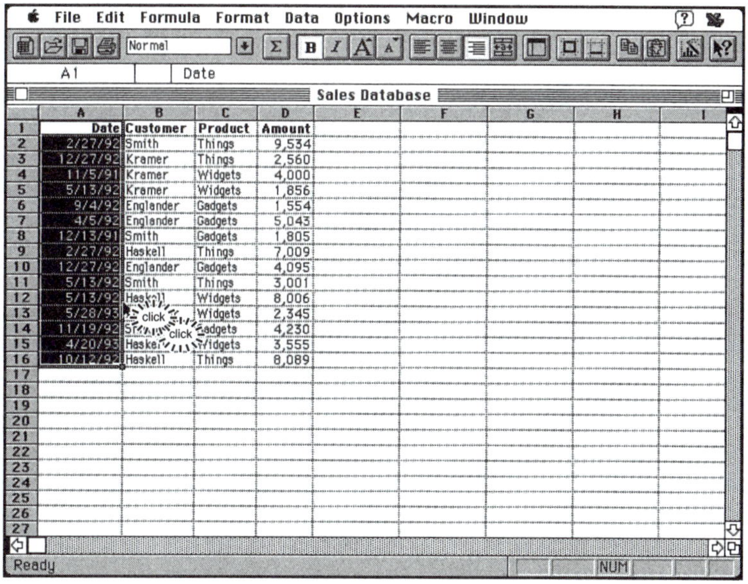


**Figure 7.1**
*Autoselecting columns.*

# New Kids on the Block

To select a block of rows, click and drag along the first row. Move the mouse pointer to the bottom edge of the selected range, hold down the Shift key, and double-click.

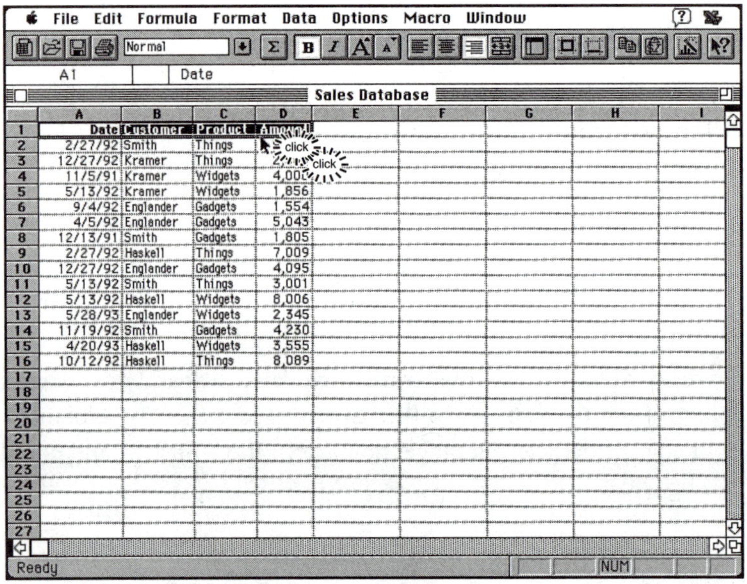


**Figure 7.2**
*Autoselecting rows.*

Sometimes, it's more efficient to select more than one range at the same time. For example, you can select all the headings, those going across and those going down, and then make them all bigger.

To select more than one range at the same time, select one range, release the mouse button, move the pointer to the first cell of the next range, hold the Command key down, and drag to the last cell. This is a technique you can impress your friends with. So practice.

Sometimes entire columns or rows have to be selected. Select a column by clicking on the column letter at the top border of the worksheet. Select a row by clicking on the row number at the left border of the worksheet.

There are many reasons for selecting the entire worksheet—it requires just one mouse click. When the entire worksheet is selected, any changes that affect the whole worksheet can be made just once.

To *Select All*, click the little juncture box to the left of the column headings and above the row headings. Watch out for the close box, lurking just above (see fig. 7.4).

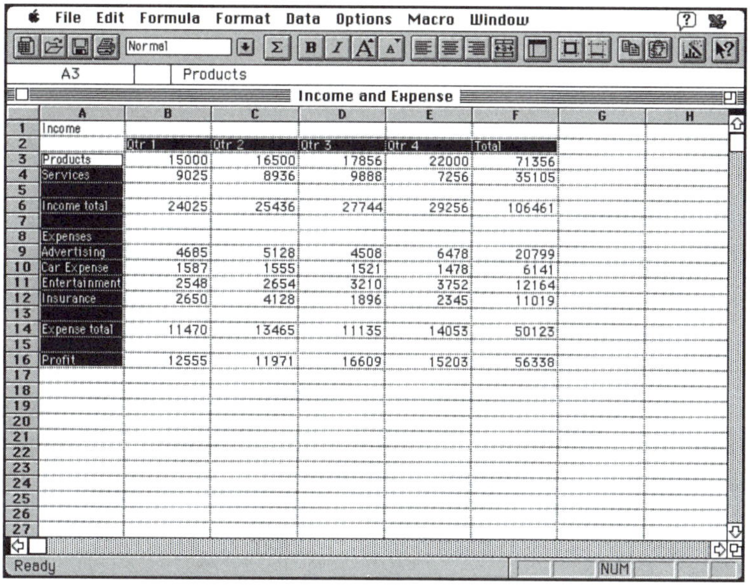


**Figure 7.3**
*Discontinuous ranges selected with the help of the Command key.*

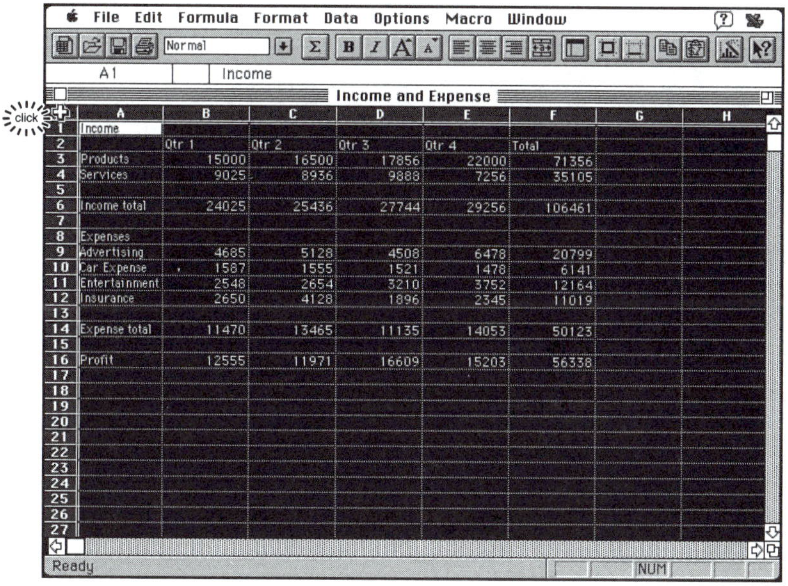


**Figure 7.4**
*Pointer on junction box.*

# Drop in Anytime

One major reason for selecting a range of cells is to move them. A great feature called *Drag and Drop* lets you move one cell or a group of cells easily from one location to another.

You can use Drag and Drop by moving the mouse pointer to an edge of the selected cell(s). When it becomes a left-leaning pointer, click and drag to the new location. You can see a gray border that shows you where the cells will land when you release the mouse pointer (see fig. 7.5).

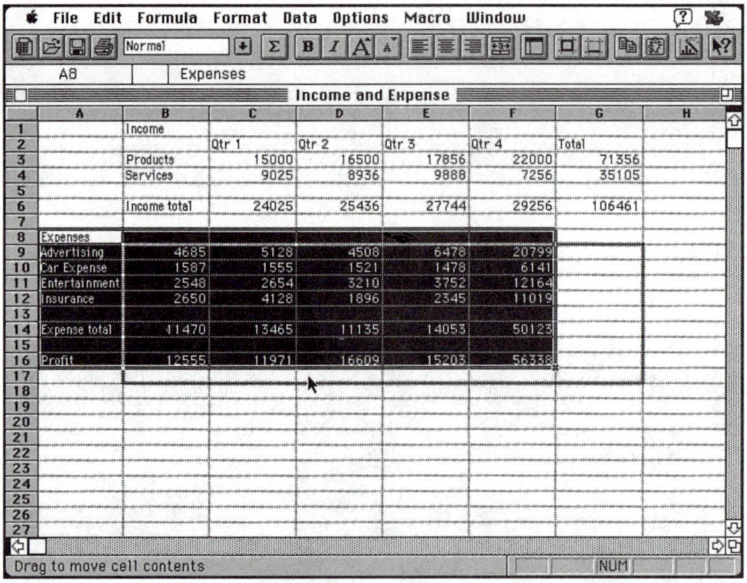


**Figure 7.5**
*Drag and Drop.*

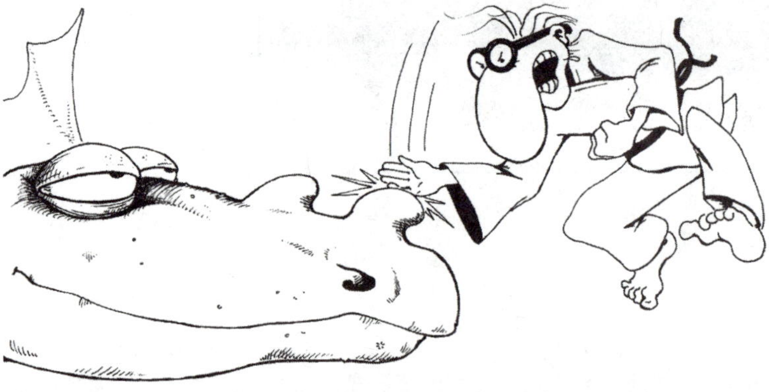

# They're Out To Get Us

Sometimes, you no longer need a range to be selected. To deselect it, just click anywhere. Whatever cell is clicked becomes the active cell, and no *cell range* is selected. To deselect a range, you can also press one of the cursor arrow keys. The active cell will be the only selected cell.

Occasionally, you need to select a different range. Just go ahead and do it. The previously selected range will no longer be selected, and the new one will be.

If you don't select as many cells as you mean to or you select too many cells, you can hold down the Shift key and click farther out or farther in. Frequently, this method lets you extend or reduce the range exactly as needed.

> It can be easy to move one or more cells with the Drag and Drop technique—by mistake! Take a deep breath, try not to panic, and use the Undo command. This is a good time to introduce the keyboard command for Undo, which is Command-Z. Memorize this one right now!

# Practice

In the next encounter, we'll look at methods that can make a worksheet look better. All of these methods require that you select one or more cells. To get ready for the next encounter, you should practice some selecting methods.

## Selecting Single Cells and Ranges

1. Select the Income total for Qtr 2 by clicking on C6. While there, double check the formula by glancing at the formula bar.

2. Press the right-arrow key until you reach the total for all four quarters in cell F6. Make sure that the formula is correct.
3. Press the up-arrow key to move to cell F4 and check the formula that sums up the Services income.
4. Select the following ranges: B3:F16, A2:E4, and F9:F12.

## The Syncopation of Shift-Click

1. Select all the numbers. Click and release the mouse button on B3.
2. Move the mouse, *without* holding down the mouse button, until the crosshair is positioned over F16.
3. Hold down the Shift key with the hand that isn't controlling the mouse and click the mouse button. The screen should look like figure 7.6.

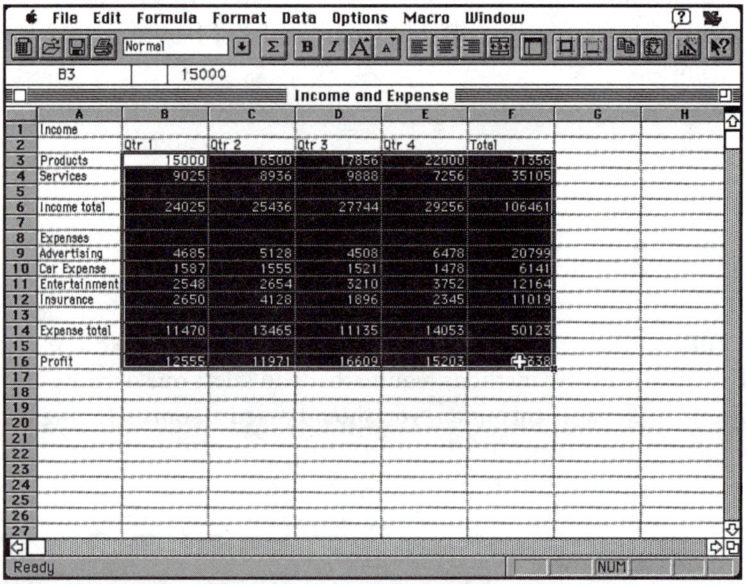


**Figure 7.6**
*Range selected.*

# Big Sky Country

Sometimes, you need to select larger ranges, so try selecting one now, just for the fun of it. How about A1:K30?

1. Click A1 to select it.
2. Click the down arrow in the vertical scroll bar until you see row 30.
3. Don't click on any cells yet, just click the right arrow in the horizontal scroll bar until you see column K.
4. Move the mouse pointer until it's hovering over K30 (Don't Click Yet) and hold down the Shift key with your other hand.
5. *NOW*, click K30.
6. Press the Tab or the Return key. Either one will move you back to the first screen.

# The Cool Cadence of Command-Click

1. Click and drag across the column headings from Qtr 1 to Total. Release the mouse button.
2. Hold down the Command key. Click on the Advertising heading, keep the mouse pointer down, and drag to the last row heading.
3. Deselect the selections by pressing the down-arrow key. What happened? Where is the cell pointer?
4. Using this same method, select the Income totals, the Expense totals, and the Profit formulas, at the same time (see fig. 7.7).

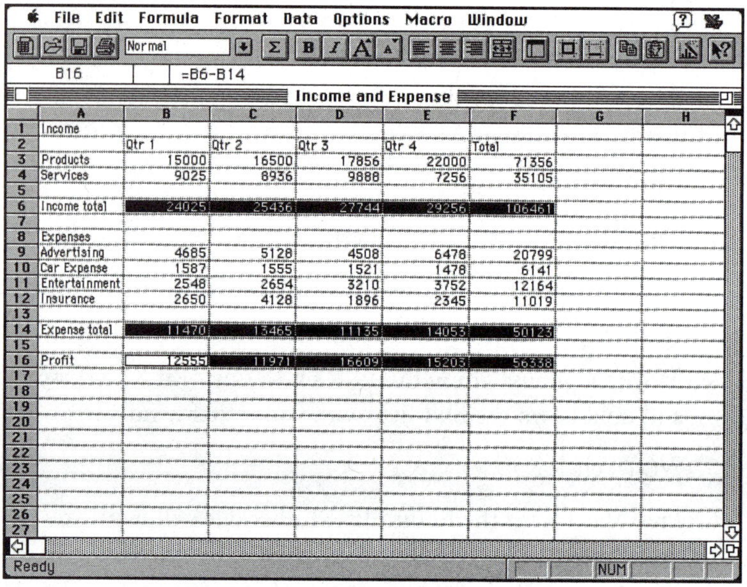


| | A | B | C | D | E | F | G | H |
|---|---|---|---|---|---|---|---|---|
| 1 | Income | | | | | | | |
| 2 | | Qtr 1 | Qtr 2 | Qtr 3 | Qtr 4 | Total | | |
| 3 | Products | 15000 | 16500 | 17856 | 22000 | 71356 | | |
| 4 | Services | 9025 | 8936 | 9888 | 7256 | 35105 | | |
| 5 | | | | | | | | |
| 6 | Income total | 24025 | 25436 | 27744 | 29256 | 106461 | | |
| 7 | | | | | | | | |
| 8 | Expenses | | | | | | | |
| 9 | Advertising | 4685 | 5128 | 4508 | 6478 | 20799 | | |
| 10 | Car Expense | 1587 | 1555 | 1521 | 1478 | 6141 | | |
| 11 | Entertainment | 2548 | 2654 | 3210 | 3752 | 12164 | | |
| 12 | Insurance | 2650 | 4128 | 1896 | 2345 | 11019 | | |
| 13 | | | | | | | | |
| 14 | Expense total | 11470 | 13465 | 11135 | 14053 | 50123 | | |
| 15 | | | | | | | | |
| 16 | Profit | 12555 | 11971 | 16609 | 15203 | 56338 | | |

**Figure 7.7**
*Selected cells.*

# Don't Get Addled Adding Columns

Select Column F and insert a column between F and E. (Just as a reminder: click one of the formulas in column F and check it in the formula bar.) You should see that the quarters are being summed up.

1. Click directly on the F up in the column heading. Choose Insert from the Edit menu.

   What was in the F column is in the G column, and the F column is empty. Do the formulas, now in Column G, still make sense?

2. Click on one of them, look at the formula bar, and check it. It should still be working.

# Kill that Column

To delete the extra column, click on the column heading at the top of the empty column and choose Delete from the Edit menu (see fig. 7.8).

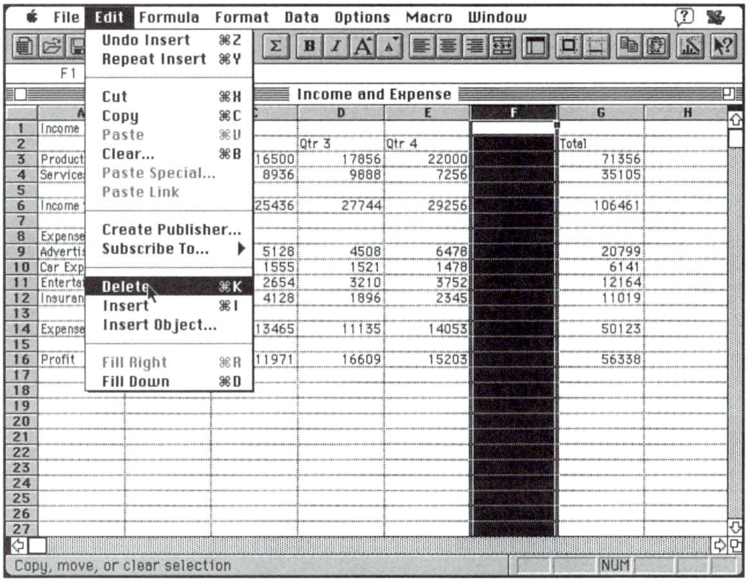


Figure 7.8
*Choosing Delete from the Edit menu.*

# Rowdy with New Rows

Before inserting a new row between the line holding the Profit and the Expense total, first look at the formula that returns the Profit. Click any of the formulas in row 16 and review the formula in the formula bar.

To add a new row, click the number 16 in the row heading and choose Insert from the Edit menu. Verify that the formula in the Profit row, which has been pushed down, is still doing what it should be doing: `=B6-B14`.

# Summary

Always select cells before attempting to type in them or change them in any way. You can use many different selection techniques (see table 7.1) on the following page. Moving to a single cell by any method selects it.

Select a range by clicking and dragging. Use the Click-Shift-Click method to quickly select larger ranges. Select discontinuous ranges by holding down the Command key while selecting the different ranges. Select columns and rows by clicking column letters and row numbers. Select the whole worksheet by clicking the area just below the close box.

### Table 7.1. A Select Group of Select Techniques

| *To Select* | *Do This* |
|---|---|
| Cell | Click it or move to it. |
| Range | Click and drag. |
| | Click and release on one end of range, hold down the Shift key, and click on the other end. |
| Discontinuous ranges | Select the first range, release the mouse button, hold down the Command key, select the second range, and so on. |
| One or more rows | Click the row number at the far left of row. |
| One or more columns | Click the column letter at the top of column. |
| Entire worksheet | Click in junction of columns and rows at the top left, under the close box. |
| Block of cells | Shift-double-click with pointer on edge of cell. |

# Exorcises

1. What is a group of cells called?
2. What do you first have to do before changing a cell?
3. What key must you press to select discontinuous ranges?
4. How do you select the entire worksheet?
5. What menu holds the Insert command?

8th Encounter

# Enhancing the Look of the Worksheet

## Goal

Gain control of basic techniques that make worksheets readable, understandable, and good looking on the screen and on the printed page.

## What You Will Need

Start with Excel running, with the Income and Expense worksheet visible, and with all the formulas completed.

## Terms of Enfearment

Formatting
Font
Typeface
Style Box
Best Fit
Alignment

# Briefing

In this encounter, we look at changing the appearance of the text and numbers. This is called *formatting.* We're preparing the worksheet to be viewed by others, printed, and distributed.

If the worksheets are meant for your eyes only, you won't need to spend much time formatting. If others will be seeing them, you'll want to spend time making them look so good you'll knock their socks off.

Try to format your documents at the end of the process, after you have entered all the text, numbers, and formulas. It's usually a waste of time to work on the formatting before everything else is formalized and complete.

There's no need to go overboard—just a few tweaks, a little maximizing the positive here, and a little de-emphasis of your not-so-great numbers there.

# Fontastic

Possibly the most important decision and the one which should be made first is which *font* or *typeface* to use. It's important because it influences the rest of the formatting decisions. For example, choosing a smaller font will allow you to have narrower columns and, therefore, more of them on the page.

Frequently, the font for the entire worksheet should be changed so that the worksheet looks as good as possible when printed.

The font Excel uses as its normal (default) choice is Geneva 10, which is good looking on screen and on printers such as inkjets but not when printed from laser printers.

Times and Helvetica are the most commonly used laser printer fonts. Laser fonts do not have city names, like New York and Chicago. Times is small, readable, and elegant. In figures 8.1 and 8.2, you can see how much more information can fit on a page after the font has been changed from Geneva 10 to Times 9.

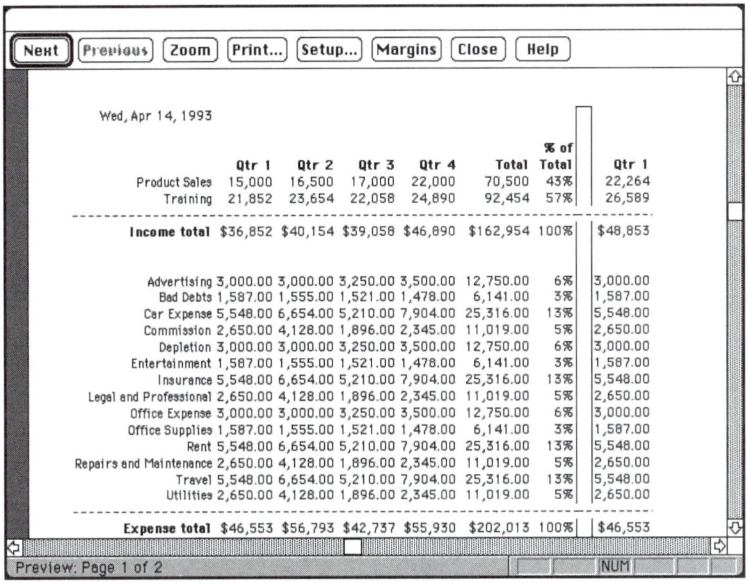


**Figure 8.1**
*Worksheet using Geneva 10.*

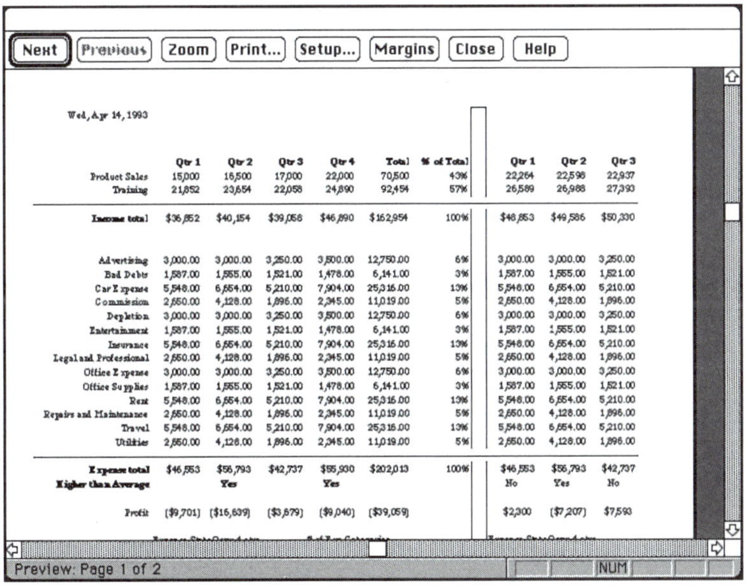


**Figure 8.2**
*Same worksheet using Times 9.*

Font and font size are controlled from the Font command on the Format menu. This dialog box lets you change fonts, font sizes, styles, and color at the same time. (If you have a color monitor, try not to get obsessive about endlessly changing colors.)

The fonts that appear in the list are the fonts that have been installed in the System of your computer. Geneva, Times, and Helvetica are all in the font package included with the Macintosh at the time of purchase.

Anywhere from 8 to 12 point type may be appropriate, depending on how much information you want to fit on the page.

You can also use the Font dialog box when you have just the headings selected, or some other smaller section selected, to experiment with different Font styles like Outline and Shadow and with color.

## You Look Fahbulous, Dahling!

Usually, you want text headings to stand out. The most common changes to headings include making them bold, larger, and aligning them to the right so that they line up with the numbers. You can go to the toolbar to give all these commands. A click on each of these tools accomplishes those changes on your selected text (see fig. 8.3). If you select a cell that is bold and right aligned, those two tools will change in appearance.

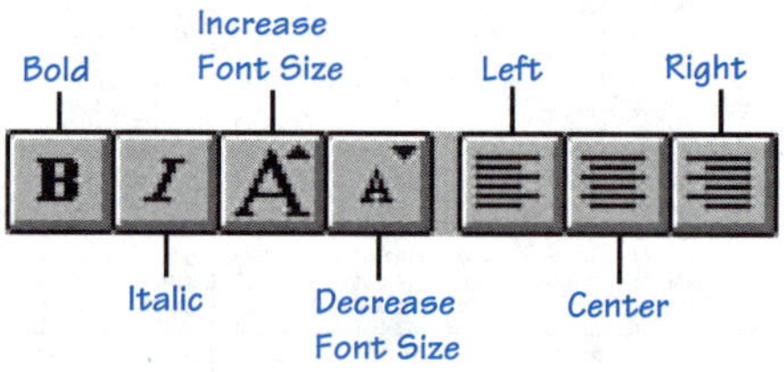


**Figure 8.3**
*Tools for formatting.*

## Makeover

You should usually enter numbers without any formatting. Type 1000 rather than $1,000.00, because you can use various formatting techniques to make your numbers look the way you want. Don't waste time typing the dollar signs and commas when you don't have to. You have more than enough to do just getting through this book! Percentages may be an exception, because typing 10% is easier than remembering to type .1 and then formatting it.

Use the *Style box* shown in figure 8.4 for the most commonly used number formats:

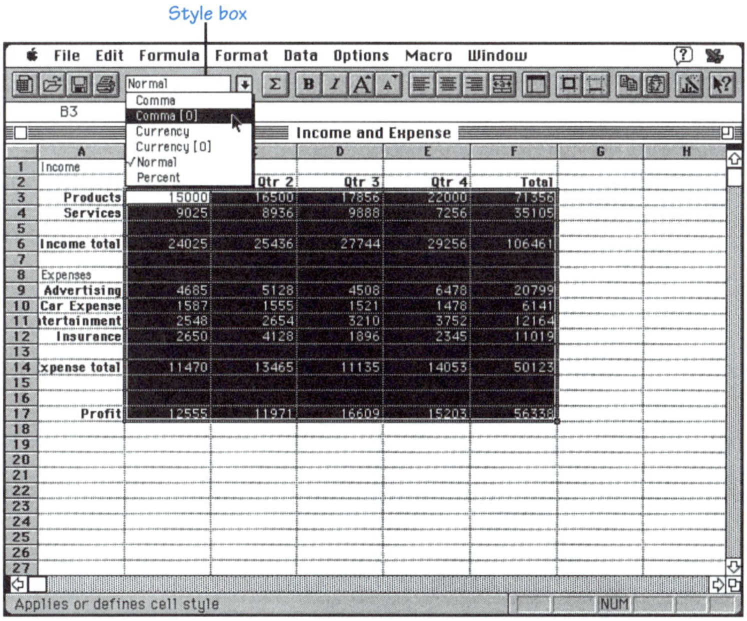


Figure 8.4
*Using the Style box.*

# Custom Tailoring

After you have decided on font and font size and have formatted your numbers, column widths should be adjusted so that each column is no wider, or narrower, than it should be.

To adjust a column's width, put the pointer on the right border of the column to the right of the column heading. When the pointer is on the border, it changes shape to a double-headed arrow (see fig. 8.5).

Click and drag the column line to the right to widen the column or left to narrow the column and then release the mouse button.

## All Together Now

To change the width of a number of columns at the same time, click and drag across the columns headings first. When you click and drag a column divider and release the mouse button, all the selected columns change at the same time (see fig. 8.5).

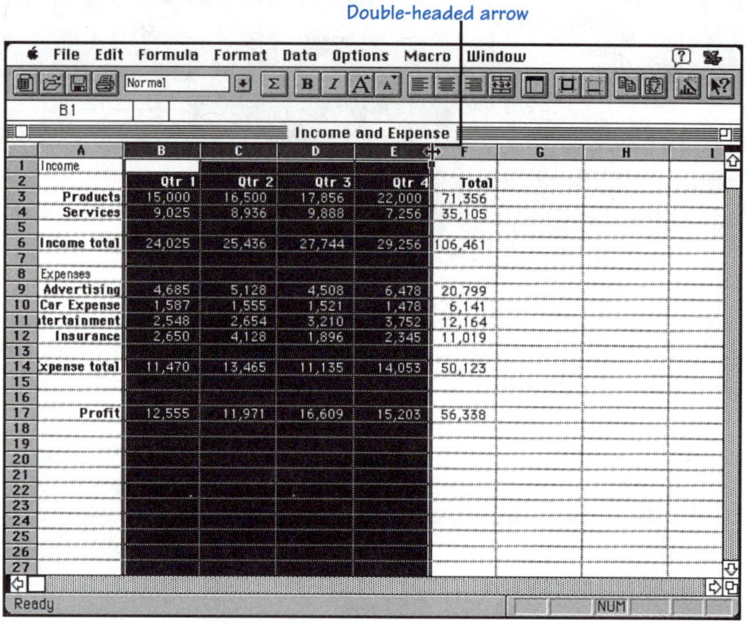


**Figure 8.5** *Four columns selected and changed at the same time.*

## Best Fit

Unlike trying to squeeze into that old tuxedo or bridesmaid dress, a column that best fits whatever is in the column has a width that's just wide enough to hold the widest item in that column; no wider, no narrower. To allow Excel to decide what would be the *best fit* for a column, double-click on a column divider rather than click-dragging it to the left or right (see fig. 8.6). It doesn't matter where the cell pointer is when doing this.

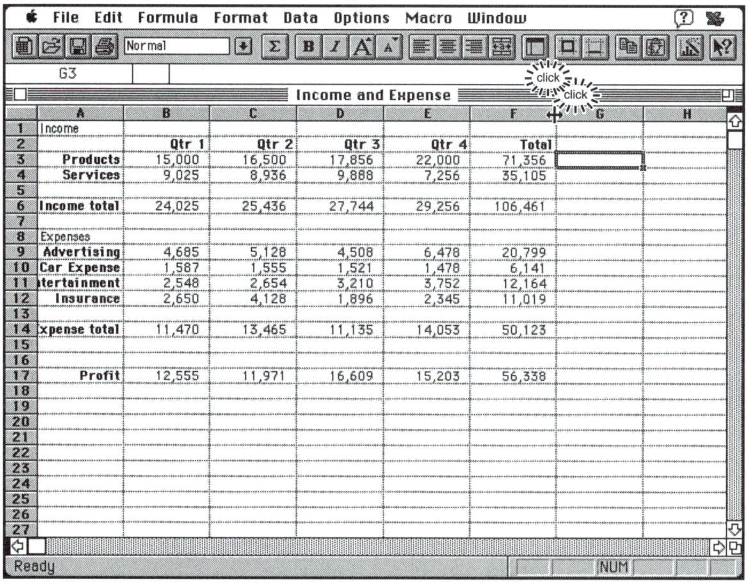


**Figure 8.6**
*Double-click for the best fit.*

If a number of columns are selected when you double-click the column divider, all of the selected columns change at the same time. Each selected column is changed individually to its best fit.

To most efficiently get all the columns to the best size, type all the data and do all your formatting. Then select the entire worksheet and double-click any column border (see fig. 8.7). All columns with data become perfectly sized. All others remain the standard width of 10 characters.

## Wuthering Heights

Row height can be changed just like column width. To do so, move the mouse pointer to the bottom border of the row, below the row number. The pointer changes to another double-sided arrow. Click and drag up to narrow; click and drag down to enlarge the row height.

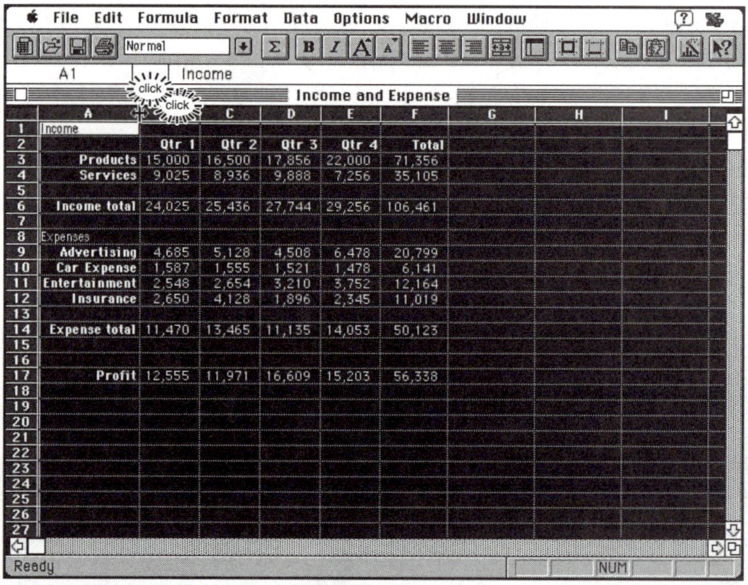


Figure 8.7
*Best fit with all the columns selected.*

## Centerpiece

To center a heading across a number of columns, type the heading into the first column. Click on the heading and drag across all the columns; then click the Center Across Columns tool (see fig. 8.8).

## Get Grid of It

To turn off the grid on the screen, choose Display from the Options menu and clear the X from the Gridlines check box (see fig. 8.9). This only affects what you see on your screen. We'll take a look at how to do the same procedure for the printout in the next encounter.

# Border Town

When the grid is turned off, certain parts of the worksheet can be accented with a border. To put a border around a group of cells or just one cell, select them (or it) and click the Outline tool. For a border along the bottom edge, select the Bottom Border tool, which is to the right of the Outline tool.

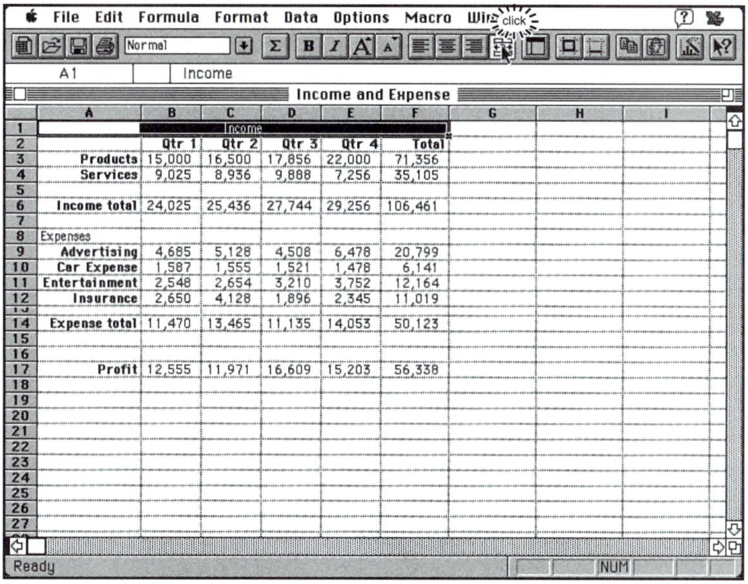


Figure 8.8
*After clicking the Center Across Columns tool.*

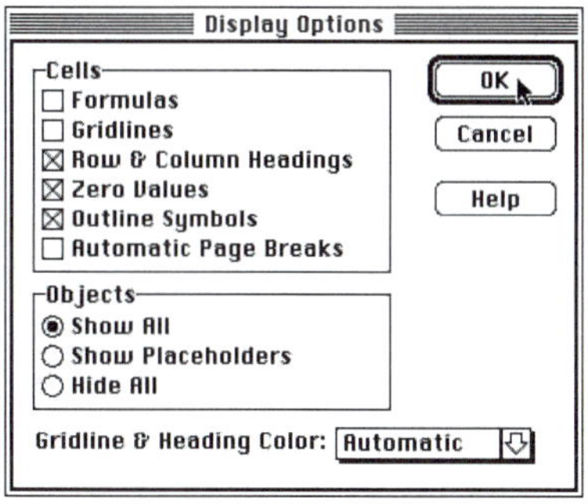


Figure 8.9
*The Options window with Gridlines cleared.*

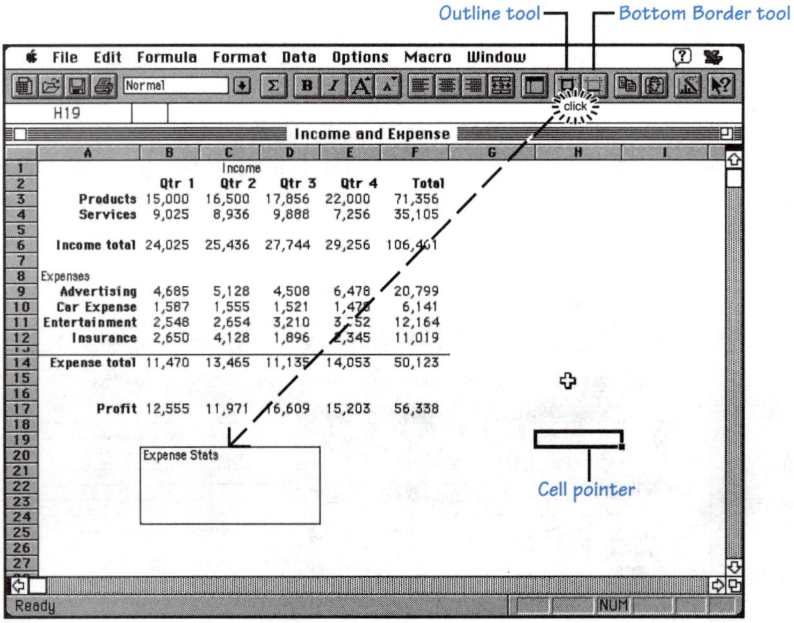


**Figure 8.10**
*The Outline tool and what it does.*

# They're Out To Get Us

## Clear the Decks

If you have been experimenting with lots of different formatting styles, the worksheet may become confusing rather than more readable. It sometimes make sense to clear out all the formatting and start again.

The Clear command on the Edit menu allows you to clear out just the formatting, not the contents of the selected cells. To return to plain text and numbers, choose Clear from the Edit menu, click the Formats button, and click OK.

If you change your mind after bolding certain cells, reselect them and click the Bold tool again to turn off the bold formatting. If you change your mind after using the Outline and Bottom Border tools, reselect the affected cells and choose Border from the Format menu (see fig. 8.11). You then can click the borders out of the boxes or change to another kind of border.

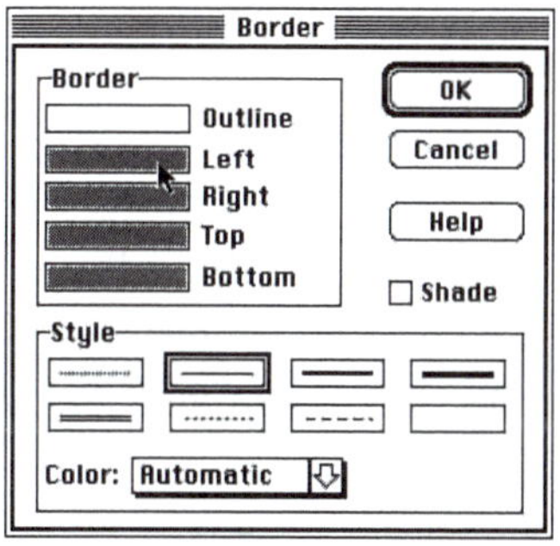


Figure 8.11
*Border choices.*

You can use the Decrease Font Size tool to reverse the Increase Font Size tool. To change the look of your numbers, choose another style from the Style box. If you format your numbers and suddenly the cells that hold the numbers are filled with pound (#####) signs as shown in figure 8.12, do not fear.

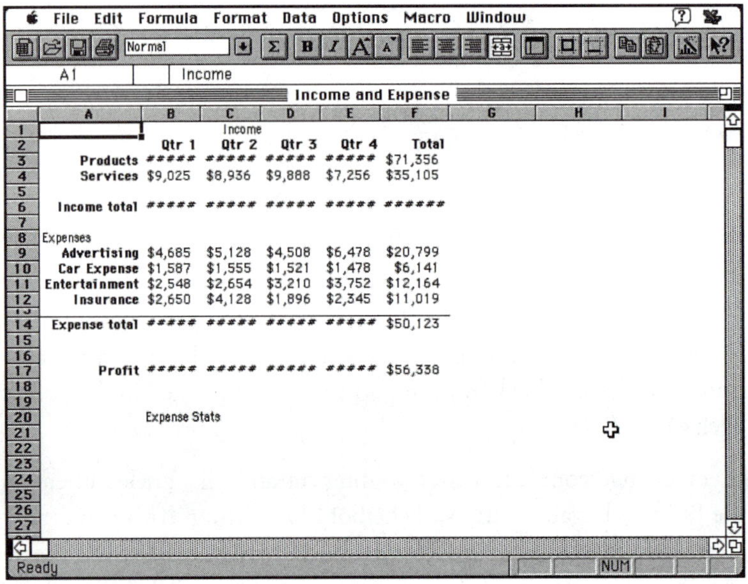


**Figure 8.12**
*Scrunched columns. (They're too narrow.)*

The numbers are still in the cells, safe and sound. The pound signs occur when the number of characters in a cell is more than can fit in the cell. Double-clicking on the column divider solves this problem immediately.

If you double-click on a column divider and the column becomes too wide, a wide text heading is probably in that column. Normally, it's fine for the heading to spill over. However, it's the one place where the double-click for Best Fit may give you a cell wider than it should be. To fix the problems, click and drag the column divider to the left to adjust the column *to fit the numbers* and not the long heading (see fig. 8.13).

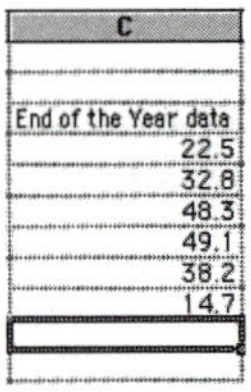


**Figure 8.13**
*Column fitting long head.*

# Practice

Begin by changing the font to Times 12:

1. Select the entire worksheet (click the juncture to the left of the columns and above the row numbers).
2. Choose Font from the Format menu and then change the Font and Font size to Times 12. You might have to scroll down your list to get to Times (see fig. 8.14). Click OK.

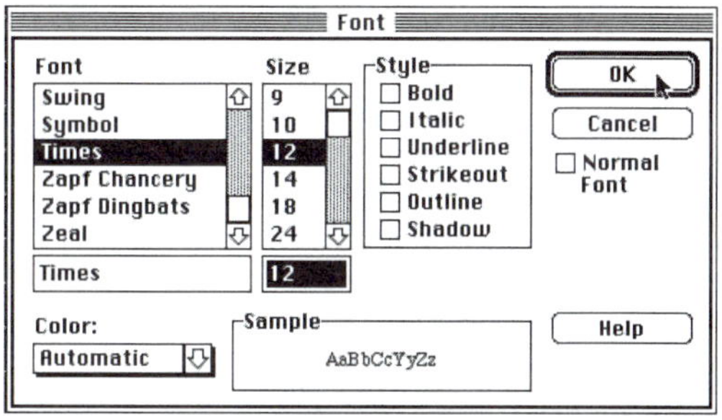


Figure 8.14
*Choosing a font.*

# Headstrong

1. To change the headings, select the column headings from Qtr 1 through Total.
2. Move the pointer up to the toolbar and click the Bold tool, the Increase Font Size tool, and the Right Align tool. Is that easy or what?
3. Do the same to the row headings, remembering to select them first.
4. Experiment with the Center Align, the Decrease Font Size, the Italic, and the Underline tools (see fig. 8.3).

# Playing the Numbers

1. Select all the numbers by clicking and dragging from the top left number just under the Qtr 1 heading to the last number down at the bottom right of your table.
2. Go up to the Style box, move the mouse pointer over the down arrow next to the style box, hold down the mouse button, and drag to Comma (0) as shown in figure 8.15.

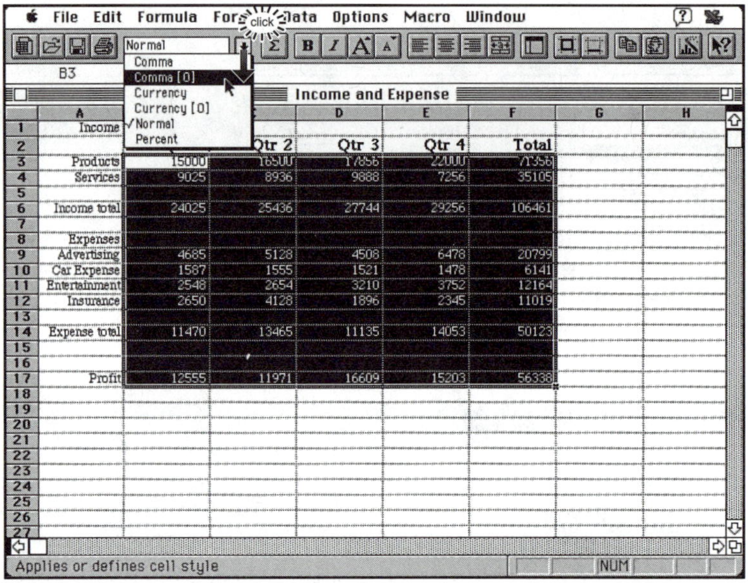


**Figure 8.15**
*Choosing the Comma (0) style from the Style box.*

# Column Capers

If the dreaded ##### appear, it's time to adjust the column width. Change all the columns in the worksheet at the same time by doing the following:

1. Select all the columns at the same time by clicking the juncture box below the close box.
2. Apply Best Fit with a double-click on any column divider. See how each column is adjusted individually?

3. To adjust the Total column, begin by clicking in any cell. (The whole worksheet is no longer selected.) Move the mouse pointer until it is on the column divider to the right and above the Total heading.
4. Click and drag to the right, just a little bit. Do the same again, only this time to the left. Keep adjusting until you like the look of the column.

## Adjust All Four Qtrs at the Same Time

To adjust the four columns that contain information on the four quarters, do the following:

1. Select Columns B:E.
2. Put the pointer on any one of the column dividers.
3. Click and drag the double-headed arrow. When you release the mouse button, all the selected columns change to the same width.
4. Return to Best Fit by double-clicking on one of the column dividers (B:E).

## Bottom Border

To add a bottom border to the rows between the numbers and formulas, do the following:

1. Select the cell directly above Income Total and drag over to the Total column. Click the Bottom Border tool (see fig 8.16).
2. Select the range above Expense total and click the Bottom Border tool again.

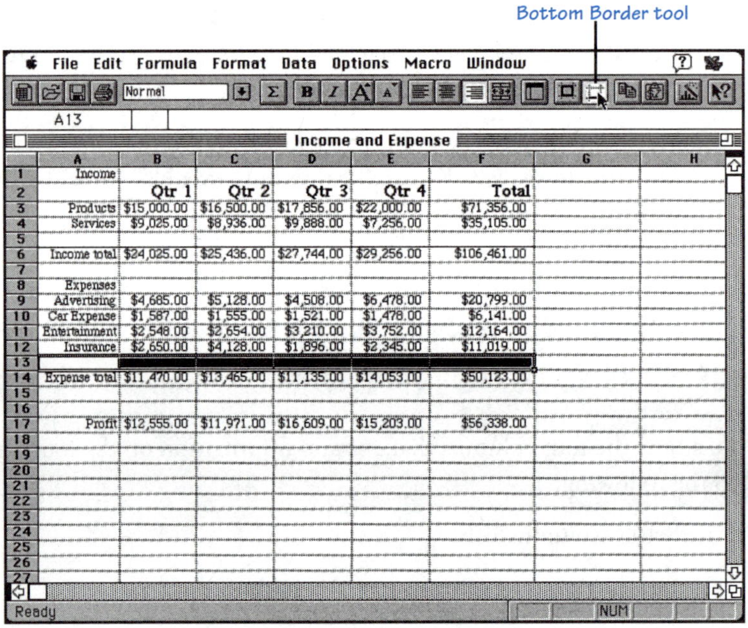


**Figure 8.16**
*A bottom border below the Expense categories.*

# Whitewash

To hide the grid on screen so that you can see the border a little better, choose Display from the Options menu and clear the box for Gridlines.

# Row Height

1. Change the row height on row 5 by moving the mouse pointer to the bottom border of the empty row.
2. Click and drag up just a little bit. Keep doing this until the number in the left section of the formula bar says `2.00`.

   Repeat these steps for row 13.

# Center Across Columns

Now that the columns are the proper width, center "Income" across them.

1. Select A1:F1. Note that "Income" is in A1.
2. Click the Center Across Columns tool.
3. Click the Bigger Font Size tool.
4. Do the Same with "Expenses."

Figure 8.17 shows your worksheet in all its glory.

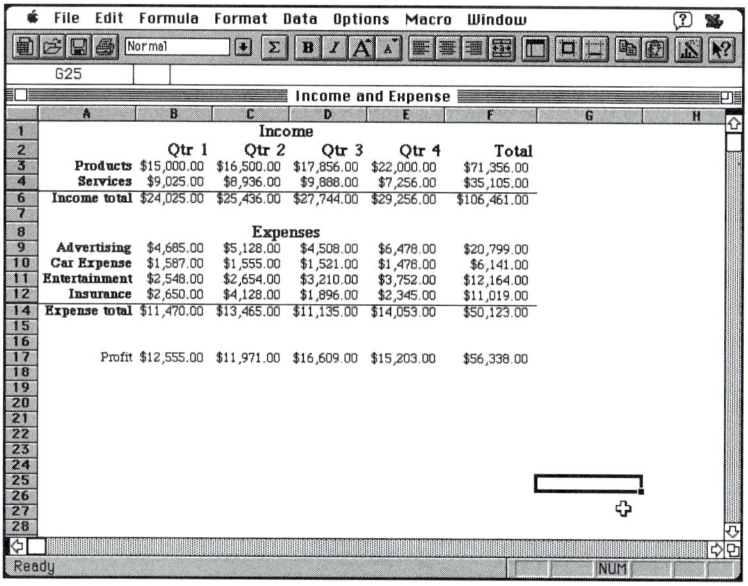


Figure 8.17
*Work in progress.*

# Summary

You've seen how you can change the worksheet from plain to interesting. You can use the Style Box, the Bold tool, the *Alignment* tools, and others on the Standard toolbar to change the look quickly and easily. You can adjust column width and row height as needed, and you can use borders to define and separate different areas.

# Exorcises

1. Name some fonts that look best when printed on a laser printer.
2. What dialog box allows you to change the style of your text from plain to shadow? Which menu is it in?
3. What should you do first: change font size or adjust column width?
4. Where do you position the mouse pointer to change the width of a single column? How do you know that Excel is ready to change the column width?
5. Describe the technique that achieves "Best Fit" for every column the same time.

9th Encounter

# Printing the Worksheet

## Goal

Learn basic techniques that enable you to print a fine-looking document.

## What You Will Need

Start with Excel running, with the Income and Expense worksheet visible, and with all the formulas and formatting completed. Document should appear ready to be printed.

## Terms of Enfearment

| | |
|---|---|
| Print Preview | Margins |
| Headers and Footers | Page Setup |
| Orientation | Default |
| Zoom button | |

# Briefing

By now, your document looks good enough to print. Well, almost good enough. You have a few more decisions to make, plus some additional activity before the printing.

Making the decision to print a document should always start with choosing *Print Preview* from the File menu. This command gives you a bird's eye view of the page(s) as they will look when printed.

Using Print Preview saves you from wasting paper and time over the long run. You can see whether the document looks the way you expect it to look on the page and can make changes without having to wait for the printout.

Excel makes certain assumptions, all of which can be changed, about how you want to print the worksheet. You can see these *default* settings in action when you first go into Print Preview mode (see fig. 9.1).

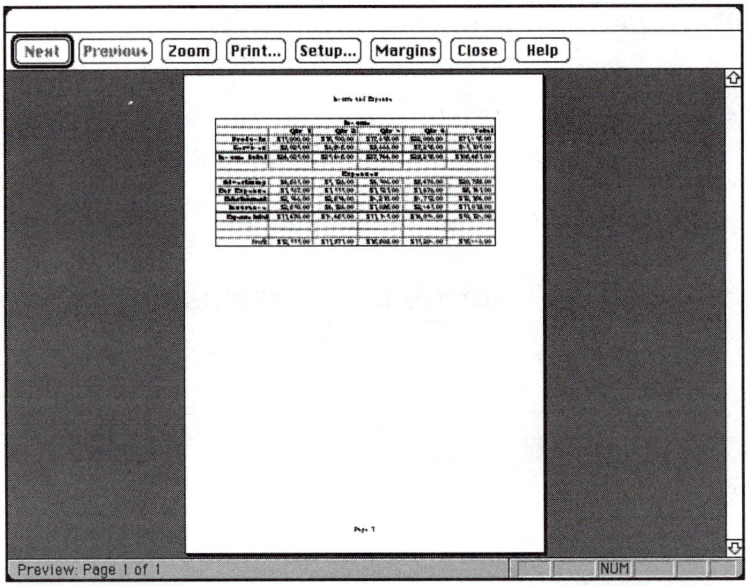


**Figure 9.1**
*Print Preview mode.*

# Default of De Preview

From the Print Preview mode, you can tell that every cell that contains any text, numbers, or formulas is printed; the row and column headings are not to print; the gridlines print; the document has *headers and footers*—the name of the file appears at the top of the page and the word "Page" followed by the page number appears at the bottom of the page—and the *orientation* is tall (portrait), rather than wide (landscape).

Figure 9.2 shows a document in Print Preview, which is set for landscape mode.

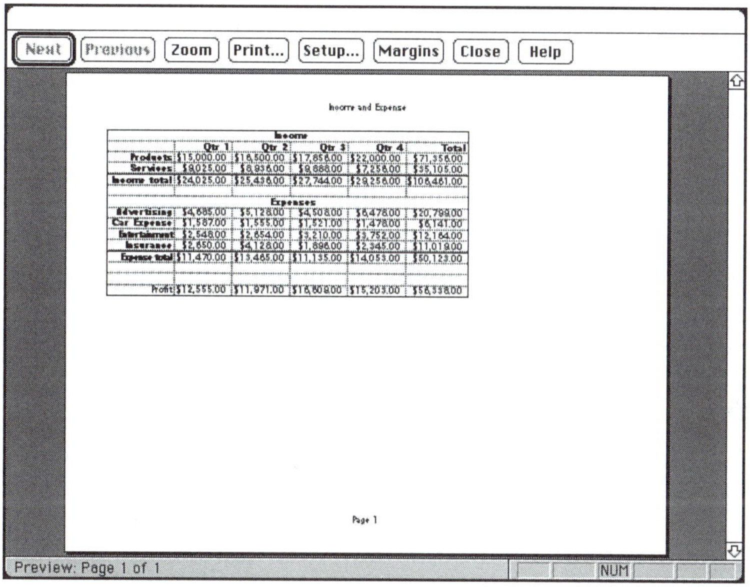


**Figure 9.2**
*Landscape mode.*

From figure 9.2, you can tell that the document is positioned at the upper, left side of the page.

# Cute as a Button

Useful is an understatement for the buttons along the top of the Preview window. You can check out different pages by clicking the Next or Previous buttons. A click on the *Zoom* button magnifies the page so that you can read it, and another click zooms back out. You can also click the pointer, which becomes a magnifying glass when hovering over the page. By clicking on a particular part of the page, you can zoom in for a closer look. Another click, and you're back to the bird's eye view. When the Margins button is clicked, dotted lines appear that indicate the margins. You can adjust the amount of white space (*margin*) around the page by dragging the selection handles at the end of the dotted lines. In the lower left of the Print Preview screen, you can see the current width as you are dragging the handle.

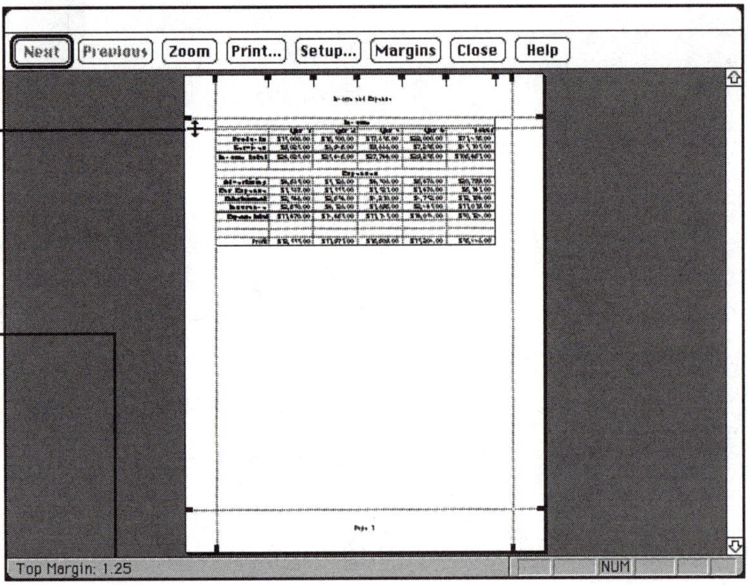


**Figure 9.3**
*The Status bar.*

# Close to the Edge

The kind of printer you're using determines how close you can print to the paper's edge. You may want to experiment with this when you're not dealing with a deadline. Fat chance of that ever happening! Start with a 1/2 inch (.50) on all four sides. See whether all your information is printed after changing to .25.

# This Is a Setup

Clicking the Setup button gives you the same window as choosing *Page Setup* from the File menu. The Setup window enables you to center the worksheet in the page, to turn the cell gridlines on or off, and to turn the row and column headings on or off.

It makes sense to print the gridlines and the row and column headings at first, but not for the final draft of a worksheet as shown in figure 9.4.

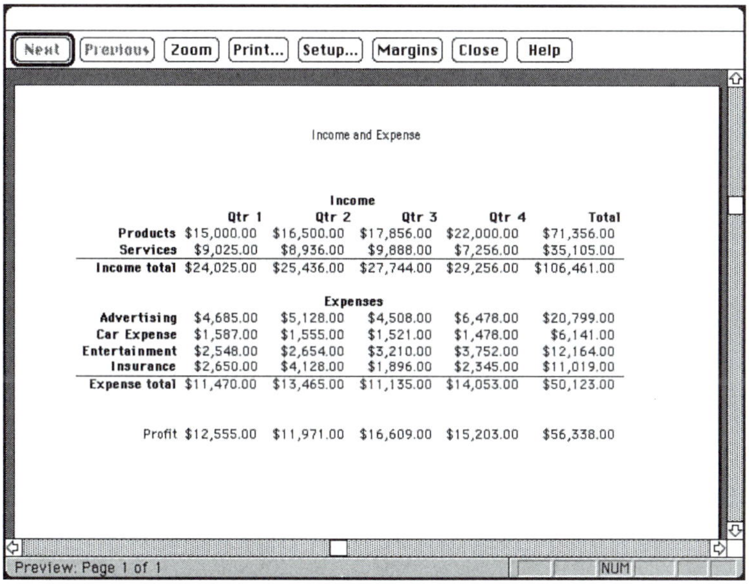


Figure 9.4
*A worksheet without gridlines and row and column headings.*

# From Head to Foot

Other buttons in the Setup window let you change the default headers and footers. The buttons in the Header and Footer window are described in

Microsoft Excel Help under "Header and Footer Codes" (see fig. 9.5). Basically, headers and footers are the same thing, but headers appear in the top margin, and footers appear in the bottom margin. Along with text, you can easily add the date, time, and page numbers to headers and footers.

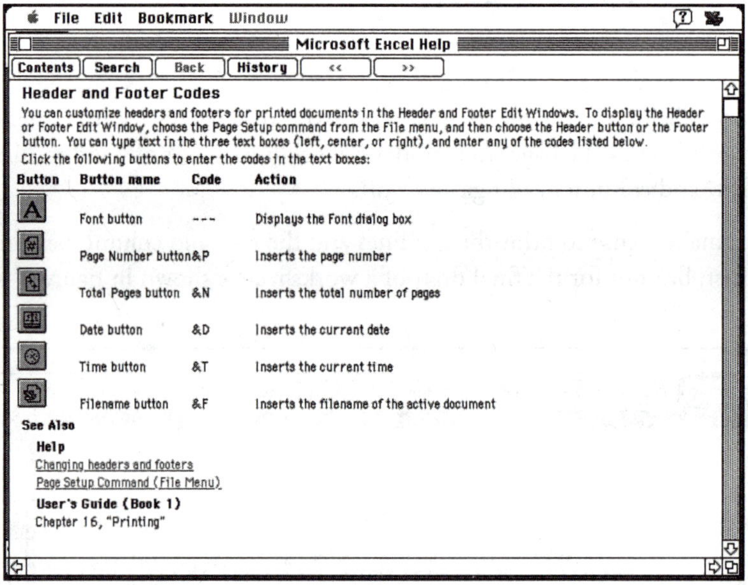


**Figure 9.5**
*Buttons in the Header and Footer windows.*

# For a Good Time . . .

The date and time change to reflect the date and time the document prints. This feature is very useful when you keep printing lots of drafts of your document, because it lets you know what's the most recent version. When it's midnight and you've just printed your 20th "final" draft, you'll thank your lucky stars for this one.

When the document looks ready to print in the Print Preview window, click the Print button, which displays the Print dialog box, just as the Print command on the File menu does.

Almost always, you just need to click Print. Sometimes, you need to ask for more copies. (Use a copier if you need more than five or six; it will be faster and cheaper.)

You might have a multiple page document and only want to print pages 3 and 4. In that case, click in the From box and type 3 and click in the To box and type 4.

# They're Out To Get Us

If you give the Print command and nothing happens, there may be a problem on the printing end.

Follow these troubleshooting steps:

1. Check that the printer is turned on.
2. Check all cables to see that they are tightly in place.
3. Choose Chooser from the Apple menu and make sure that the proper printer driver and port are selected. The port is the place (sort of a hole) in the rear of the computer that the printer cable plugs into.

On occasion, Print Preview shows you something totally unexpected. Maybe the page looks blank, or just some cells or a row or two are showing. Other times, Print Preview shows more than you want to print of the worksheet. This can really be discombobulating. When Print Preview does show you something different than you want to print, do the following:

1. Click the Close button to leave Print Preview.
2. In the worksheet, select the range that you want to print.
3. Go to the Options menu and choose Set Print Area. This tells Excel to print only the selected area.

If you give the Print command and then change your mind, you can cancel the printing by holding down the Command key and pressing the Period key (.).

## Where Did That Dotted Line Come From?

After you see a document in Print Preview or after printing, Excel adds funny lines to the screen that represent page breaks. Don't worry about them for now. We'll talk about them a little later.

# Practice

## Getting Ready To Print

If you do not know which port on your Macintosh holds the printer cable, get up and look at the back of the computer.

1. Trace the connection between the printer and your computer and take note of the icon above the port holding the cable.
2. If you are on a network and the connection isn't obvious, ask one of the local gurus to show you which cable hooks your computer to the printer.

Also ask the following questions:

- Is there more than one printer I can use?
- Where are the printers physically located?
- Which ones are appropriate for me to use?
- Which printer is the best quality and fastest?

## Choosing the Chooser

Make certain that your Macintosh knows which printer you are planning to use by doing the following:

1. Choose Chooser from the Apple menu.

2. Click the icon on the left that represents the kind of printer you are using.
3. Choose a particular printer on the right side of the window.
4. You may have to indicate which port on the computer holds the cable coming from the printer. The icon should match the one you noted earlier.
5. Close the Chooser window.

# Bird's Eye View

1. Choose Print Preview from the File menu.
2. Zoom in to look at the Header at the top of the page by moving the magnifying glass to the center top of the page and clicking.

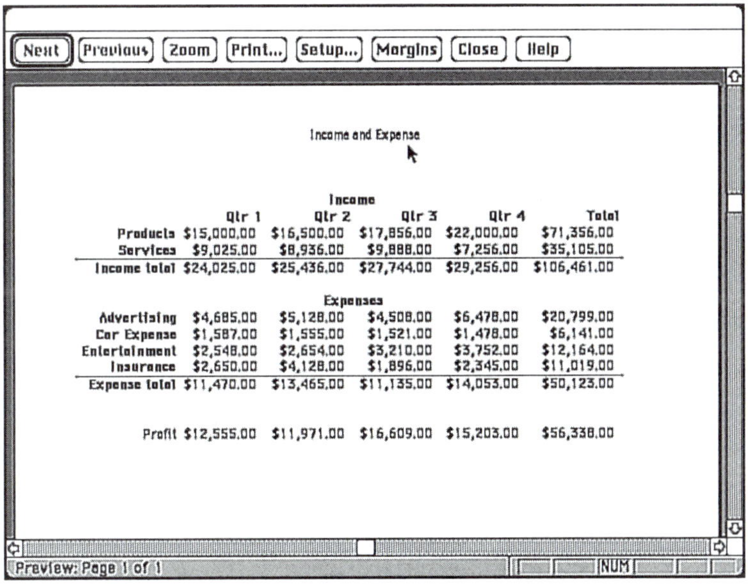


Income and Expense

Income

| | Qtr 1 | Qtr 2 | Qtr 3 | Qtr 4 | Total |
|---|---|---|---|---|---|
| Products | $15,000.00 | $16,500.00 | $17,856.00 | $22,000.00 | $71,356.00 |
| Services | $9,025.00 | $8,936.00 | $9,888.00 | $7,256.00 | $35,105.00 |
| Income total | $24,025.00 | $25,436.00 | $27,744.00 | $29,256.00 | $106,461.00 |

Expenses

| | | | | | |
|---|---|---|---|---|---|
| Advertising | $4,685.00 | $5,128.00 | $4,508.00 | $6,478.00 | $20,799.00 |
| Car Expense | $1,587.00 | $1,555.00 | $1,521.00 | $1,478.00 | $6,141.00 |
| Entertainment | $2,548.00 | $2,654.00 | $3,210.00 | $3,752.00 | $12,164.00 |
| Insurance | $2,650.00 | $4,128.00 | $1,896.00 | $2,345.00 | $11,019.00 |
| Expense total | $11,470.00 | $13,465.00 | $11,135.00 | $14,053.00 | $50,123.00 |
| Profit | $12,555.00 | $11,971.00 | $16,609.00 | $15,203.00 | $56,338.00 |

Figure 9.6
*Print preview window, zoomed in on default Header.*

3. Click anywhere in the text to zoom back out.

4. Look at the footer by clicking once on the bottom center of the page. It should say, `Page 1`.
5. Click the Zoom button to zoom in and out. Notice that it gives you less control over which part of the page comes into view.
6. Note that the gridlines are showing, but there are no row and column headings.

## Going Nowhere

Click the Next button and notice that nothing happens. In fact, the grayness of the button indicates that nothing happens unless the document has more than one page. In that case, you could turn to the next page, which would activate the Previous button.

## Changing Margins

1. Click the Margins button. Note the horizontal and vertical dotted lines that appear around the page and the little rectangles at the ends of the lines, which are called selection handles.
2. Move your pointer over either selection handle on the horizontal line at the top of the document. Note how the pointer changes to a double-sided arrow.
3. Click and drag down a small distance. When you release the mouse button, the page redraws with a larger top margin.
4. Note the column markers across the top of the page. Drag one or more of them to a new position to see how the column widths change. Return the column to an appropriate width.

# This Is a Setup

1. Click the Setup button (see fig. 9.7).

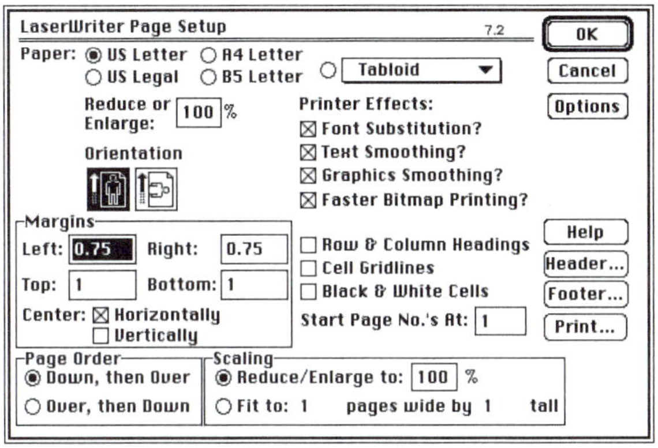


**Figure 9.7**
*The Page Setup dialog box.*

2. Select the second orientation button (the one on the right) and click OK. See how the page is now wider than it is long. This is called Wide (landscape) orientation and it is useful for printing worksheets with a lot of columns. You want to think of this option automatically as the number of columns increases.
3. Click the Setup button again.
4. Select the first orientation button to return the document to Tall (Portrait) orientation.
5. Click the Center Horizontally check box down near the bottom left.
6. Clear the Gridlines box over on the left side and click OK. Now we're talking!

You are again in Print Preview. This is definitely an easy way to center the document on the page without worrying about how to adjust the margins. Also note how the document looks more professional without the gridlines (see fig. 9.8).

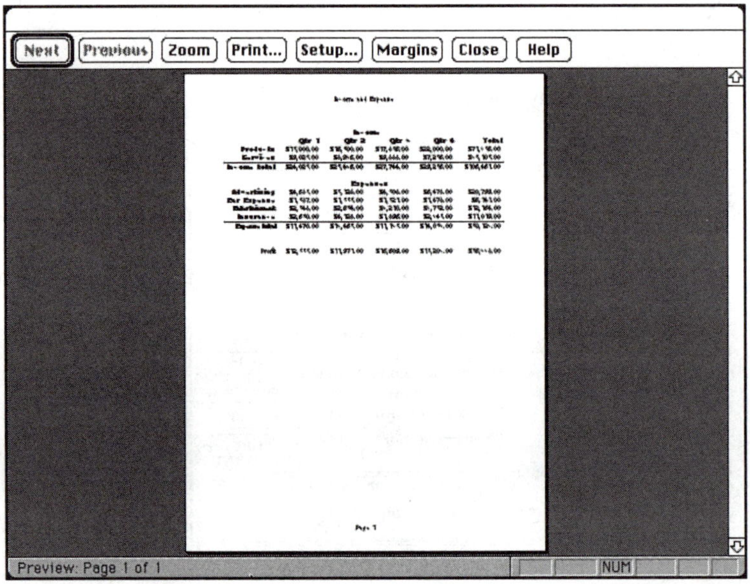


Figure 9.8
*Bird's Eye view.*

# Do Let It Go to Your Head

Click the Setup button again and then click the Header button. Observe &F in the center, which is the code that stands for the filename. If you follow along with this practice session, you will change the header as in figure 9.9 to create a new header (see fig. 9.10).

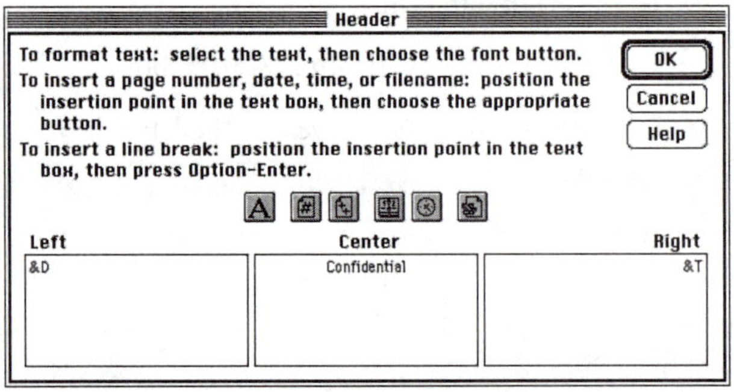


Figure 9.9
*The Header window*

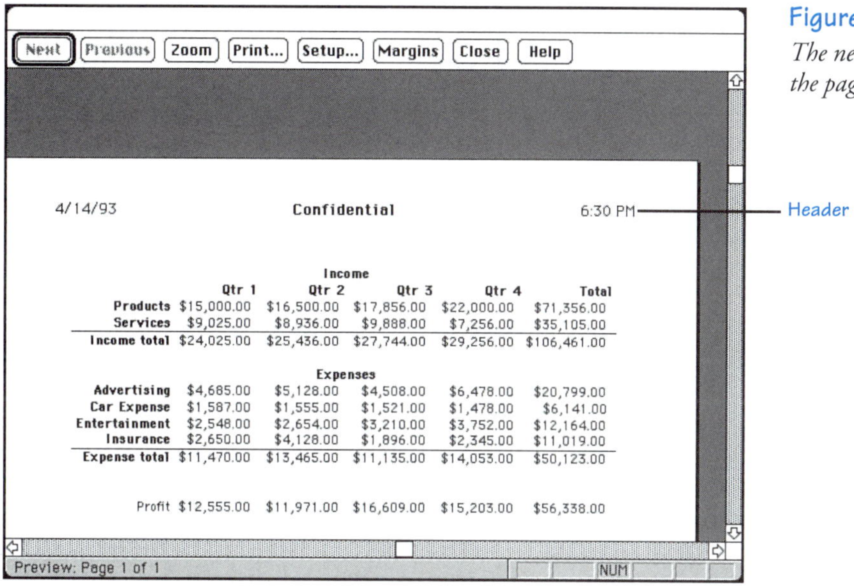


**Figure 9.10**
*The new header on the page.*

# Take All the Help You Can Get

1. Notice the Help button. Click it to see explanations of the icons.
2. Find the date and time icons, just to show yourself what they look like; then close the help window with a click on the close box.
3. Read the instructions along the top of the Header window.
4. Make sure that the insertion point is blinking in the left text box.
5. Click the Date (fourth from the left) icon. Notice that it looks like a little desk calendar.
6. `&D` should appear in the text box. Click and drag across `&D` to select it and then click the A. This is the font button. It brings up the Font dialog box (see fig. 9.11).

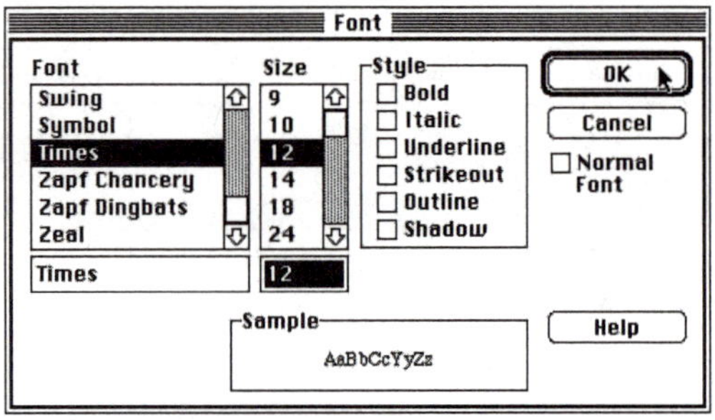


Figure 9.11
*The Font dialog box*

# Fonting It

1. Choose Times 12 and click OK.
2. Select &F in the Center section and type *Confidential.* Click and drag across it.
3. Click the font button again, choose Times 14, click the Bold check box, and click OK.
4. Click in the right text box and then click the Times (fifth) icon.
5. Select the &T which appears, click the font tool (A), and choose Times 12.
6. Click OK.

# Playing Footsie

Now make your Footer print Page 1 of 1 by doing the following:

1. Click the Footer button in the Page Setup dialog box (see fig. 9.12).

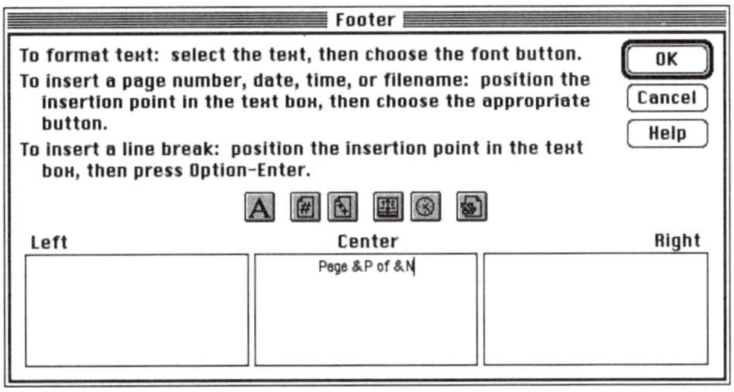


Figure 9.12
*The Footer window.*

2. Click at the end of the default footer, press the spacebar once, type "of," press the spacebar again, and click the third icon.
3. Select the entire item and click the Font tool (A). Change it to Times 10.
4. Click OK until you are back to the Print Preview window.

## Review Print Preview

1. Zoom in on the Header and the Footer. If you like what you see, you're ready to print.
2. Otherwise, click the Setup button and go back into the Header or Footer windows and make the necessary changes.
3. If you're in the Print Preview window, click the Print button to bring up the Print window. All you have to do now is click the Print button again and your document becomes hard copy.

   If you are not in Print Preview mode when you want to print, you can also choose Print from the File menu and click the Print button.

# Summary

The Print Preview command lets you see what the worksheet looks like when it's printed. You can click a button to go into the Page Setup window from Print Preview, create headers and footers, and give commands that have an impact on the look of the page. After making changes, you should use Print Preview again until you reach worksheet perfection.

# Exorcises

1. Where's the Print Preview command?
2. Where's the command that turns off the gridlines on the printed page?
3. What's landscape orientation?
4. How do headers and footers relate to the margins?

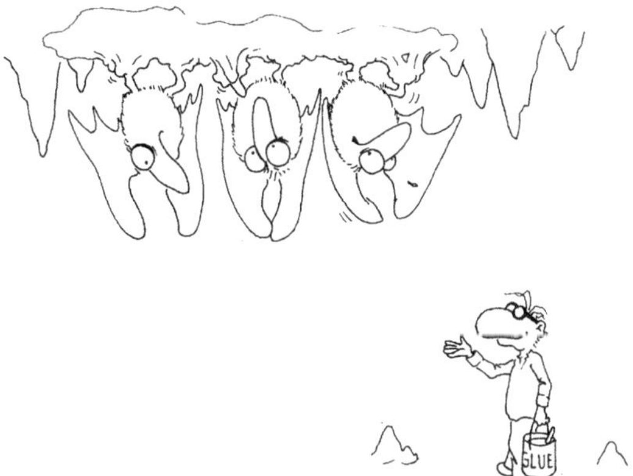
GLUE

10th Encounter

# Using Absolute Reference

## Goal

Master the difference between two different kinds of formulas that use relative and absolute reference; learn when and how to use the Reference command.

## What You Will Need

Start with Excel running, with the Income and Expense worksheet visible and with all the formulas completed.

## Terms of Enfearment

Absolute reference
Paste Format
Wrap Text
#DIV/0!

# Briefing

In this encounter, you're going to create more formulas that are different in an important way from the ones you've already produced. Until now, all the formulas you've created and copied have automatically adjusted to work properly in their new positions. Take a look at the examples of relative referencing shown in figures 10.1 and 10.2:

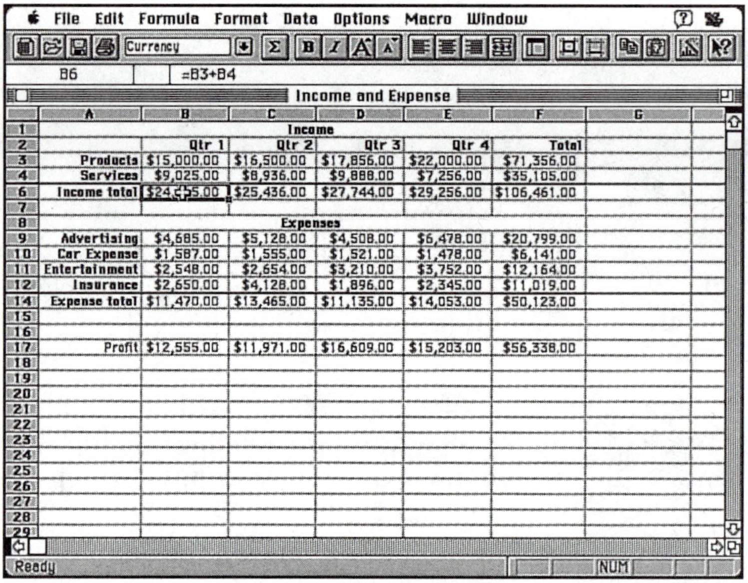


**Figure 10.1**
*Formula in column B.*

Note how the formula at the bottom of the second column relates to the numbers above it, as does the formula at the bottom of the first column (which we copied to create the second formula with the Autofill method).

Although Autofill is the fastest and easiest technique, we could have copied the original formula using a number of different methods, and the results would have been exactly the same.

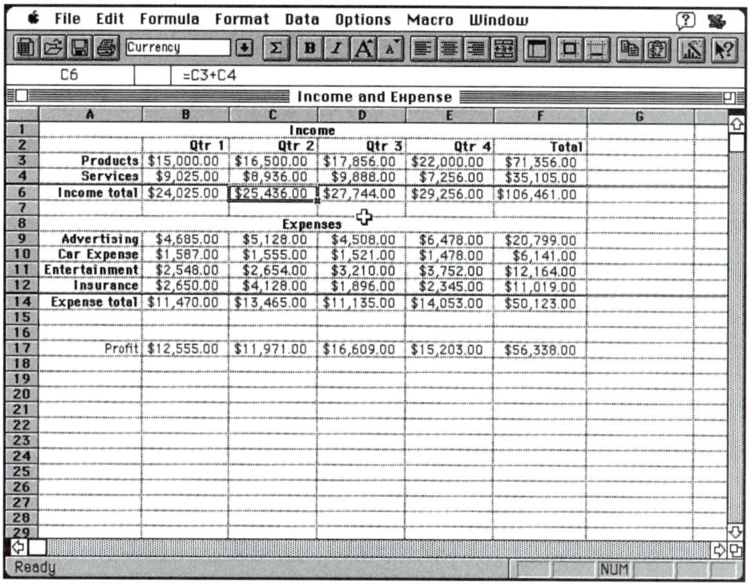


Figure 10.2
*Formula in column C.*

The cells referred to in the original formulas, once copied, have changed during the copying period so that they work *relative* to their new positions.

When you copy a formula in column B that refers to B3, the B in the cell reference changes to C when it's in column C. This automatic adjustment makes a lot of sense and happens so naturally you wouldn't even have to think about it—if it worked all the time.

About 85 to 90% of the formulas you create can be copied across formulas and rows, and the formula on the 90th column and the 50th row works. Sometimes, it doesn't work, and the result can be confusing if you're not first clear about the concept of relative referencing.

# Exit Relative, Enter Absolute

Figure 10.3 shows an example of a formula that won't copy properly. In this case, relative referencing is inappropriate.

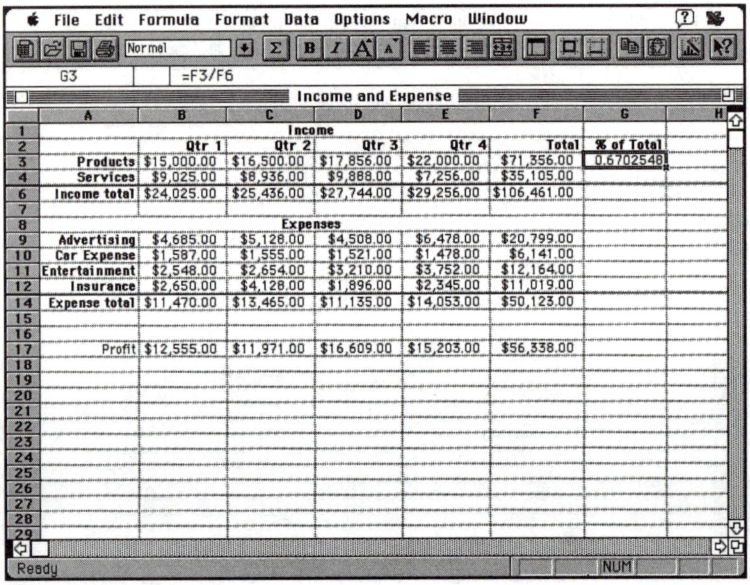


**Figure 10.3**
*Percent of total formula.*

You're asking Excel to tell you what percentage the first Income category is of the Income total. To get this number, you have to divide the income category by the income total.

## Copy Cat

Think about copying this formula down the column. If both of the cells referred to in this formula adjust one cell down, the cell referring to the Income total adjusts down one cell and ends up referring to the wrong cell—one that's empty.

In a case like this, you want to create a different kind of formula in which you prevent the relative referencing from happening. In effect, you want to tell Excel, "When I copy this formula, *don't adjust* this cell reference."

You can do this with a special code right in the formula. The code you use, which tells Excel not to adjust the cell reference when copying the formula, is the dollar sign. The cell reference looks like this: $A$1, instead of A1. This is called *absolute* rather than relative referencing.

You can type the dollar signs (Shift-4), or you can use the Reference command from the Formula menu to add the dollar signs to a cell reference in the formula bar. After it's copied, the formula should read `=F4/$F$6` (see fig. 10.4). You're probably thinking the dollar sign makes absolutely no sense as a code for absolute reference. You're right, but whatcha gonna do?

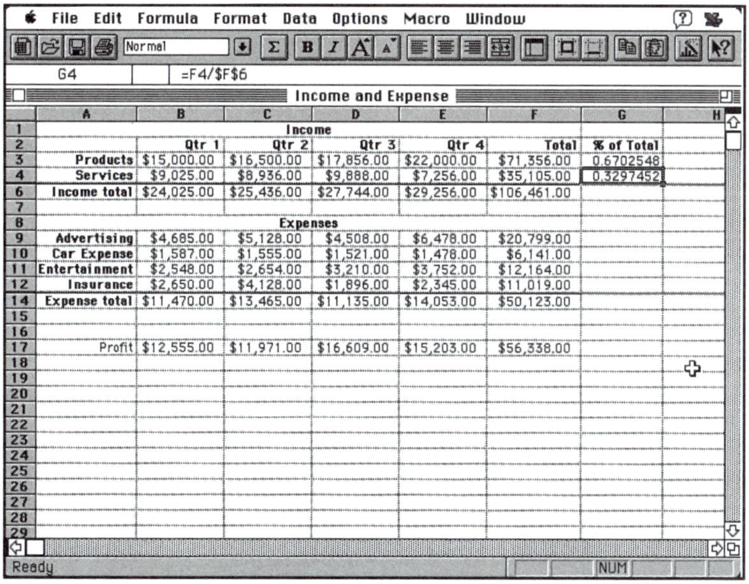


| | A | B | C | D | E | F | G |
|---|---|---|---|---|---|---|---|
| 1 | | | Income | | | | |
| 2 | | Qtr 1 | Qtr 2 | Qtr 3 | Qtr 4 | Total | % of Total |
| 3 | Products | $15,000.00 | $16,500.00 | $17,856.00 | $22,000.00 | $71,356.00 | 0.6702548 |
| 4 | Services | $9,025.00 | $8,936.00 | $9,888.00 | $7,256.00 | $35,105.00 | 0.3297452 |
| 6 | Income total | $24,025.00 | $25,436.00 | $27,744.00 | $29,256.00 | $106,461.00 | |
| 7 | | | | | | | |
| 8 | | | Expenses | | | | |
| 9 | Advertising | $4,685.00 | $5,128.00 | $4,508.00 | $6,478.00 | $20,799.00 | |
| 10 | Car Expense | $1,587.00 | $1,555.00 | $1,521.00 | $1,478.00 | $6,141.00 | |
| 11 | Entertainment | $2,548.00 | $2,654.00 | $3,210.00 | $3,752.00 | $12,164.00 | |
| 12 | Insurance | $2,650.00 | $4,128.00 | $1,896.00 | $2,345.00 | $11,019.00 | |
| 14 | Expense total | $11,470.00 | $13,465.00 | $11,135.00 | $14,053.00 | $50,123.00 | |
| 15 | | | | | | | |
| 16 | | | | | | | |
| 17 | Profit | $12,555.00 | $11,971.00 | $16,609.00 | $15,203.00 | $56,338.00 | |

**Figure 10.4**
*Formula after it's copied*

# Non-Paste Makes Waste

Along with creating formulas, you also need a new heading above them. After typing the new heading, it's obvious that it needs to be formatted like the other headings in its row.

You can use the *Paste Formats* tool to copy just the formatting of the other headings into the cell holding the new heading. This is a heavy-duty time saver that does a whole bunch of formatting in one pass. To use this tool, select a cell with the formatting you want and click the Copy tool. Next select the cell(s) with the text you want formatted and click the Paste Formats tool (see fig. 10.5).

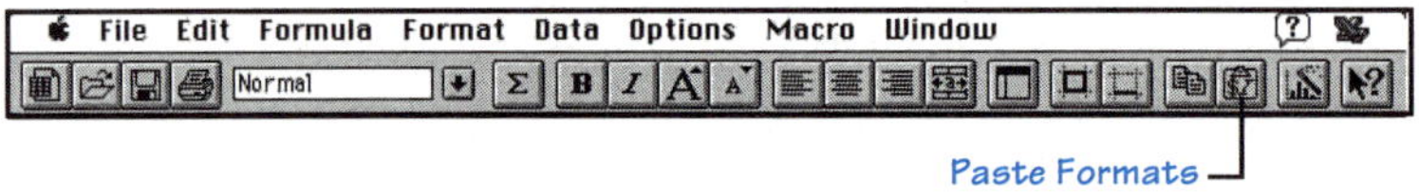


**Figure 10.5**
*Paste Formats tool.*

# Gift Wrap

If a heading gets too long, you have the lovely *Wrap Text* command (choose Alignment from Format) to make it fit into a narrower space (see fig. 10.6). This command adjusts the row height so that a long heading can wrap within one cell. First narrow the column, select the row holding the headings, and turn on Wrap text.

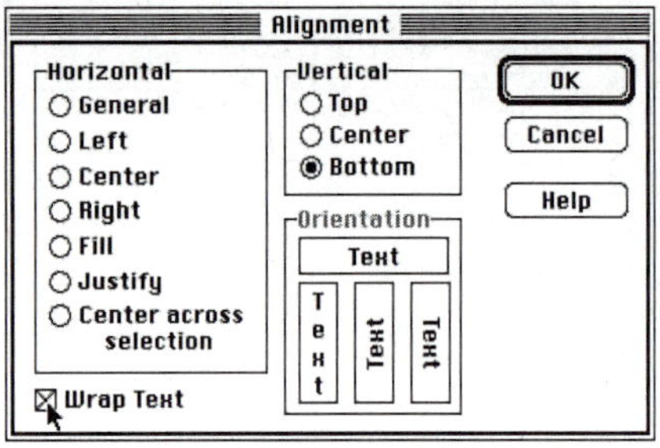


**Figure 10.6**
*Alignment dialog box.*

# They're Out to Get Us

Sometimes, a newly entered formula doesn't do what you expect. Rather than seeing the kind of number you want to see, you see *#DIV/0!* This immediately arouses fear deep inside even the most courageous Excel users. Actually, it's no big deal.

When this happens, immediately click on the cell holding the error message and look at the formula bar. Excel is telling you that the formula in this cell is attempting to divide a cell with another cell that's empty or contains a zero (0). Sometimes, this is genuinely a mistake that you must fix. Other times, the cell that is empty or contains a zero is only temporarily that way. If this is the case, you can ignore the error message.

## Bad Formula

Sometimes, you may not get an error message, but the formula still isn't a good formula. You, however, assume that it's a good formula and believe the number you see in the cell. This can have disastrous consequences if that number is important—like thinking you owe the I.R.S. $5,000 when you really owe them $10,000!

The only way you can be certain that your formulas are doing what you want is by checking and double checking them.

# Practice

Start by saving the worksheet with a different name for this practice session:

1. Choose Save As from the File menu.
2. Type *Inc &Exp w/% of total* in the `Save Worksheet as:` box.
3. Make sure that you are saving it into the Fear Excel No More folder and click the Save button.

Income and Expense is now safe and sound on the hard drive while you are working on this new copy with a different name.

## Getting Comfortable

For this practice session, we have changed the worksheet's font to Geneva 12 and the number format to Comma (0) so that the pictures of the screen will be as readable as possible. We have also turned the gridlines back on.

Here are reminders, if you want to do the same:

1. Select the whole worksheet and choose Font from the Format menu.
2. Select the numbers and choose Comma (0) from the Style box.
3. Choose Display from Options and click in the Gridlines check box.

## Paste Formats

Type the new heading and then copy the formatting of one of the other headings, by doing the following:

1. Select the cell to the right of the Total heading.
2. Type *Percent of Total* and press the left-arrow key to move the cell pointer to the Total heading.
3. With the Total heading selected, click the Copy tool. You should see the marching ants around Total.
4. Move the cell pointer back to the new heading.
5. Click the Paste Formats tool.

## Wrap Text

Now this heading is too wide. It doesn't look right next to the others. It would look much better formatted as shown in figure 10.7.

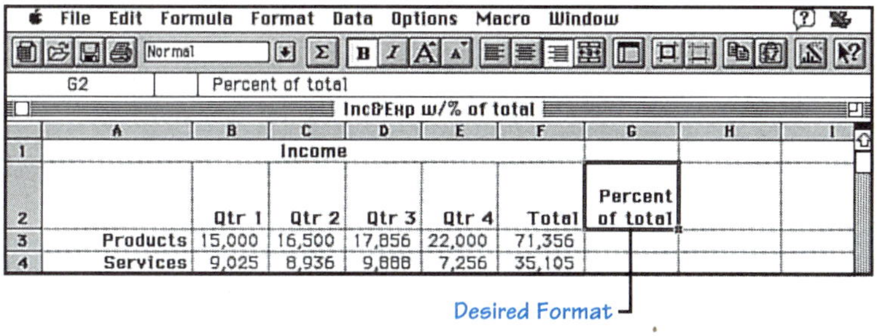


**Figure 10.7** *The wrapped heading.*

1. To make your heading wrap, narrow the column so that it fits the words "of Total."
2. Select the whole row by clicking on the row number.
3. Select Alignment from the Format menu, click the Wrap text check box, and click OK.

# A Calculated Risk

Now you're going to create the formula to get your percent of total. The first time you'll create it without adding the special code and copy it so that you see the error message. Then you'll fix the formula and recopy it.

1. Select the cell under the new heading (Percent of Total).
2. Type an equal sign (=).
3. Click the Total cell to the left.
4. Type a forward slash (/).
5. Click the cell holding the Income total.
6. Enter the formula by clicking the Enter box.
7. Go up to the Style box and choose Percent (see fig. 10.8).

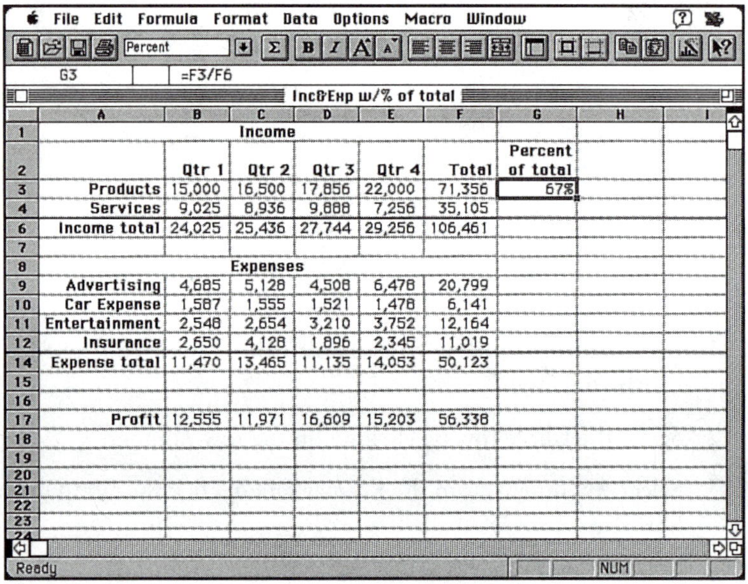


**Figure 10.8**
*The percent of total formula.*

# Bad Copy

This formula works for this cell, but it won't work for the cell below this one once it's copied.

1. Position the pointer on the fill handle. Wait until you have the bold cross hair and then click and drag down one cell. You should see the error value as shown in figure 10.9.

2. Click on the cell holding the error message and look at the formula bar. See how both cells in the formula you copied have adjusted down one cell so that one of them is referring to an EMPTY CELL.

3. Just to avoid confusion, clear out the bad formula by pressing the BackSpace key and Return.

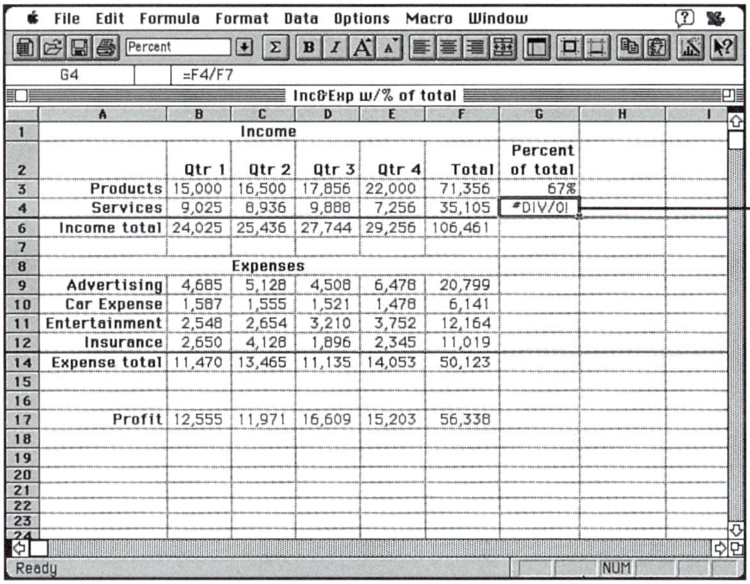


| | A | B | C | D | E | F | G |
|---|---|---|---|---|---|---|---|
| 1 | | | Income | | | | |
| 2 | | Qtr 1 | Qtr 2 | Qtr 3 | Qtr 4 | Total | Percent of total |
| 3 | Products | 15,000 | 16,500 | 17,856 | 22,000 | 71,356 | 67% |
| 4 | Services | 9,025 | 8,936 | 9,888 | 7,256 | 35,105 | #DIV/0! |
| 6 | Income total | 24,025 | 25,436 | 27,744 | 29,256 | 106,461 | |
| 7 | | | | | | | |
| 8 | | | Expenses | | | | |
| 9 | Advertising | 4,685 | 5,128 | 4,508 | 6,478 | 20,799 | |
| 10 | Car Expense | 1,587 | 1,555 | 1,521 | 1,478 | 6,141 | |
| 11 | Entertainment | 2,548 | 2,654 | 3,210 | 3,752 | 12,164 | |
| 12 | Insurance | 2,650 | 4,128 | 1,896 | 2,345 | 11,019 | |
| 14 | Expense total | 11,470 | 13,465 | 11,135 | 14,053 | 50,123 | |
| 15 | | | | | | | |
| 16 | | | | | | | |
| 17 | Profit | 12,555 | 11,971 | 16,609 | 15,203 | 56,338 | |

Error Value

**Figure 10.9**
*Error value.*

# Fix the Formula

To change the first formula so that when you copy it the reference to the Income total does not shift down, do the following:

1. Select the formula and click in the formula bar right after the cell reference that refers to the Income total.
2. Choose Reference from the Formula menu.
3. Look at the formula bar to see the dollar signs added to the cell reference.
4. Enter the formula after the dollar signs appear by pressing the Enter key.

# Play It Again, Sam

1. Position the pointer on the fill handle. After the pointer changes to the bold crosshair, click-drag down one cell.
2. Click on the formula and look at it in the formula bar. See how F6 has remained F6, while F3 has adjusted the way it should (see fig 10.10).
3. Do the same for the expense categories (see fig 10.11).
4. Use Autofill to copy the formula down. Position the pointer on the fill handle. After the pointer changes to the bold crosshair, click-drag down to the final expense category.

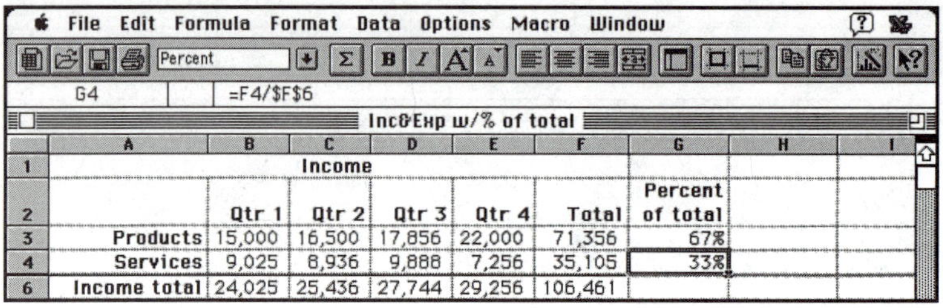


| | A | B | C | D | E | F | G | H | I |
|---|---|---|---|---|---|---|---|---|---|
| 1 | | | Income | | | | | | |
| 2 | | Qtr 1 | Qtr 2 | Qtr 3 | Qtr 4 | Total | Percent of total | | |
| 3 | Products | 15,000 | 16,500 | 17,856 | 22,000 | 71,356 | 67% | | |
| 4 | Services | 9,025 | 8,936 | 9,888 | 7,256 | 35,105 | 33% | | |
| 6 | Income total | 24,025 | 25,436 | 27,744 | 29,256 | 106,461 | | | |

**Figure 10.10** *The formula with absolute reference.*

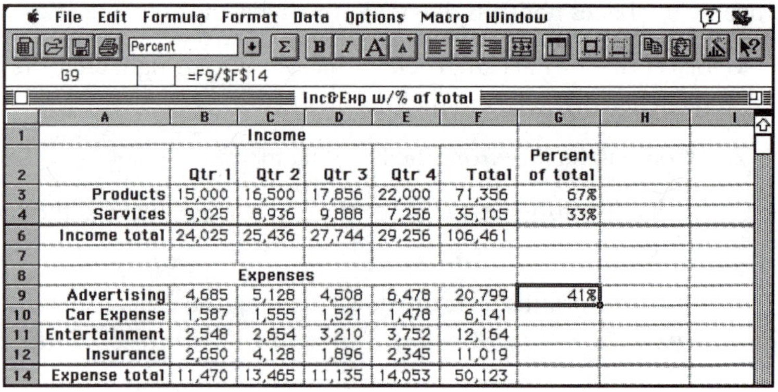


| | A | B | C | D | E | F | G | H | I |
|---|---|---|---|---|---|---|---|---|---|
| 1 | | | Income | | | | | | |
| 2 | | Qtr 1 | Qtr 2 | Qtr 3 | Qtr 4 | Total | Percent of total | | |
| 3 | Products | 15,000 | 16,500 | 17,856 | 22,000 | 71,356 | 67% | | |
| 4 | Services | 9,025 | 8,936 | 9,888 | 7,256 | 35,105 | 33% | | |
| 6 | Income total | 24,025 | 25,436 | 27,744 | 29,256 | 106,461 | | | |
| 7 | | | | | | | | | |
| 8 | | | Expenses | | | | | | |
| 9 | Advertising | 4,685 | 5,128 | 4,508 | 6,478 | 20,799 | 41% | | |
| 10 | Car Expense | 1,587 | 1,555 | 1,521 | 1,478 | 6,141 | | | |
| 11 | Entertainment | 2,548 | 2,654 | 3,210 | 3,752 | 12,164 | | | |
| 12 | Insurance | 2,650 | 4,128 | 1,896 | 2,345 | 11,019 | | | |
| 14 | Expense total | 11,470 | 13,465 | 11,135 | 14,053 | 50,123 | | | |

**Figure 10.11**

# Run for the Border

Temporarily widen the rows with bottom borders so that it'll be easier to add the bottom border to the new column:

1. Click and drag from the row above to the one below the narrowed row. Be sure not to click-drag with the double-headed arrow.
2. Choose Row Height from the Format menu and click the Use Standard Height check box (see fig. 10.12).

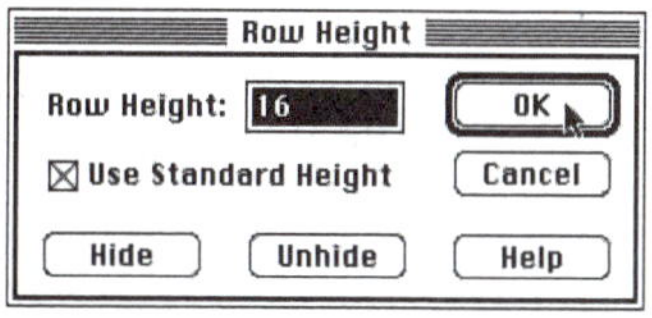


**Figure 10.12**
*Use Standard Height.*

3. Use Autofill to copy the bottom borders and the total formulas over to the Percent of total column (see fig. 10.13). (Do this once for Income and again for Expenses.)

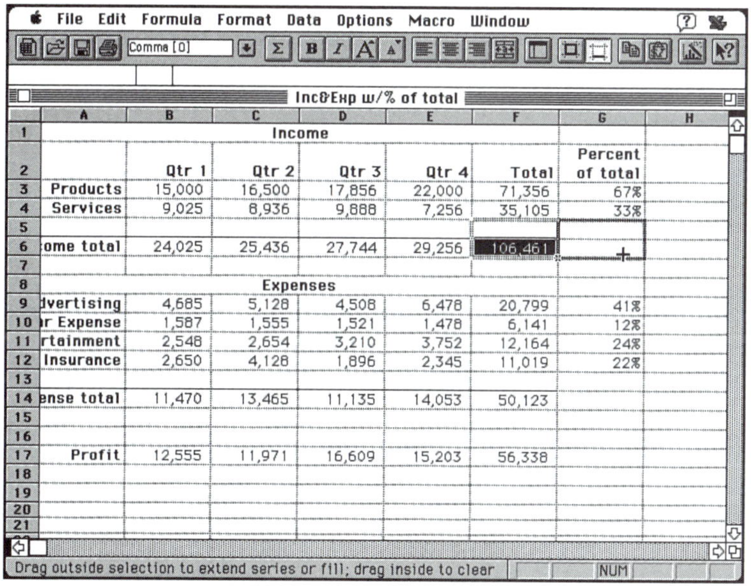


**Figure 10.13**
*Autofill copies both border and formula*

4. Apply the Percent format to the Total Percent formulas, using the Style box.
5. Narrow the rows again.

# Center Headings

1. To recenter the Income heading, select from A1 to G1.
2. Click the Center Across Columns tool twice (once returns it to the left; again causes the heading to move to the center of the selected columns).
3. Do the same for Expenses: selecting the range first and then using the tool.

# Put That Away!

Figure 10.14 shows your finished worksheet.

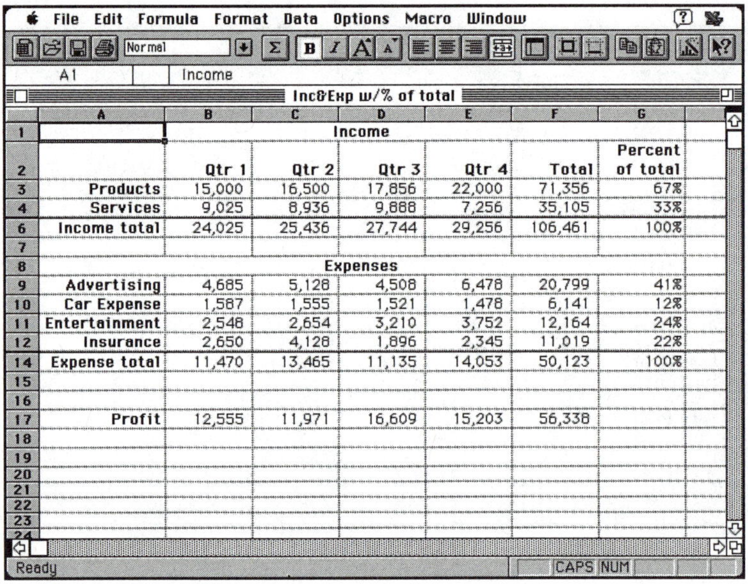


| | A | B | C | D | E | F | G |
|---|---|---|---|---|---|---|---|
| 1 | | | | Income | | | |
| 2 | | Qtr 1 | Qtr 2 | Qtr 3 | Qtr 4 | Total | Percent of total |
| 3 | Products | 15,000 | 16,500 | 17,856 | 22,000 | 71,356 | 67% |
| 4 | Services | 9,025 | 8,936 | 9,888 | 7,256 | 35,105 | 33% |
| 6 | Income total | 24,025 | 25,436 | 27,744 | 29,256 | 106,461 | 100% |
| 7 | | | | | | | |
| 8 | | | | Expenses | | | |
| 9 | Advertising | 4,685 | 5,128 | 4,508 | 6,478 | 20,799 | 41% |
| 10 | Car Expense | 1,587 | 1,555 | 1,521 | 1,478 | 6,141 | 12% |
| 11 | Entertainment | 2,548 | 2,654 | 3,210 | 3,752 | 12,164 | 24% |
| 12 | Insurance | 2,650 | 4,128 | 1,896 | 2,345 | 11,019 | 22% |
| 14 | Expense total | 11,470 | 13,465 | 11,135 | 14,053 | 50,123 | 100% |
| 15 | | | | | | | |
| 16 | | | | | | | |
| 17 | Profit | 12,555 | 11,971 | 16,609 | 15,203 | 56,338 | |
| 18 | | | | | | | |
| 19 | | | | | | | |
| 20 | | | | | | | |
| 21 | | | | | | | |
| 22 | | | | | | | |
| 23 | | | | | | | |
| 24 | | | | | | | |

**Figure 10.14**
*Your worksheet.*

It's that time again. Choose Quit from the File menu and save your changes.

# Summary

Sometimes, a formula is not suitable for copying if it causes a cell reference to adjust to its new location when it shouldn't. In these cases, you need to add dollar signs to the cell reference before copying the formula. The dollar signs are a special code that keeps the cell reference unchanged—no matter how many cells it gets copied into.

The Paste Format button lets you copy the formatting but not the contents of cells. The Wrap Text command, found in the Alignment dialog box, is used to wrap long headings in one cell.

# Exorcises

1. What should you do when you see a cell holding the message `DIV/0!`?
2. Explain relative referencing.
3. Explain absolute referencing.
4. How can you put the dollar signs in a formula without typing them directly?

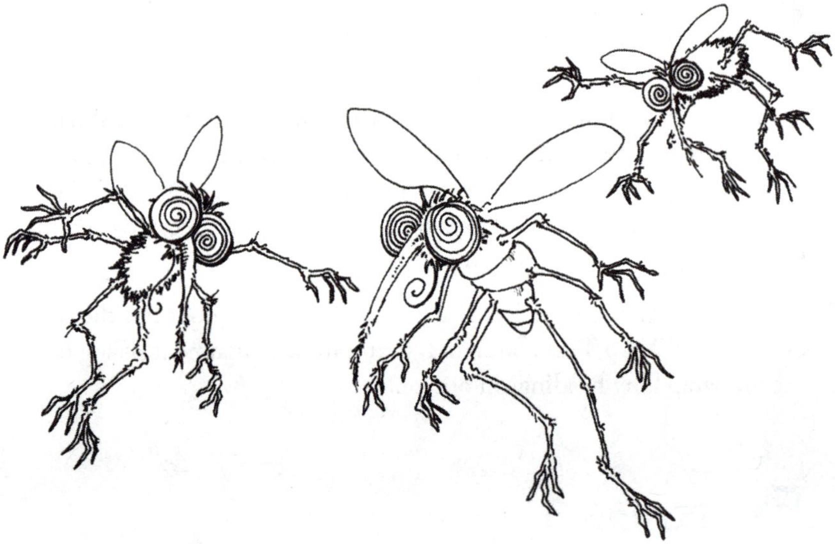

11th Encounter

# Our Favorite Functions

## Goal

Master the most frequently used functions, the Paste Function command, and a technique that allows your formulas to stretch to include newly inserted numbers.

## What You Will Need

Start with Excel running, with the *Inc & Exp w/% of total* worksheet visible and with all the formulas and formatting completed.

## Terms of Enfearment

| | |
|---|---|
| Command syntax | MAX( ) |
| Argument | MIN( ) |
| Paste Function | COUNT( ) |
| AVERAGE( ) | TODAY( ) |

# Briefing

In this encounter, you're going to learn about some way cool functions. A *function* is a built-in routine that performs one or more calculations for a special purpose. For example, if you need to find the average for a column of numbers, you can create a formula that adds those numbers together and then divides the sum by however many numbers are in the column. This could be a real pain in the neck: If you added more numbers, the formula would have to be adjusted.

# Just an Average Kind of a Day

Fortunately, it's not necessary to create that type of formula because Excel provides the *AVERAGE* function. All you have to do is tell Excel that you want an average and then give it the range of cells that holds the numbers. Excel does the rest.

Of course, you have to ask nicely, or rather, properly. The formula must look just right. This is called the *command syntax*.

Fortunately, asking properly won't be difficult, because you already know how to use the AVERAGE function. Really, you do. It works just like the SUM function, which totals a range of numbers without your having to click on each and every cell. Because SUM is the most popular function, it gets its very own Autosum tool on the toolbar, which you've been using.

One of the reasons the Autosum tool is so great to use is that it creates the formula properly, each and every time:

- It starts with an equal sign.
- Its range of numbers is inside parentheses.
- The first cell is separated from the last cell in the range by a colon.
- There are no spaces from the beginning of the formula to the end.

The range inside the parentheses is called an *argument.* The argument tells the function what to do; as in "Add up these numbers!" Besides the Autosum tool, you also can find the SUM function in a list along with all the other functions.

The *Paste Function* command, found in the Formula menu, brings up a list of all the functions and their syntax. You can use this list to pop a function into a formula without typing it and to see how the formula has to look to work properly.

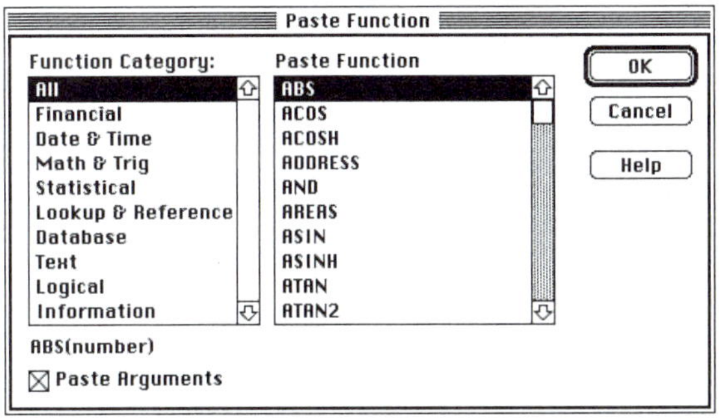


**Figure 11.1**
*Paste Function dialog box.*

## Getting to the (Square) Root of the Matter

Along with SUM and AVERAGE are a few other functions that work the same way and are very useful. The *MAX* function looks at a range and tells you which is the highest number. The *MIN* function looks at a range and tells you which is the lowest number. The COUNT function tells how many cells in the range hold numbers.

SUM is a Math function. There are more than 40 other Math functions, including one that figures the square root of a number (SQRT) and another that figures the squared sum of a range of numbers (SUMSQ).

AVERAGE, MAX, MIN, and *COUNT* are statistical functions. More than 50 other statistical functions deal with lamdas and degrees, probability, and other very down-to-earth, common-sense matters.

Along with the Math and Statistical functions, there are seven other categories of functions, including Date, Logistical, Financial, and so on.

The best way to deal with this abundance is to know that the functions are there if you should need them. Most people live their entire worksheet lives using only the functions we're looking at here and still live happily and productively.

# Here Today . . .

With that piece of advice out of the way, take a look at one of the useful Date functions called TODAY. The TODAY function lets you have a cell that always shows the current date, no matter when the worksheet is open. You can format the date to look anyway you want it to look.

### Table 11.1. Your Date's Appearance

| *In the Date's Format* | *In the Cell* |
|---|---|
| mmmm | January |
| mmm | Jan |
| dddd | Monday or Tuesday or . . . |
| ddd | Mon or Tue or . . . |
| mm | 01 |
| dd | 01 |
| m | 1 |
| d | 1 |
| YY | 93 |
| yyyy | 1993 |
| mm/dd/yy | 01/04/93 |
| dddd, mmmm d, yyyy (yes, commas, spaces, dashes, and so on allowed in format) | Monday, January 4, 1993 |

If you want to see the full date in a cell, first enter the date. You can type it, use the *TODAY* function, or use the keyboard shortcut Command—(hyphen). Choose Number from the Format menu and type a custom format into the Code box (see figs. 11.2 and 11.3).

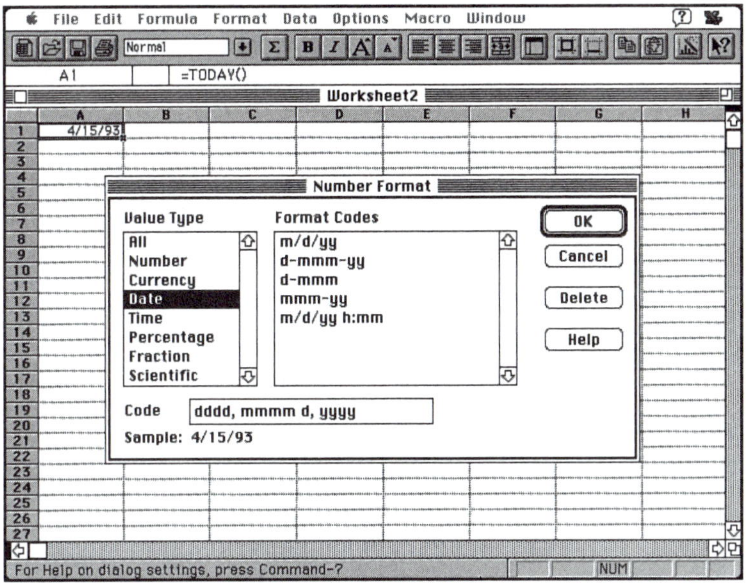


Figure 11.2
*Custom date format in Code box.*

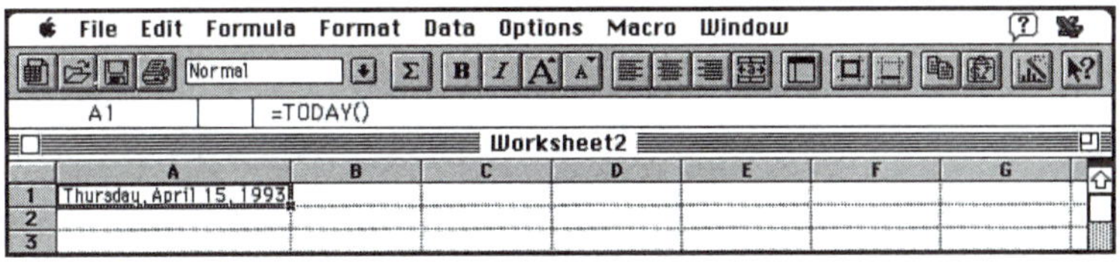


Figure 11.3
*=TODAY() formatted.*

The TODAY function is a very unusual one because it doesn't have anything between the parentheses. Nevertheless, the cell must hold exactly `=TODAY()` for you to see the date (no spaces are in the formula).

The TODAY function enables you to perform date arithmetic. For example, you may have a worksheet that is tracking your invoices. One of the invoices is dated March 6. Today is April 15. If you want Excel to tell you how old that invoice is, you can create a formula as shown in figure 11.4.

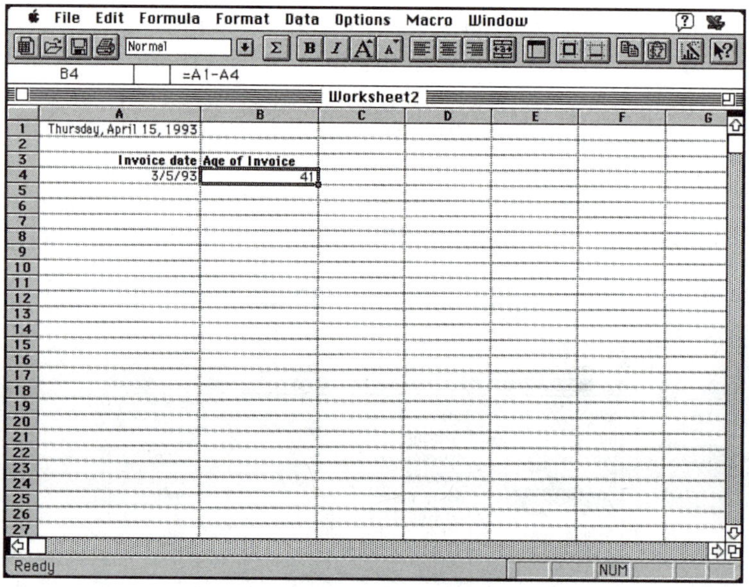


**Figure 11.4**
*Just how old is that invoice?*

At any time, whether it be days, weeks, or (hopefully not) months, Excel is still able to tell you how old that invoice is because the cell holding the TODAY function has been automatically updated to the current date.

# They're Out To Get Us

Sometimes, when you use the Autosum button, Excel gets the range wrong. This is why it's important to always double check the range inside the parentheses before entering the formula.

The range is selected when Excel puts the formula up in the formula bar. If it's incorrect, click and drag across the correct cells, and the incorrect range is replaced by the range you've just selected.

# Practice

In this session, you will put together a section in your worksheet so that you can have more information on your expenses. You want to be able to add more expense categories when necessary. You also want a constantly updated list of the average, highest, and lowest amounts and a count of how many expenses are actually in the list at any time.

First, save the worksheet with a new name:

1. Choose Save As from the File menu.
2. Type *Inc & Exp w/stats.*
3. Make sure that Fear Excel No More is the current folder.
4. Click the Save button.

## Workworkwork

1. Type *Expense Stats Over 4 Qtrs* starting at B19 and *# of Exp Categories* starting in E19 (see fig. 11.5).
2. Select them and click the bold tool.

## To the Right of Average

1. Select the cell to the right of the cell that holds the Average heading (C20).
2. Choose Paste Function from the Formula menu. Note the list of catcgorics on thc left and click a few.

As you click, the list on the right changes. If you see a function that looks interesting, click it once to see its command syntax at the bottom of the dialog box.

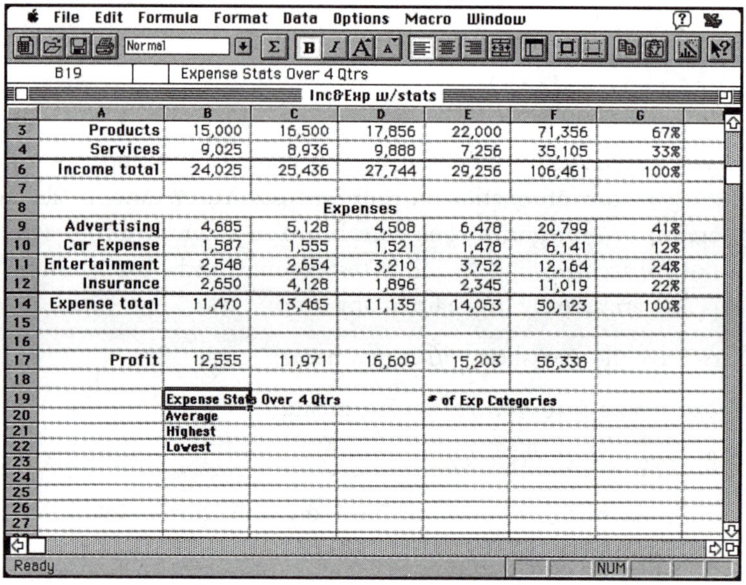


**Figure 11.5** *Headings for the statistical area.*

3. Click `All` at the top of the category list on the right.
4. Scroll down the list on the right until you see AVERAGE.
5. Go back over to the list on the left and click `Statistical`. Now see how AVERAGE is one of the first in the list on the right (see fig. 11.6).
6. Click Average once.
7. Clear the Paste Arguments check box as shown in figure 11.6.
8. Click OK.
9. Look at the formula bar (see fig. 11.7).

   Excel wants to know what range of cells to average.

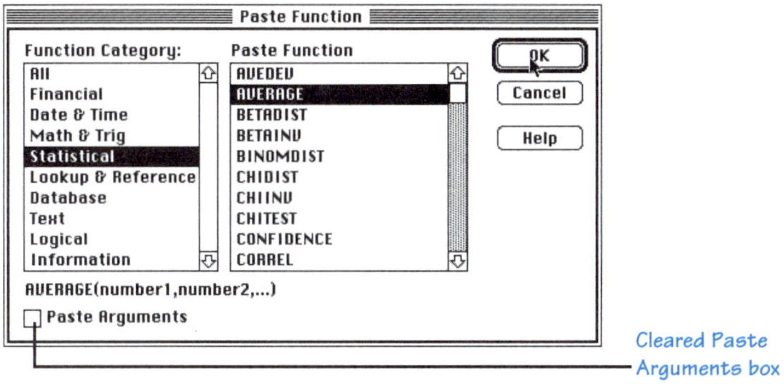


**Figure 11.6**
*Cleared check box in the Paste Function window.*

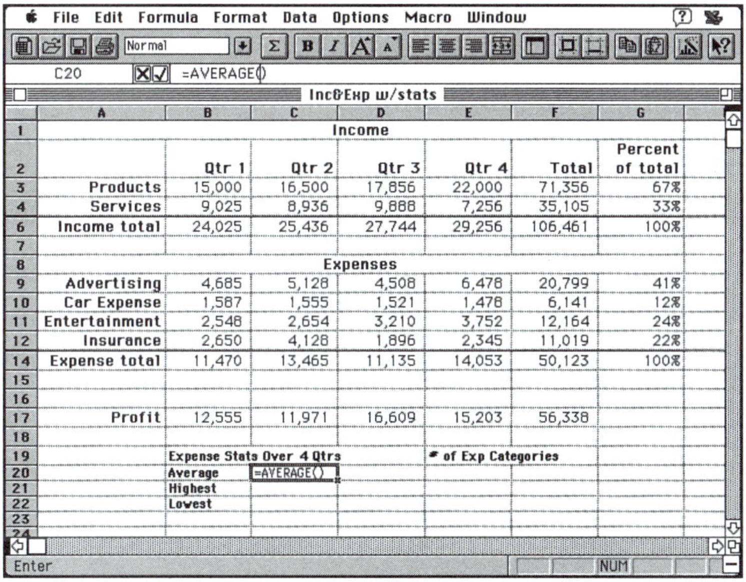


**Figure 11.7**
*The AVERAGE function in the formula bar.*

10. Click on the Qtr 1 Expense total and drag over to Qtr 4 (B14:E14).

    The formula should look like `=AVERAGE(B14:E14)`.

11. Press the Return key to enter the formula and move down one cell.

# To the Max and Min

1. Choose Paste Function again.
2. This time, rather than scrolling down to get to MAX in the list, type the letter M. Note how the highlight moves down the list to the first function that begins with that letter.

   This is a cool technique for traversing through lists. Keep going down until you reach MAX and then double-click it, which is the same as clicking MAX once and then clicking OK.
3. Look at the formula bar and again drag from the Qtr 1 Expense total to Qtr 4.
4. Enter the formula (see fig. 11.8).

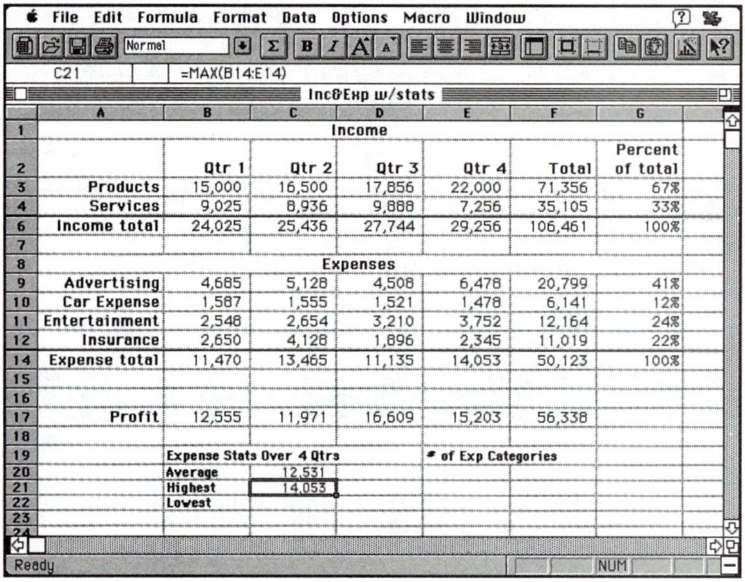


**Figure 11.8** *The completed formula for Highest Expense total.*

5. Move down one cell and create the formula for the lowest number—`=MIN(B14:E14)`.

## Holding You a-COUNT-able

1. Move to E21. Remember to double check your active cell by glancing at the formula bar.
2. Choose Paste Function and double-click COUNT on the right. The range is different this time. You want to click on the top expense amount for Qtr 1 and drag down to the row below the last expense. (B10:B14) is the range you want. Because B14 is a narrow row, you might find it easier to type the range this time.

Having a formula to count four measly categories is no big deal currently. You can see, at a glance, how many there are. On the other hand, in real life, there are usually more than we care to think about.

## Keeping the Formula Stretchable

The selection of this range, which includes an extra row at the bottom, ensures that this formula will work no matter how many more expense categories you add (see fig. 11.9). *As long as we insert new rows within the range in the formula, the formula will stretch to include them.*

All functions that use a range inside the parentheses, including the SUM function, work this way. Try to set up your formulas this way whenever there is the smallest chance new columns or rows will be added.

## Live for Today

To put today's date into cell A1, do the following:

1. To insert a new row at row 1, select row 1 (click the row number) and choose Insert from the Edit menu.
2. Select A1.
3. Choose Paste Function from the Formula menu.

4. Click Date & Time on the left.
5. Choose TODAY on the right with a double-click.

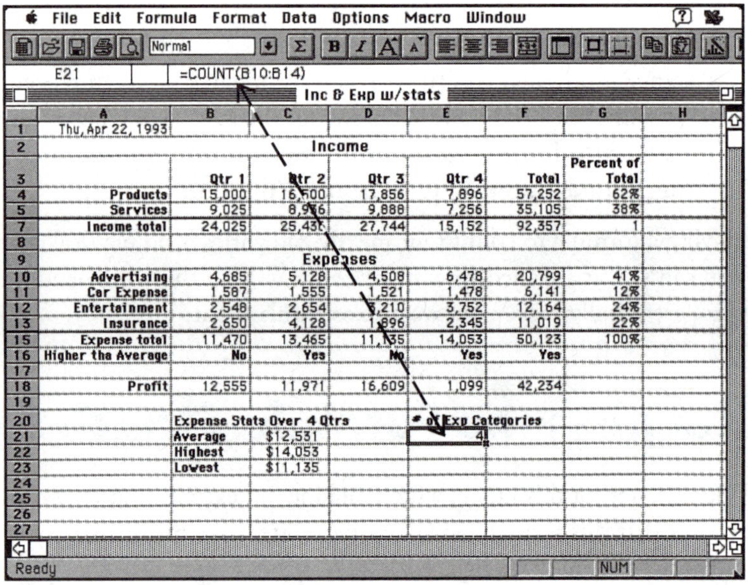


Figure 11.9
*The completed formula for counting the number of expenses.*

# Format the Date

When you enter the formula, the current date appears in A1 with a month/day/year format.

1. Make sure that A1 is still selected.
2. Choose Number from the Format menu.
3. Note that Date is selected on the left, because Excel already knows it's a date. You can see what the built-in formats on the right make TODAY look like. Just click on them one at a time and look at the bottom of the dialog box. Choose whichever you prefer or type a custom date format in the Code box.

# Summary

Hundreds of functions let you wrest information from numbers and analyze them to death. You'll probably never use most of them, but others are invaluable to just about everybody's work, like the SUM function. Paste Function is the command that lets you paste a function into a cell.

# Exorcises

1. Which menu holds the Paste Function command?
2. Describe one technique that enables you to move swiftly down the Paste Function list.
3. How many categories of functions are there?
4. What's the name of the function that tells you the lowest number of a group of numbers?
5. What function would you use to find the latest date in a column full of dates?

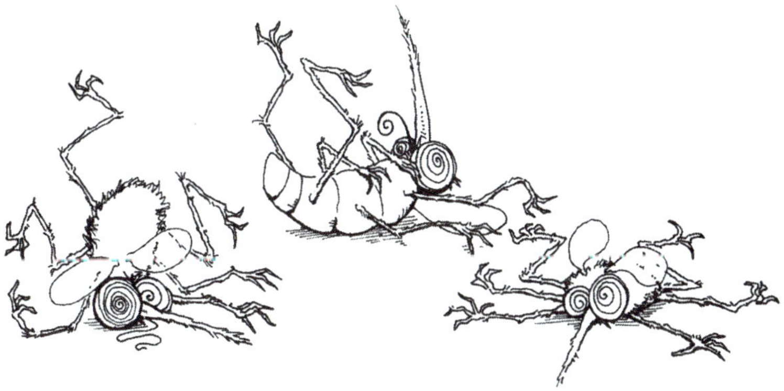

12th Encounter

# Working with Large Documents

## Goal

Learn techniques that make it easier to work with large spreadsheets on the screen and to print them so that they are understandable.

## What You Will Need

Start with Excel running, with the Inc & Exp w/stats worksheet visible, and with all previous encounters and exorcises completed.

## Terms of Enfearment

| | |
|---|---|
| Arrange | Print Titles |
| Insert | Page breaks |
| Delete | Scaling |
| Freeze Panes | |

# Briefing

In this encounter, you explore a number of techniques that let you work with large worksheets, on-screen and when printing.

First, when creating large worksheets, you can often copy sections of headings to new areas. You can use the Copy command on the Edit menu or the Copy tool to copy selected ranges. To add the copied cells to a new area, choose the Paste command from the Edit menu or press the Enter key.

After giving the Copy command, the message in the Status bar says, `Select destination and Press Enter or Choose Paste`. You can either choose Paste from the Edit menu or press the Enter key at this point. If you choose Paste, the selected range you just copied will remain in the clipboard, so you can continue to paste the copied range into other areas of the worksheet. Pressing the Enter key only gives you one copy.

As your worksheets become longer than one screen, and you need to look at rows that are lower down, the headings at the top of the columns scroll upward and eventually disappear. The same thing happens as you scroll to distant columns. The row headings scroll to the right and disappear as well.

# Dazed and Confused

Soon, you have no idea what the numbers mean, which can lead to feelings of insecurity and a total loss of self-esteem. The same situation happens when you need to compare cells that aren't close enough to each other to be on the same screen at the same time. You have to go back and forth between them to make sense of their relationship, and soon it's just not worth the effort.

# Here Comes the Cavalry

Fortunately, you can use a number of methods to end the confusion.

On-screen, you can create windows into the same document and arrange them on different parts of the screen. The New Window command found on the Window menu lets you make a copy of your document that you can view on-screen. You can make as many copies as you want, but two versions of the same document at the same time are usually enough. The important thing to understand about this command is that you're still working with *just* one document. Excel tells you by temporarily adding :1 to the original worksheet and naming the new window with the same name plus :2 (see fig. 12.1).

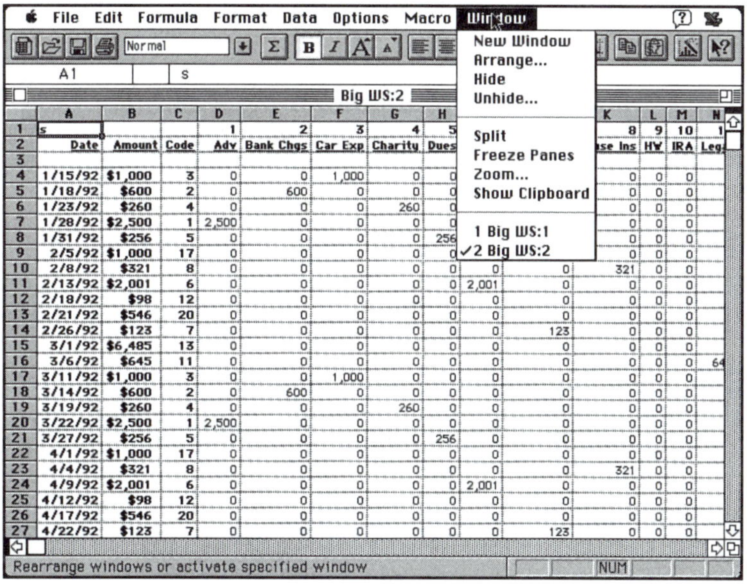


Figure 12.1
*The Window menu.*

# A Perfect Arrangement

You can go back and forth between the two windows by choosing one or the other from the list at the bottom of the Window menu, but this doesn't solve your problem. You need to be able to see different parts of the worksheet simultaneously. The *Arrange* command, also on the Window menu, provides a dialog box in which you can tell Excel to make the two windows smaller and to put them next to each other (see fig. 12.2).

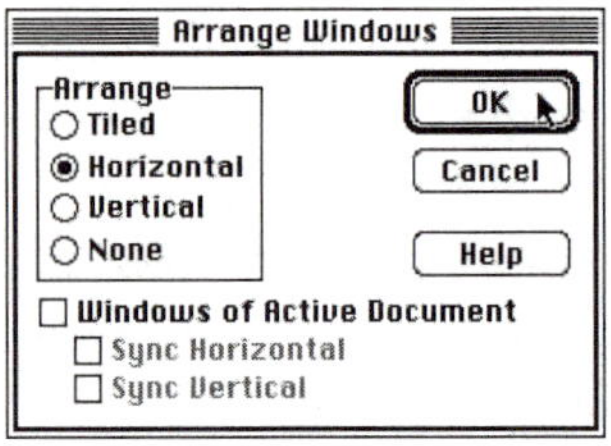


**Figure 12.2**
*Arrange Windows dialog box.*

The Arrange command lets you ask for different kinds of arrangements. You can look at different arrangements until you find one you like. When the worksheets are arranged to your satisfaction, you can scroll in each window to see different parts of the same worksheet (see fig. 12.3).

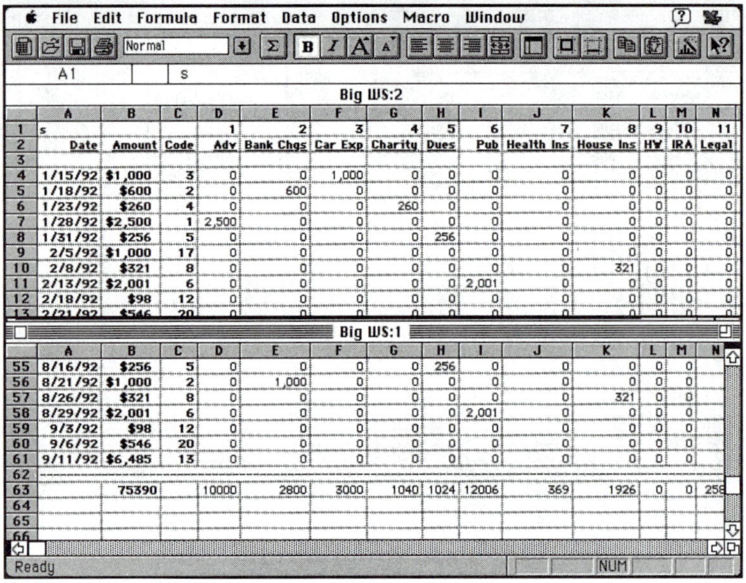


**Figure 12.3**
*One document with two open windows.*

# We *Do* Do Windows

You can also freeze the columns and rows so that they stay in position. Again, it's the Window menu that holds the *Freeze Panes* command. When you choose this command, the headings freeze in place until you give the Unfreeze command.

The position of the active cell tells Excel where to enforce the freeze, which occurs above and to the left of the active cell.

To scroll all over the worksheet without losing sight of your headings, select the cell below the column headings and to the right of the row headings (see fig. 12.4).

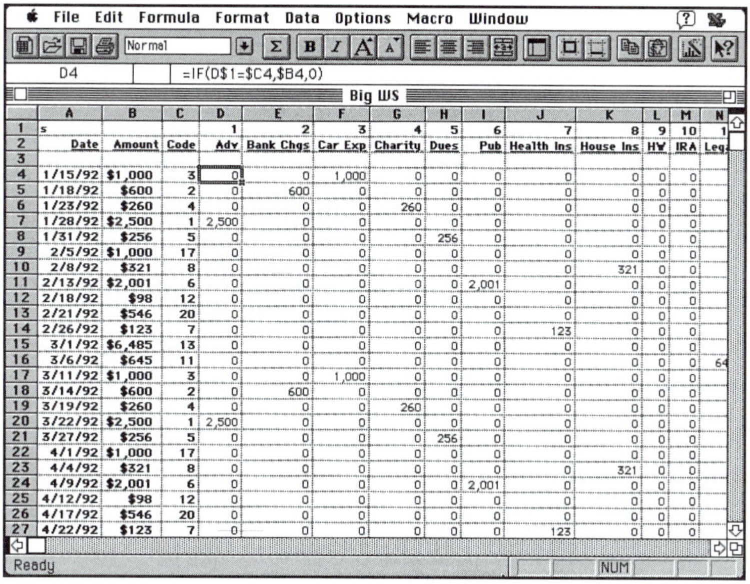


**Figure 12.4**
*The right position for the cell pointer.*

Choose Freeze Panes from the Window menu.

# Print Titles

Now, you need to tell Excel which rows and columns to show at the top and left side of every page when printing.

First, select the column(s) and row(s) you want to appear on the top and left side of the pages. Remember that holding down the Command key lets you select columns and rows at the same time; to select a column or row, click the column letter or the row number.

After selecting the column(s) and row(s), choose Print Titles from the Options menu. The dialog box confirms the columns and rows that are selected (see fig. 12.5). All you have to do is click OK. However, if you have chosen too many or too few, you can fix it here.

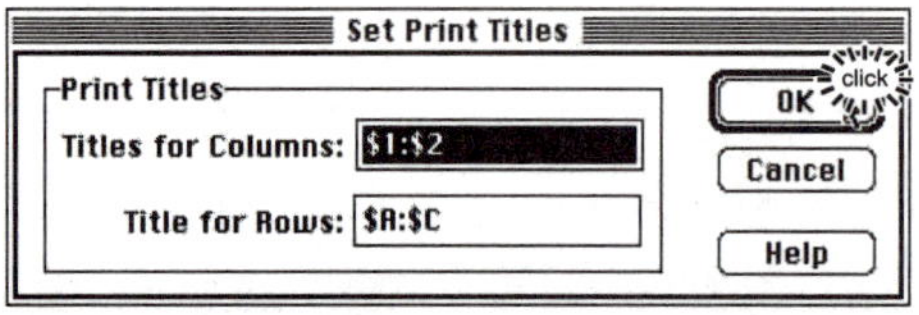


**Figure 12.5**
*Print titles chosen.*

# They're Out To Get Us

Usually, you don't get the design quite right the first time, so you have to *insert* or *delete* columns and rows. To insert a row, select the entire row just below where you want a new row and choose Insert from the Edit menu. To insert more than one row, do the same and drag down the number of rows you want inserted.

Inserting columns works the same way, only you select the column to the right of where you want the new column and choose Insert from the Edit menu.

To delete columns or rows, select what you want to delete and choose Delete from the Edit menu.

## Page Breaks

Sometimes, you may disagree with Excel's decision about where to end a page. We can see what's going on in Print Preview by zooming in on the bottom of each page.

If one or more pages stop at a row that doesn't make sense, click the Close button to get back to the worksheet.

## Breaking and Entering

Next, select the row directly below the row you want to be the final one. Choose Set Page Break from the Options menu, and you should see a dotted line representing the page break (see figs. 12.6 and 12.7). If it's still not in the right place, choose Remove Page Break and try again. To set both a row and column break at the same time, select one cell below and to the right of the cell that represents the bottom right of the page, before giving the Set Page Break command.

You can only set page breaks above, not below, the page break Excel puts in your document. This is *not* a method to get more rows on the page.

## Very Important Advice

If you need more rows on the page, rather than controlling exactly where the page breaks, print on legal size paper, use a smaller font, and make the margins smaller.

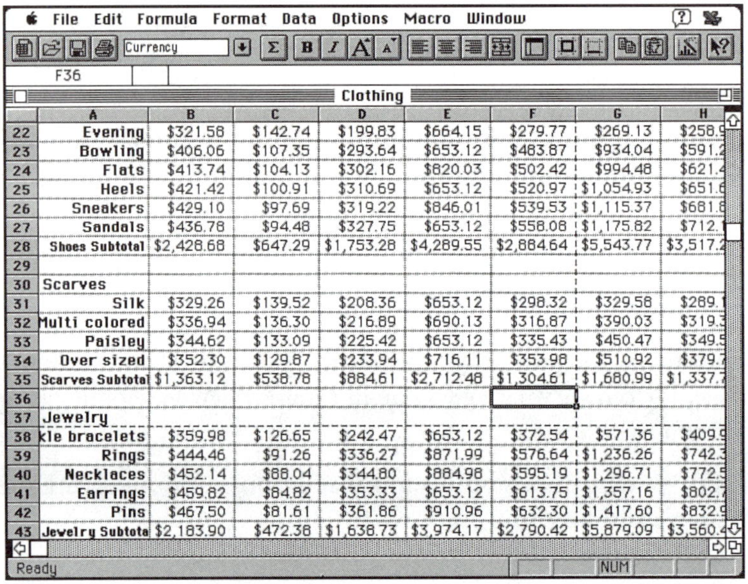


| | A | B | C | D | E | F | G | H |
|---|---|---|---|---|---|---|---|---|
| 22 | Evening | $321.58 | $142.74 | $199.83 | $664.15 | $279.77 | $269.13 | $258.9 |
| 23 | Bowling | $406.06 | $107.35 | $293.64 | $653.12 | $483.87 | $934.04 | $591.2 |
| 24 | Flats | $413.74 | $104.13 | $302.16 | $820.03 | $502.42 | $994.48 | $621.4 |
| 25 | Heels | $421.42 | $100.91 | $310.69 | $653.12 | $520.97 | $1,054.93 | $651.6 |
| 26 | Sneakers | $429.10 | $97.69 | $319.22 | $846.01 | $539.53 | $1,115.37 | $681.8 |
| 27 | Sandals | $436.78 | $94.48 | $327.75 | $653.12 | $558.08 | $1,175.82 | $712. |
| 28 | Shoes Subtotal | $2,428.68 | $647.29 | $1,753.28 | $4,289.55 | $2,884.64 | $5,543.77 | $3,517.2 |
| 29 | | | | | | | | |
| 30 | Scarves | | | | | | | |
| 31 | Silk | $329.26 | $139.52 | $208.36 | $653.12 | $298.32 | $329.58 | $289. |
| 32 | Multi colored | $336.94 | $136.30 | $216.89 | $690.13 | $316.87 | $390.03 | $319.3 |
| 33 | Paisley | $344.62 | $133.09 | $225.42 | $653.12 | $335.43 | $450.47 | $349.5 |
| 34 | Over sized | $352.30 | $129.87 | $233.94 | $716.11 | $353.98 | $510.92 | $379.7 |
| 35 | Scarves Subtotal | $1,363.12 | $538.78 | $884.61 | $2,712.48 | $1,304.61 | $1,680.99 | $1,337.7 |
| 36 | | | | | | | | |
| 37 | Jewelry | | | | | | | |
| 38 | kle bracelets | $359.98 | $126.65 | $242.47 | $653.12 | $372.54 | $571.36 | $409.9 |
| 39 | Rings | $444.46 | $91.26 | $336.27 | $871.99 | $576.64 | $1,236.26 | $742.3 |
| 40 | Necklaces | $452.14 | $88.04 | $344.80 | $884.98 | $595.19 | $1,296.71 | $772.5 |
| 41 | Earrings | $459.82 | $84.82 | $353.33 | $653.12 | $613.75 | $1,357.16 | $802.7 |
| 42 | Pins | $467.50 | $81.61 | $361.86 | $910.96 | $632.30 | $1,417.60 | $832.9 |
| 43 | Jewelry Subtota | $2,183.90 | $472.38 | $1,638.73 | $3,974.17 | $2,790.42 | $5,879.09 | $3,560.4 |

**Figure 12.6**
*Before choosing Set Page Break.*

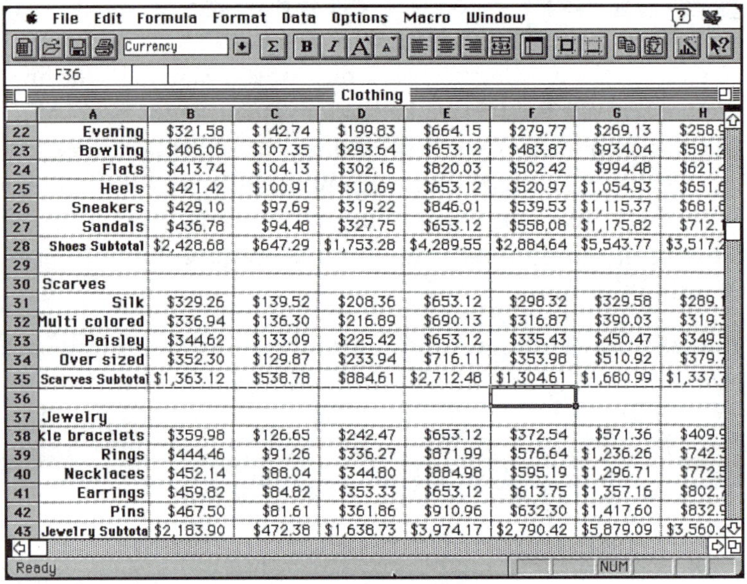


| | A | B | C | D | E | F | G | H |
|---|---|---|---|---|---|---|---|---|
| 22 | Evening | $321.58 | $142.74 | $199.83 | $664.15 | $279.77 | $269.13 | $258.9 |
| 23 | Bowling | $406.06 | $107.35 | $293.64 | $653.12 | $483.87 | $934.04 | $591.2 |
| 24 | Flats | $413.74 | $104.13 | $302.16 | $820.03 | $502.42 | $994.48 | $621.4 |
| 25 | Heels | $421.42 | $100.91 | $310.69 | $653.12 | $520.97 | $1,054.93 | $651.6 |
| 26 | Sneakers | $429.10 | $97.69 | $319.22 | $846.01 | $539.53 | $1,115.37 | $681.8 |
| 27 | Sandals | $436.78 | $94.48 | $327.75 | $653.12 | $558.08 | $1,175.82 | $712. |
| 28 | Shoes Subtotal | $2,428.68 | $647.29 | $1,753.28 | $4,289.55 | $2,884.64 | $5,543.77 | $3,517.2 |
| 29 | | | | | | | | |
| 30 | Scarves | | | | | | | |
| 31 | Silk | $329.26 | $139.52 | $208.36 | $653.12 | $298.32 | $329.58 | $289. |
| 32 | Multi colored | $336.94 | $136.30 | $216.89 | $690.13 | $316.87 | $390.03 | $319.3 |
| 33 | Paisley | $344.62 | $133.09 | $225.42 | $653.12 | $335.43 | $450.47 | $349.5 |
| 34 | Over sized | $352.30 | $129.87 | $233.94 | $716.11 | $353.98 | $510.92 | $379.7 |
| 35 | Scarves Subtotal | $1,363.12 | $538.78 | $884.61 | $2,712.48 | $1,304.61 | $1,680.99 | $1,337.7 |
| 36 | | | | | | | | |
| 37 | Jewelry | | | | | | | |
| 38 | kle bracelets | $359.98 | $126.65 | $242.47 | $653.12 | $372.54 | $571.36 | $409.9 |
| 39 | Rings | $444.46 | $91.26 | $336.27 | $871.99 | $576.64 | $1,236.26 | $742.3 |
| 40 | Necklaces | $452.14 | $88.04 | $344.80 | $884.98 | $595.19 | $1,296.71 | $772.5 |
| 41 | Earrings | $459.82 | $84.82 | $353.33 | $653.12 | $613.75 | $1,357.16 | $802.7 |
| 42 | Pins | $467.50 | $81.61 | $361.86 | $910.96 | $632.30 | $1,417.60 | $832.9 |
| 43 | Jewelry Subtota | $2,183.90 | $472.38 | $1,638.73 | $3,974.17 | $2,790.42 | $5,879.09 | $3,560.4 |

**Figure 12.7**
*After choosing Set Page Break.*

To fit more columns on the page, along with changing the font and margins, you can also change the number formatting. Perhaps, you can change the numbers from Currency format to Comma (0). This would reduce the width of those columns holding numbers by 4 characters ($.00) Try Best Fit again (double-click on column divider).

# A Whale of a Scale

You can also use the Reduce/Enlarge and *Scaling* commands in the Page Setup dialog box. Both of these commands let you fit more columns and rows than Print Preview first shows.

Try typing *95%* first in the Reduce/Enlarge box. Check Print Preview. If the document still doesn't fit, try *90%*, then *85%*, and so on.

Use the Scaling command when your document is slightly larger than the page. With this command, you can tell Excel to scale down a 1.25 page document until it fits on one page (see fig. 12.8). Be sure to carefully proof the printed document for anything that doesn't look right.

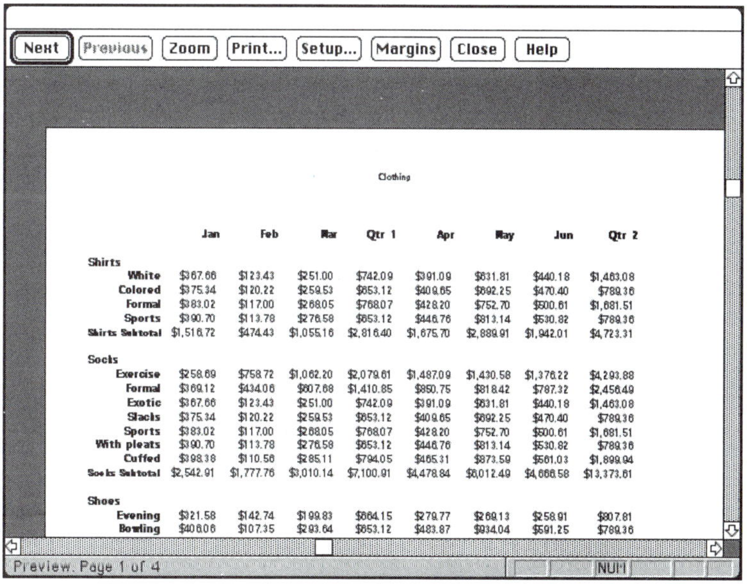


**Figure 12.8**
*A scaled-down document.*

Suppose that your worksheet is two pages long and two pages wide. Excel assumes that you want to first print going down and then across (see fig. 12.9). If this doesn't make sense, click the Over and then the Down button in the lower left corner of the Page Setup dialog box (see fig. 12.10).

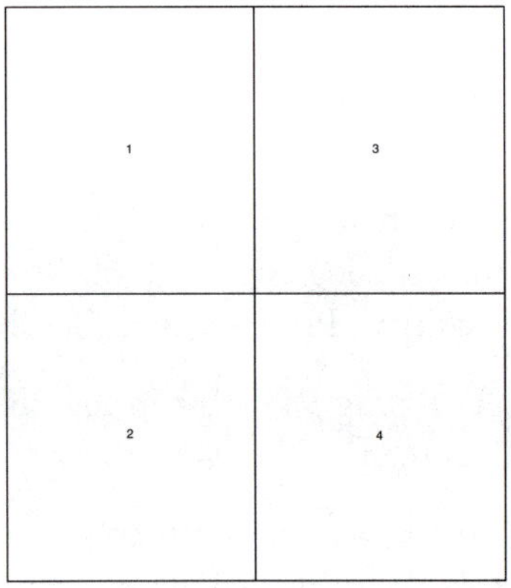


**Figure 12.9**
*Down, then across.*

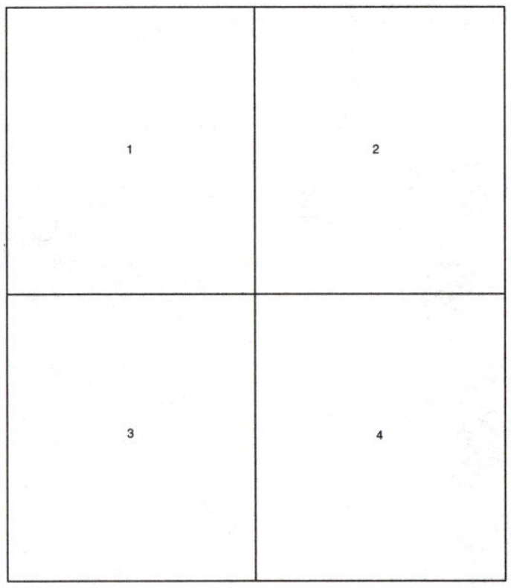


**Figure 12.10**
*Over, then down.*

# Practice

In this session, you make your Income and Expense worksheet larger by making it cover two years instead of one and by adding more expense categories.

To start with a new copy of the worksheet, choose Save As from the File menu, type a new filename—Inc & Exp 2 Yrs—make sure that it's in the right folder, and click the Save button.

# The More the Merrier

To add more expense categories, start by expanding row 14:

1. Click and drag from row 13 to 15.
2. Move the pointer to the bottom edge of row 15 and double-click with the double-sided arrow pointer. This will make all three rows a standard height.
3. Click on row number 14 (where the border is) and drag down 10 rows. Watch the formula bar rather than counting the rows (see fig. 12.11).

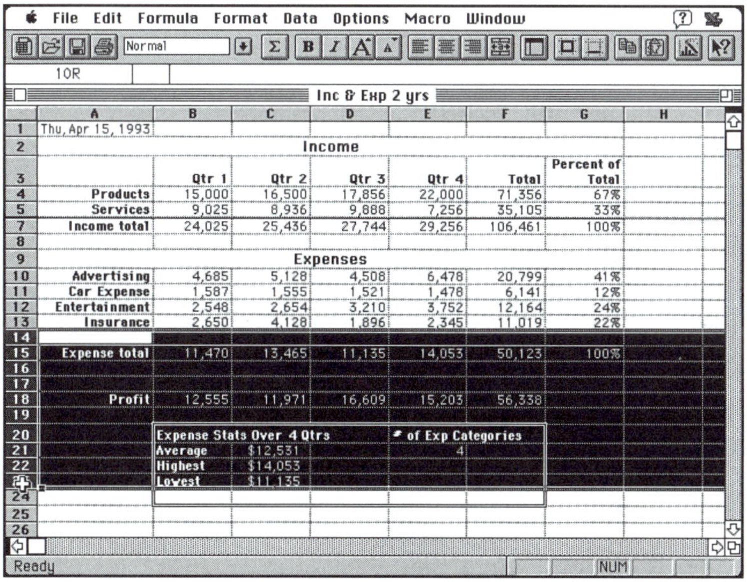


**Figure 12.11**
*10 rows selected.*

4. Choose Insert from the Edit menu.

## Type Type Type

Figure 12.12 shows the new category listing. Type the new categories and adjust the column width to fit the new categories. You are shortening the long ones as your worksheet gets larger.

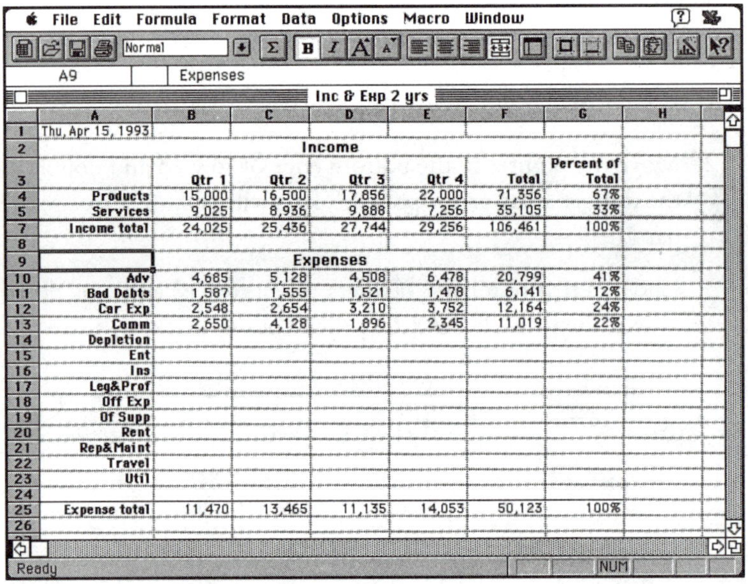


| | A | B | C | D | E | F | G |
|---|---|---|---|---|---|---|---|
| 1 | Thu, Apr 15, 1993 | | | | | | |
| 2 | | | Income | | | | |
| 3 | | Qtr 1 | Qtr 2 | Qtr 3 | Qtr 4 | Total | Percent of Total |
| 4 | Products | 15,000 | 16,500 | 17,856 | 22,000 | 71,356 | 67% |
| 5 | Services | 9,025 | 8,936 | 9,888 | 7,256 | 35,105 | 33% |
| 7 | Income total | 24,025 | 25,436 | 27,744 | 29,256 | 106,461 | 100% |
| 8 | | | | | | | |
| 9 | | | Expenses | | | | |
| 10 | Adv | 4,685 | 5,128 | 4,508 | 6,478 | 20,799 | 41% |
| 11 | Bad Debts | 1,587 | 1,555 | 1,521 | 1,478 | 6,141 | 12% |
| 12 | Car Exp | 2,548 | 2,654 | 3,210 | 3,752 | 12,164 | 24% |
| 13 | Comm | 2,650 | 4,128 | 1,896 | 2,345 | 11,019 | 22% |
| 14 | Depletion | | | | | | |
| 15 | Ent | | | | | | |
| 16 | Ins | | | | | | |
| 17 | Leg&Prof | | | | | | |
| 18 | Off Exp | | | | | | |
| 19 | Of Supp | | | | | | |
| 20 | Rent | | | | | | |
| 21 | Rep&Maint | | | | | | |
| 22 | Travel | | | | | | |
| 23 | Util | | | | | | |
| 24 | | | | | | | |
| 25 | Expense total | 11,470 | 13,465 | 11,135 | 14,053 | 50,123 | 100% |
| 26 | | | | | | | |

**Figure 12.12**
*Expense categories.*

## Fill Down the Formulas for Total and Percent of Total

Select both the Total and Percent of Total formulas in F13 and G13 and move the pointer to the fill handle on the Percent of Total formula. Click-drag down to the row holding the last category (see fig. 12.13).

You don't have to put new numbers in for the new categories, but you can if you want to.

## Copy the First Section (Year 1)

1. To select what you want to copy, click on Qtr 1 (B3) and drag diagonally down to the bottom row of your statistical area and over to the last column (see fig. 12.14).

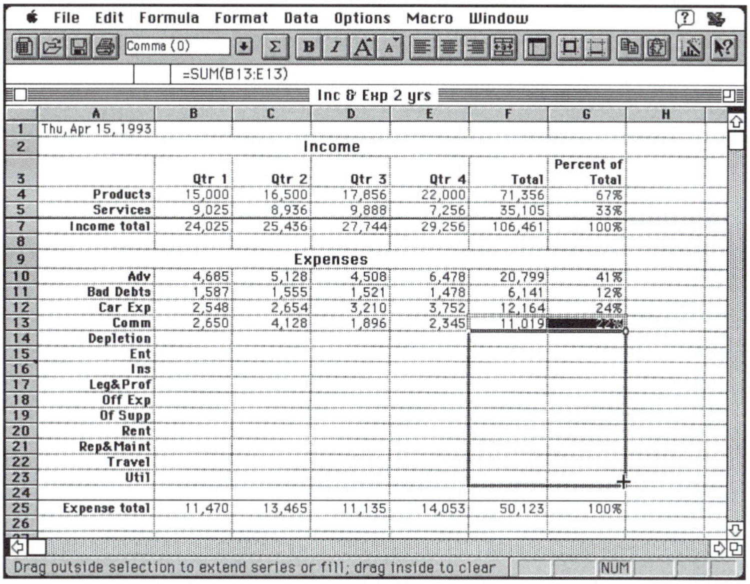


**Figure 12.13** *Formulas copied down.*

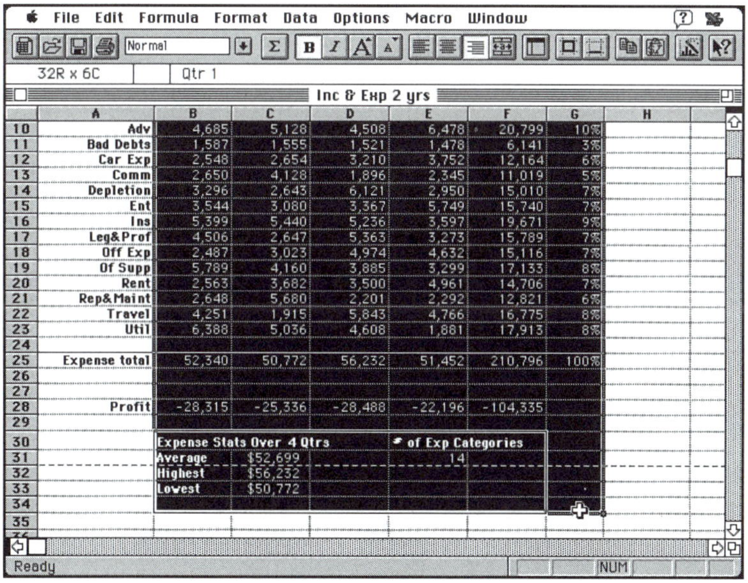


**Figure 12.14** *The section selected.*

2. Click the Copy tool.
3. Click to select I3.
4. Press Enter and voilà, you have a new section for Year 2.

## Cleaning House

Now, you have some cleaning up to do.

1. Change Income in A2 to Income 92—click in the formula bar and add 92 after Income.
2. Click I2 and type *Income 93.*
3. Do the same with the Expense headings.
4. Adjust all column widths appropriately.
5. Use the Center Across Columns tool on the new Income and Expenses headings. Remember to first select the rows you want the headings centered across.
6. Select all of the numbers (except the percents), choose Number from the Format menu, click Number on the left, and choose the third format (`#,##0`). This is a very narrow format.
7. Column H, which is separating the two years, needn't to be so wide. Make it narrower by dragging the column divider to the left until the formula bar says 1.00 (see fig. 12.15).

## Lost in the Ozone

1. Scroll over to the end of Year 2 in Column O.
2. Notice that you no longer see the headings in column A (unless you have a monitor larger than 13 inches).
3. Scroll down to the bottom of Expenses. Notice how the row headings scroll up and out of view (ditto on the monitor message).

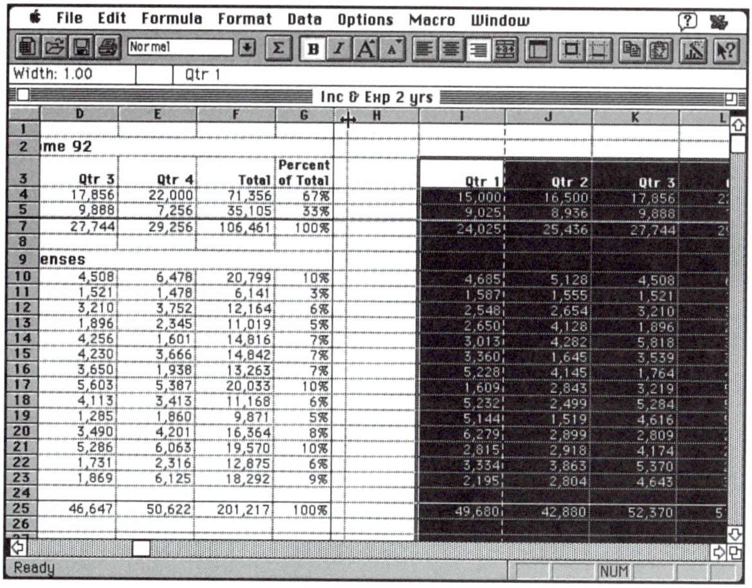


**Figure 12.15**
*The narrowed column.*

4. Scroll back to the first screen and select B4, just under Qtr 1.

   Note that this is an important juncture. You are under the column headings and to the right of the row headings.

5. Choose Freeze Panes from the Window menu (see fig. 12.16).

6. Note how the new scroll bars disappear and that a darker line shows where the panes have been frozen.

7. Scroll until you see only Column A and the columns for Year 2. What a concept!

# A Heading on Every Page

1. See whether this Freeze Panes command has also given you headings on every page. Choose Print Preview from the File menu.

2. Check the top of each page. There are no headings.

3. Click the Close button.

4. Now you need to make a few minor changes. Delete row 1. Click the row number and choose Delete from the Edit menu. You don't need the date there any more because you can add a dynamic date to the Header or Footer. (A dynamic date changes according to the day it's printed.)

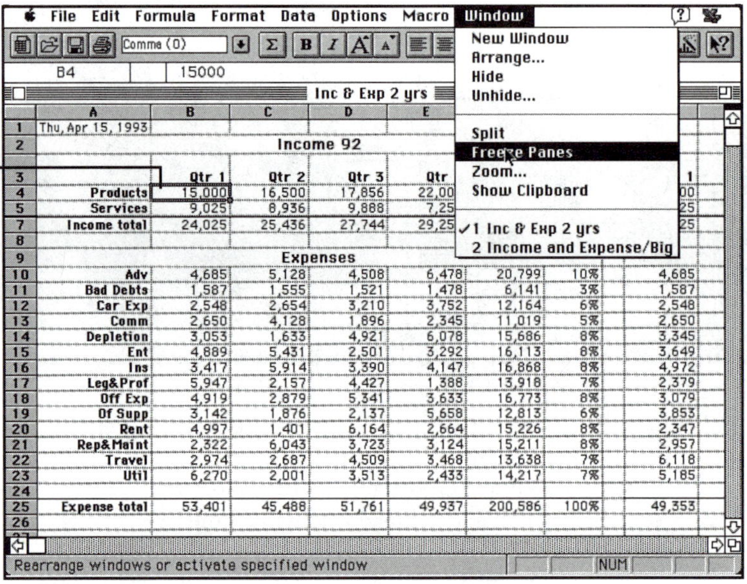


**Figure 12.16**
*Choose Freeze Panes.*

5. Delete a row between Expense total and Profit.

6. Delete the empty row below Profit.

# Print Titles

Even though you can see headings on-screen, they're not going to print after page 1 without one more step:

1. Tell Excel which rows and headings are to appear on every page: Click on row 1 and drag down one row to row 2. Hold down the Command key and click Column A.

2. Choose Set Print Titles from the Options menu (see fig. 12.17). Click OK.

3. Look at Print Preview again and turn the pages. Now you'll see headings on every page (see fig. 12.18). If you don't like where the pages are breaking, go back to "They're Out to Get Us" for instructions.

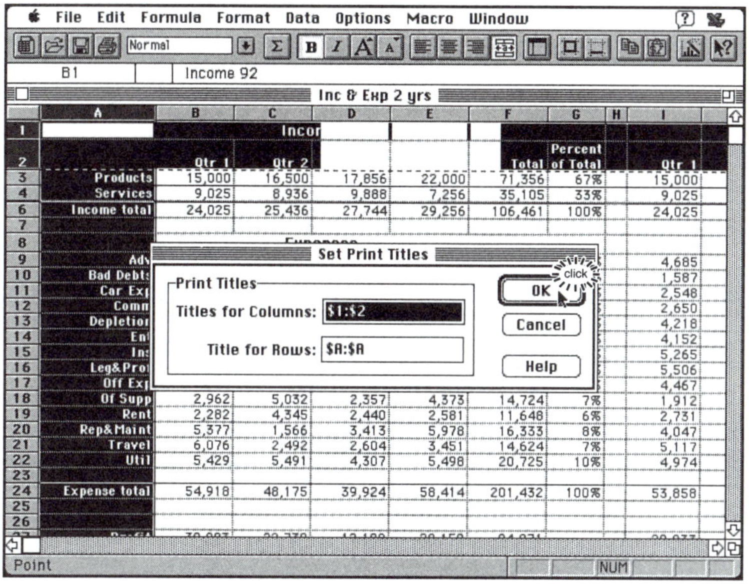

**Figure 12.17**
*Select these ranges.*

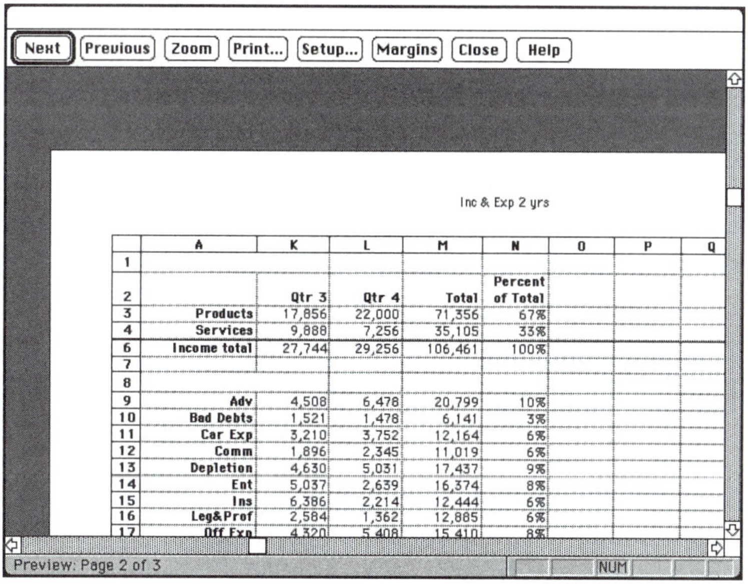

**Figure 12.18**
*Headings where they should be on page 2.*

## Back to the Beginning

1. Choose Unfreeze Panes from the Window menu and return to A1.
2. Choose Quit from the File menu, save your changes, and take a well deserved break.

## Summary

When a document becomes larger than the screen or page, you can use a number of methods to avoid confusion:

- On-Screen: The New Window command gives you a new temporary window for the same document. The Freeze Panes command freezes columns and rows in their place on the left and top sides of the window.
- For Printing: The Print Titles command lets you print headings on every page.

## Exorcises

1. What cell should you select before giving the Freeze Panes command?
2. What menu holds the Arrange command? The Print Titles command?
3. Where do you find the listing of all open windows?
4. What steps can you take to fit more of your worksheet on a page?
5. What command lets you tell Excel to fit your worksheet onto one page, even though it is 1 1/2 pages? What dialog box is it in?
6. What command is the opposite of Freeze Panes?

13th Encounter

# Linking Worksheets

## Goal

Learn techniques for creating worksheets that are linked together by formulas.

## What You Will Need

Knowledge of simple formulas.

## Terms of Enfearment

Source worksheets
Dependent worksheets
Zoom box
Links command

# Briefing

Frequently, it makes sense to keep track of information about related items on different worksheets. You may supervise a number of salespeople, manage three divisions, or have responsibility for two departments.

In this encounter's example, you have been tracking sales for three salespeople, each having their own worksheet. You want to create a summary sheet to track sales for all three salespeople.

You also want to change and add to the information in the individual worksheets and have the summary worksheet update itself automatically with the new, changed information. This can happen when formulas in the summary sheet can look at the individual sheets and grab numbers from them.

The worksheets that hold the original information are called *source* worksheets because they hold the numbers the summary worksheet needs. The summary sheet is the *dependent* worksheet (see fig. 13.1).

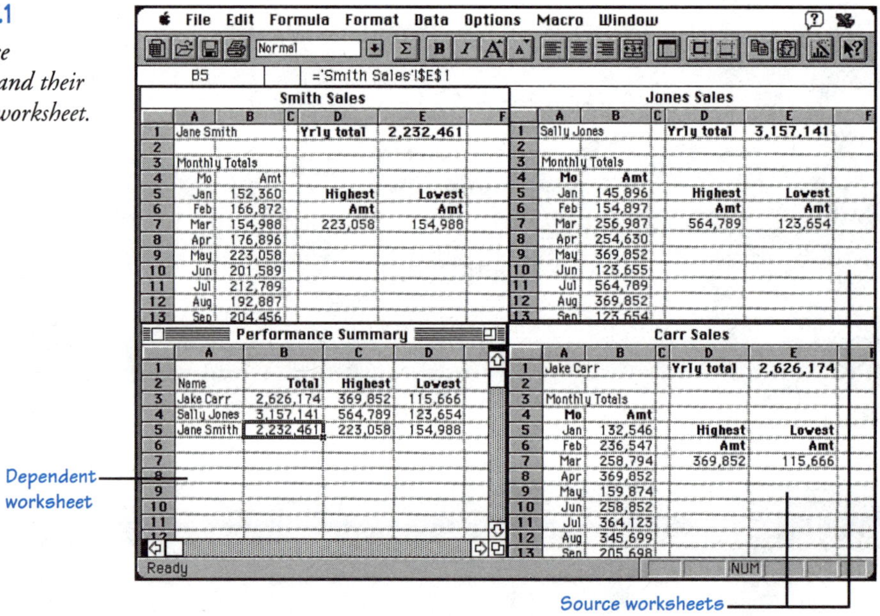


**Figure 13.1**
*Three source worksheets and their dependent worksheet.*

Start the process by opening the source worksheets. Spend some time making sure that they are set up in the same way. This makes the next step easier. Think about how you want to compile the information on the dependent worksheet. Keep the design as simple as possible.

Whenever you have more than one document open, you can see their names listed at the bottom of the Window menu. You can move any of them to the top of the pile by choosing them from this list.

## A Marriage of Convenience: Hooking Two Worksheets Together

When you have the source worksheets and dependent worksheets all open, you can use the Arrange command on the Window menu to see them all at the same time. Any time you want one of the windows to return to full size, click the *Zoom box* (upper right corner of the window). Click it again to shrink the window back down and put it in its place.

The actual link is a formula in the dependent worksheet that refers to the supporting worksheet. If you had to type the formula, you would have to remember some weird stuff, but you don't. You can click it in, just like all the formulas you have created. Only this time, to create the link, click on a cell in another worksheet.

To create a linking formula, select the cell in the dependent worksheet where you want the information from the source worksheet to appear (in the example, you would select cell B3 of the Performance Summary worksheet). As always, start the formula by typing an equal sign. Next, select the supporting worksheet (Carr Sales) with one click, click again on the cell holding the information (E1), and finally enter the formula in the dependent worksheet (see fig. 13.2).

This is what the formula is saying to Excel: "From the worksheet with this name, go get the contents of this cell." After the link has been created, keep all the linked worksheets in the same folder.

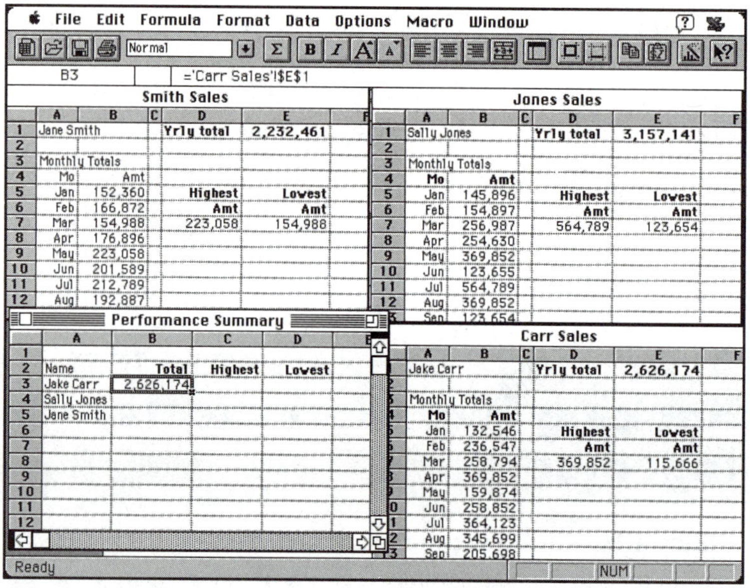


**Figure 13.2**
*The completed formula.*

# Close All

When you have more than one worksheet open and need to close them, you can make the File menu offer a Close All command by holding down the Shift key before opening the File menu. Close changes to Close All.

# Open Dependent Worksheet First

Always open the dependent worksheet first. Then use the *Links* command on the File menu (see fig. 13.3) to open the source worksheets in one step, rather than one at a time. To open them at the same time, press and hold down the Shift key while clicking once on each of them.

When you open a dependent worksheet before opening the source worksheets, Excel asks whether it should look at the source worksheets (see fig. 13.4). It wants to see whether the source worksheets have been changed since the last time the dependent worksheet was saved.

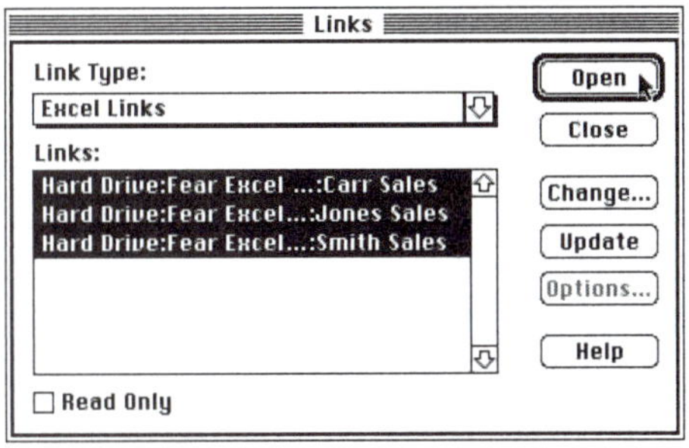


Figure 13.3
*The Links window.*

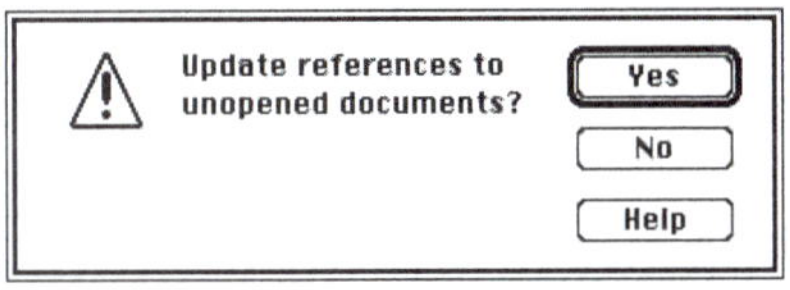


Figure 13.4
*Results when opening the dependent worksheet first.*

# You Don't Mind if We Call Your References. . .

If you are also planning to open the source worksheets, you can click the No button, because when these worksheets open, the update automatically happens. Otherwise, you should click the Yes button.

Generally, it's a good idea to keep all the associated worksheets open when you are working on one or more of them. Also get in the habit of closing and saving the summary sheet last. By following these two procedures, you know the summary sheet will be updated.

When you close a dependent worksheet, Excel asks whether you want to save changes, even if you have not made changes. This happens because Excel recalculates the dependent worksheet whenever it's opened and thinks it's been changed. There's no harm in clicking Yes to this question.

## They're Out To Get Us

If a source worksheet is renamed or moved from the folder it was in when the link was made, the link is in trouble.

The best (easiest) solution is start them all off in the same folder before creating the link and don't move or rename linked files.

If you've changed the name of a source worksheet after creating the link, you'll probably see the dialog box in figure 13.5.

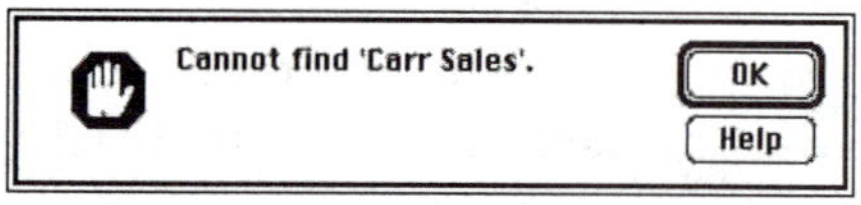


Figure 13.5
*Where is that file?*

Click the OK button and then choose Links from the File menu. Click the former name and click the Change button. Find the new file name in the file list and double-click. This tells Excel to change the link to the different name.

## Hot Links, No Sauerkraut

If you move a source worksheet to another folder and then open the dependent worksheet without updating your cell references, the cell holding your formula might hold an error value: `#REF!`. This message says that a cell in the formula is no longer valid—it isn't valid because Excel can't find it.

To fix this, choose Links from the File menu and select the name of the moved file. Click the Change button, find the file in the new location, and double-click it.

# Practice

## Keeping Up with the Joneses

In this session, you will create Jones Sales (see fig. 13.6)and copy it for the other sales people.

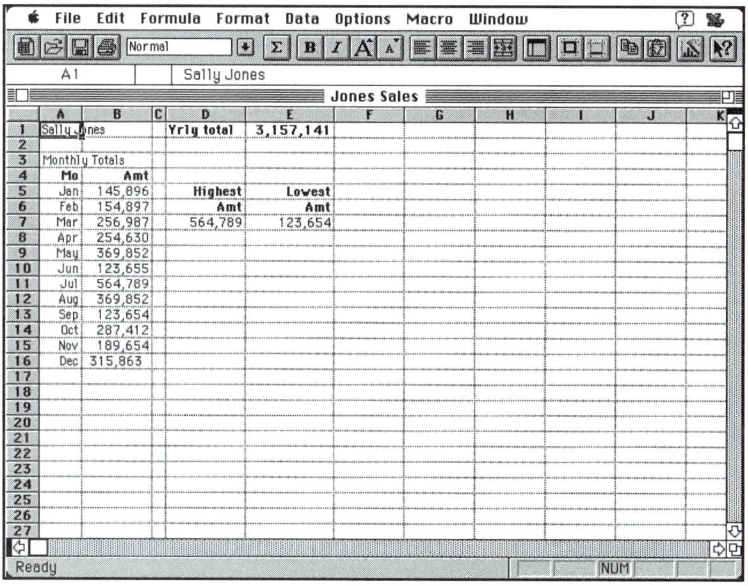


**Figure 13.6** *The Jones Sales worksheet.*

1. Click the New Worksheet tool if you don't have a new worksheet visible. Type *Jan* in A5.
2. Remember Autofill? Here's a perfect opportunity to practice it. Put the pointer on the fill handle. When it becomes a crosshair, click and drag down the column while watching the formula bar for Dec. When it appears, release the mouse button.

3. Type the numbers next.

   Notice how the total for the column is not at the bottom of the column. The worksheet police will not knock on your door if you want to total a column above, rather than below.

4. Put the formula for the yearly total in E1.
5. Get your total by clicking the AutoSum tool and selecting the range: Click the top number. **Don't** release the mouse button. Keep the mouse button held down and drag down the column. Don't release the mouse button until you've reached one cell below the final number.
6. Keep trying until you get it right and then enter it (see fig. 13.7).

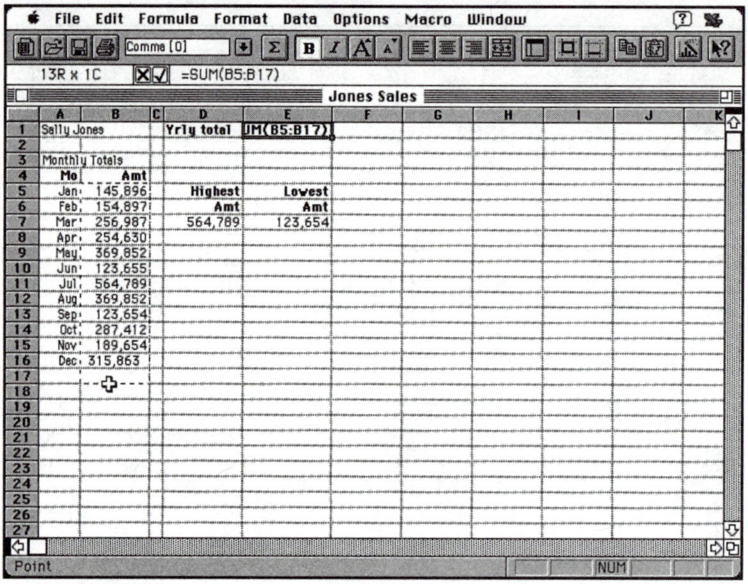


**Figure 13.7**
*Total formula with range selected.*

7. Use the MAX and MIN functions with the same range for the other two formulas under Highest and Lowest Amounts.
8. Format the worksheet to your satisfaction. Don't forget those neat tools (Bold, etc.).
9. Click the Save tool and call this worksheet Jones Sales.

# Four (Work)Sheets to the Wind

1. To make a copy, choose Save As from the File menu, call it Smith Sales, and click Save.
2. Replace Jones's name with Smith's name, change the numbers, and click the Save tool.
3. Choose Save As and name this third worksheet for the third salesperson Carr.
4. Make the necessary changes for Carr and click the Save tool again.
5. Click the New worksheet tool so that you can create the dependent worksheet.
6. Type the three names in column A.
7. Click the Save tool, call this worksheet Performance Summary, and click the Save button.

# OpenOpenOpen

1. Click the Open Worksheet tool and double-click Jones Sales.
2. Again click the Open Worksheet tool and double-click Smith Sales.

## What's Out There

1. Look at the Window menu. Note the list of open documents at the bottom.
2. Choose Arrange Tiled from Window.
3. Now look at all the worksheets simultaneously. It's likely that they're not arranged exactly as they are in the picture, so move them around until you like the way they look.

   Remember, you move a window by dragging the Title bar. You resize a window by dragging the size box.

## Gold Links

1. Activate the Performance Summary worksheet by clicking on it. Note how the title bar appears on the active worksheet (see fig. 13.8).

Figure 13.8
*Active Title bar.*

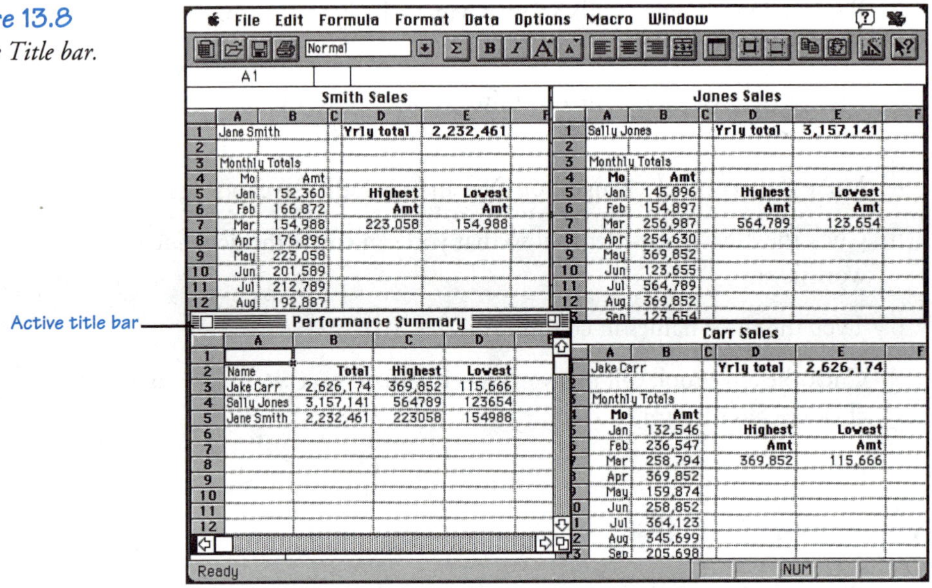


2. Click on the cell that should hold Carr's total (B3).
3. Type an equal sign (=).
4. Click on the worksheet named Carr Sales. This first click alerts Excel that you want to create a formula that involves Carr Sales.
5. Click on the Carr Sales worksheet in the Yrly total cell (E1).
6. Enter the formula (see fig. 13.9).

Performance Summary should still be the active worksheet.

1. Select the cell holding the formula if it's no longer the active cell.
2. Look at the formula bar. What does it say?

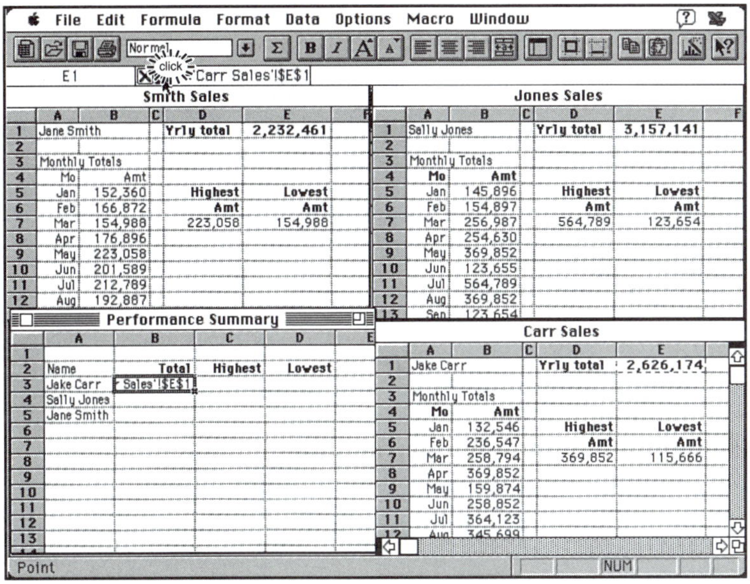

Figure 13.9
*Click on the Enter box.*

3. Move the cell pointer down and pull in the next formula. Type an equal sign (=); click the worksheet named Jones Sales; click on the cell holding the yearly total; enter the formula.
4. Do the same for Smith.
5. Save and close all four documents, closing Performance Summary last.

# Open Up, Nice and Easy

1. To open them all up again in two steps, first open Performance Summary.
2. Choose Links from the File menu.
3. Click the first file name, hold down the Shift key, and click each of the others until they're all selected.
4. Click the Open button.

## Play Time

1. Make some changes to the numbers in the sales people's worksheets. Note how Performance Summary is updated immediately.
2. Practice making more links.

## Time Flies When . . .

1. Close Performance Summary and save the changes.
2. Chose Quit from the File menu. As Excel closes the worksheets, it will ask about saving changes. Click the Yes button.

# Summary

Worksheets can be linked together by formulas so that one worksheet depends on another, called the source worksheet.

The formulas can be created by pointing to the formula in the source worksheet after starting the formula in the dependent worksheet.

The Links command enables you to open all the source worksheets at the same time. It's a good idea to keep all the source worksheets and the dependent sheet in the same folder and not to change their names after the link is made. If a move or a name change occurs, select the original file in the Links dialog box and use the Change button to move to the new file and re-create the link with a double-click.

# Exorcises

1. Which sheet holds the linking formula: the source or the dependent worksheet?
2. Which menu shows all open files?

3. If a window isn't full size, what part do you click on to zoom it up to full size?
4. Which key do you hold down to select all the source documents in the Links dialog box?
5. Which menu holds the Links command?
6. Which menu holds the Arrange command?
7. Keeping linked files in the same folder is not important. True or False?

14th Encounter

# Using Excel as a Database

## Goal

Master techniques for creating worksheets that track information and find records that share certain characteristics.

## What You Will Need

Excel running.

## Terms of Enfearment

| | |
|---|---|
| Field | Data Form command |
| Record | Criteria |
| Sort command | Set Database command |

# Briefing

It's best to think of Excel as the right software for financial analysis and number crunching. If your main goal is to keep track of information, a database program is better. If you need any complicated reporting on your information, a database like FileMaker Pro is a better choice. For example, if you need to generate mailing labels, it's a big deal in Excel but much simpler in FileMaker Pro

However, if your information needs are simple and if you're not ready to learn another program, you can start with Excel and switch to a database in the future.

When using Excel to track information, you're still be using the same old worksheets. You're just using different commands and features, many of which are on the Data menu.

We also set up the worksheet in a specific way as shown in figure 14.1: The first row contains the field headings; each column is a *field*; each row is a *record.* The database includes the row holding the field headings and the rows containing the data.

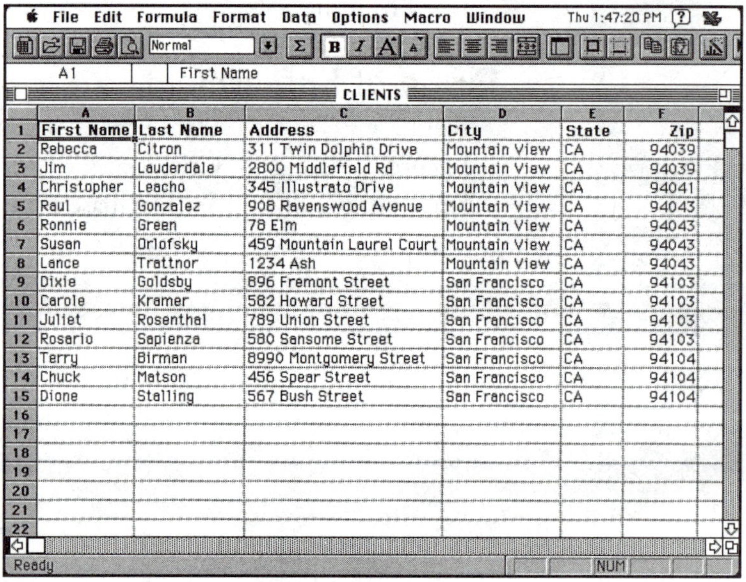


| | A | B | C | D | E | F |
|---|---|---|---|---|---|---|
| 1 | First Name | Last Name | Address | City | State | Zip |
| 2 | Rebecca | Citron | 311 Twin Dolphin Drive | Mountain View | CA | 94039 |
| 3 | Jim | Lauderdale | 2800 Middlefield Rd | Mountain View | CA | 94039 |
| 4 | Christopher | Leacho | 345 Illustrato Drive | Mountain View | CA | 94041 |
| 5 | Raul | Gonzalez | 908 Ravenswood Avenue | Mountain View | CA | 94043 |
| 6 | Ronnie | Green | 78 Elm | Mountain View | CA | 94043 |
| 7 | Susan | Orlofsky | 459 Mountain Laurel Court | Mountain View | CA | 94043 |
| 8 | Lance | Trattnor | 1234 Ash | Mountain View | CA | 94043 |
| 9 | Dixie | Goldsby | 896 Fremont Street | San Francisco | CA | 94103 |
| 10 | Carole | Kramer | 582 Howard Street | San Francisco | CA | 94103 |
| 11 | Juliet | Rosenthal | 789 Union Street | San Francisco | CA | 94103 |
| 12 | Rosario | Sapienza | 580 Sansome Street | San Francisco | CA | 94103 |
| 13 | Terry | Birman | 8990 Montgomery Street | San Francisco | CA | 94104 |
| 14 | Chuck | Matson | 456 Spear Street | San Francisco | CA | 94104 |
| 15 | Dione | Stalling | 567 Bush Street | San Francisco | CA | 94104 |
| 16 | | | | | | |
| 17 | | | | | | |
| 18 | | | | | | |
| 19 | | | | | | |
| 20 | | | | | | |
| 21 | | | | | | |
| 22 | | | | | | |

**Figure 14.1.** *Clients listing—labeled.*

# Out of Sorts

Actually, you can sort any rows or columns, even without using the database commands. This command, however, is definitely associated with tracking data. After all, when using Excel to track information, you frequently want to sort the records.

You can sort by one, two, or three columns (keys). Why not sort by City, then ZIP code, and finally by Last Name?

The first step in sorting is, as always, selecting what you want to sort (see fig. 14.2).

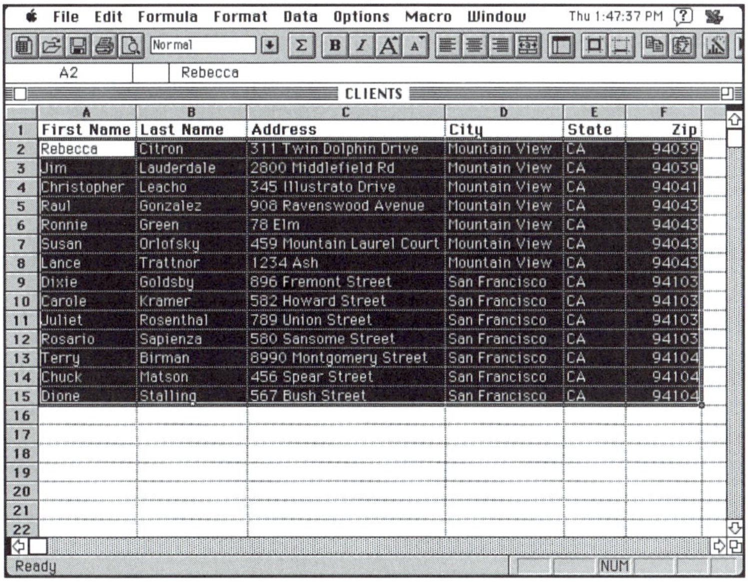


**Figure 14.2**
*Records selected for sorting.*

Note how the field headings aren't selected. You don't want to get them mixed in with the records. The next step is giving the *Sort* command, which is found on the Data menu (see fig. 14.3).

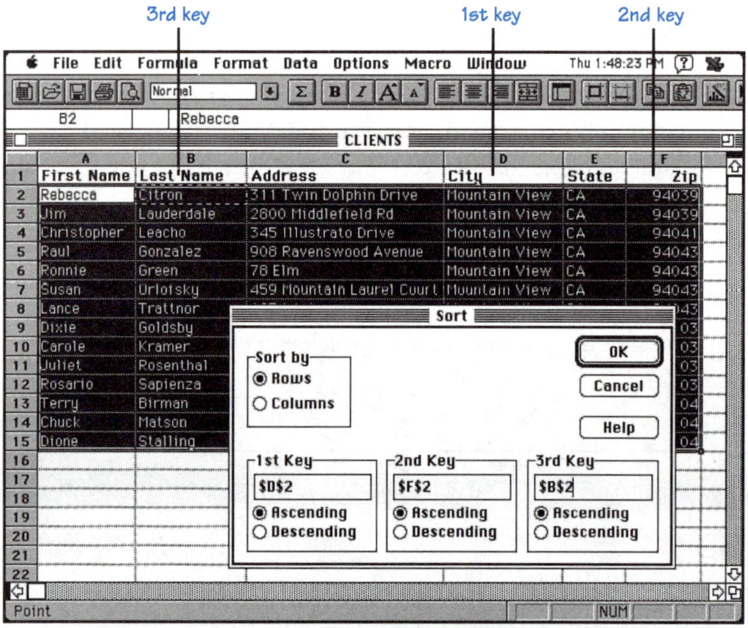


**Figure 14.3**
*The Sort window.*

Note how the cell references in the Sort key boxes refer to the first cell in the column you want to sort by. After you sort, all the people from Mountain View are together and listed before the people from San Francisco. Within each city, the records are sorted by ZIP code, and within each ZIP code, the records are sorted by last name (see fig. 14.4).

# Data Form

To add new records, delete records, and find and change records based on your criteria, you can do it directly in the database, or you can use the *Data Form* command, which is fairly convenient.

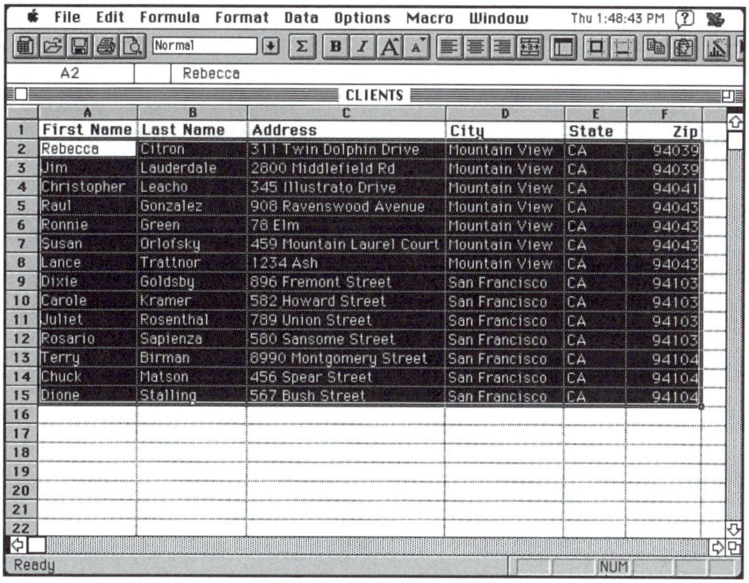

| | First Name | Last Name | Address | City | State | Zip |
|---|---|---|---|---|---|---|
| 2 | Rebecca | Citron | 311 Twin Dolphin Drive | Mountain View | CA | 94039 |
| 3 | Jim | Lauderdale | 2800 Middlefield Rd | Mountain View | CA | 94039 |
| 4 | Christopher | Leacho | 345 Illustrato Drive | Mountain View | CA | 94041 |
| 5 | Raul | Gonzalez | 908 Ravenswood Avenue | Mountain View | CA | 94043 |
| 6 | Ronnie | Green | 78 Elm | Mountain View | CA | 94043 |
| 7 | Susan | Orlofsky | 459 Mountain Laurel Court | Mountain View | CA | 94043 |
| 8 | Lance | Trattnor | 1234 Ash | Mountain View | CA | 94043 |
| 9 | Dixie | Goldsby | 896 Fremont Street | San Francisco | CA | 94103 |
| 10 | Carole | Kramer | 582 Howard Street | San Francisco | CA | 94103 |
| 11 | Juliet | Rosenthal | 789 Union Street | San Francisco | CA | 94103 |
| 12 | Rosario | Sapienza | 580 Sansome Street | San Francisco | CA | 94103 |
| 13 | Terry | Birman | 8990 Montgomery Street | San Francisco | CA | 94104 |
| 14 | Chuck | Matson | 456 Spear Street | San Francisco | CA | 94104 |
| 15 | Dione | Stalling | 567 Bush Street | San Francisco | CA | 94104 |

Figure 14.4
*The records sorted.*

# Criteria

When you give Excel *criteria*, you're asking it to find records that share one or more characteristics; for example, you could ask Excel to find all records in which the Amount field is greater than 1000 or in which the Customer field is equal to Smith.

# Set Database

Before using the Data Form command, you have to tell Excel where your database resides on the worksheet. You select the field headings and records and give the *Set Database* command, which causes Excel to name the selected range Database (see fig. 14.5). After the range is named, whenever it's selected, you see its name in the formula bar (see fig. 14.6). Wow, that formula bar is a hard-working, multipurpose, well-rounded bar.

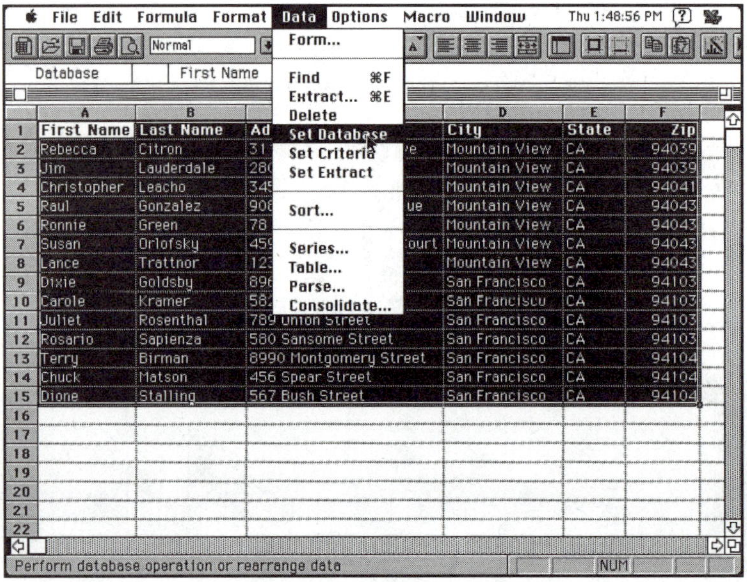


Figure 14.5
*The Set Database command from the Data menu.*

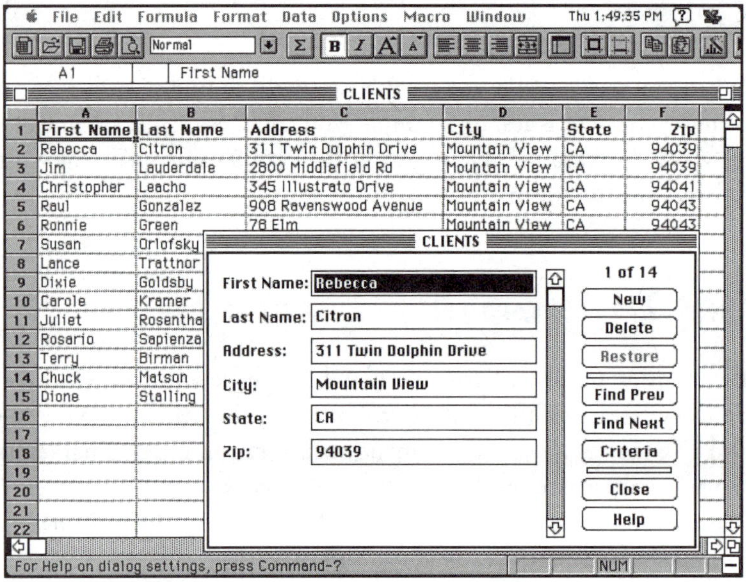


Figure 14.6
*The Form window.*

## I'm Just Browsing

Giving the Data Form command after setting the database displays the Form window. Browse through your records by clicking in the scroll bar moves through the entire database.

When you find a record you need to change, select a field by clicking on it and type the new information. Press the Return key when you're finished changing a record. You can also move from field to field by pressing the Tab key.

Add new records by clicking the New button. You'll get an empty record. Type the new information, tabbing from field to field. When you're finished with the new record, pressing the Return key adds the new record to the bottom of the database and gives you another empty record. You can add another new record at this point. You can delete the current record (the one showing in the form) by clicking the Delete button. You'll get a warning and a chance to change your mind.

## The Criteria Window

Rather than looking through all the records and stopping at ones you need to examine, you can ask Excel to show you only certain ones. To specify those records that share a certain characteristic (fulfill certain criteria), click on the Criteria button, which switches to an empty form (see fig. 14.8). You're now in a Criteria window where you can type the criteria into the correct field. Get in the habit of checking to see whether you're in Form or Criteria mode.

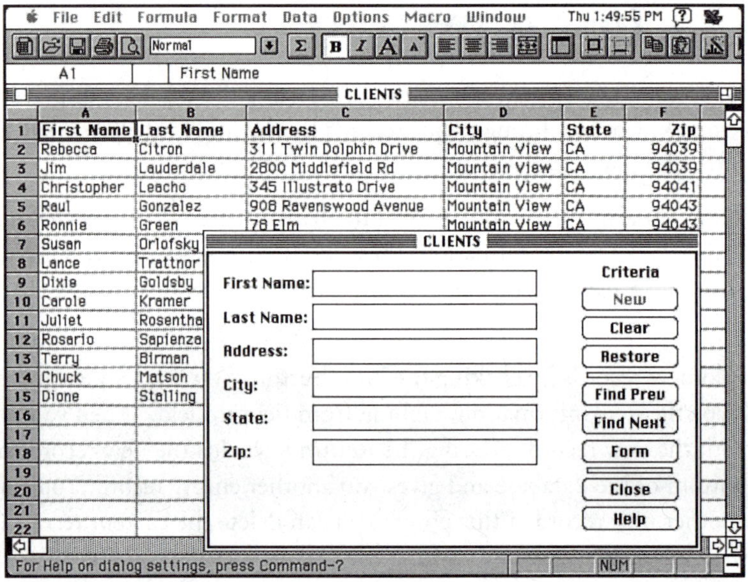


**Figure 14.7**
*Criteria window.*

# Symbols of Success

Table 14.1 shows the symbols to use when typing your criteria.

### Table 14.1. Criteria Symbols

| *Symbol* | *Description* | *Example* |
|---|---|---|
| > | Greater than | >1000 |
| < | Less than | <6/1/92 |
| >= | Greater than or equal to | >=1/1/93 |
| <= | Less than or equal to | <=5500 |

After typing the criteria, press the Return key. Now you're back in the Form (as opposed to the Criteria) window. At the top right, Excel indicates the number of records in the subset along with the total. Click Find Next and Find Previous to go through the subset of records. Excel beeps at you when you reach the first and last records in the subset.

To again explore all records, click or drag in the scroll bar.

# They're Out To Get Us

Suppose that you have multiple columns of information in each record and want to sort the records. You select all the columns on screen and give the Sort command. Unfortunately, more columns are lurking on the next screen.

The problem with making a mistake like this is that you may not realize the error until later, upon realizing one part of a record doesn't match the other part. Actually, it's better to realize it's happened, rather than blithely believing that your data is fine.

If you're fortunate enough to recognize your mistake immediately, choose Undo Sort from the Edit menu. If your realization comes too late for the Undo command, but you haven't saved the file since the bad sort, close it *without saving the changes.* Now open it again. This is a sort of reverse reincarnation. The file looks like it did the last time you saved it.

If you don't recognize your error until after you've saved it, you'll have to get the copy you backed up the day before. (You do back up important files every day, don't you?) Backing up involves storing copies of important files on another disk. At times like this, you'll bless your good habits or curse your lack of them.

You can do several things to avoid this problem in the first place:

1. Slow down! Get in the habit of double checking that you selected everything you needed to select.
2. While selecting what needs to be sorted, use the Autoselect method you learned earlier. This method selects blocks of data. Select the first column from top row to bottom row, move the mouse pointer to the right edge of the selected range, hold down the Shift key, and double-click.

# Define Name

This is an impressive stunt. You can name the range the first time you select it for sorting and thereafter use the Goto command to select the named range.

The Define Name command on the Formula menu lets you assign a name to a cell or range of cells that are selected (see fig. 14.8). No spaces are allowed in the name.

When a range is selected that has a name, the name shows in the formula bar. You can use the Goto command to select a named range because the Goto list (from the Formula menu) includes all named ranges (see fig. 14.9).

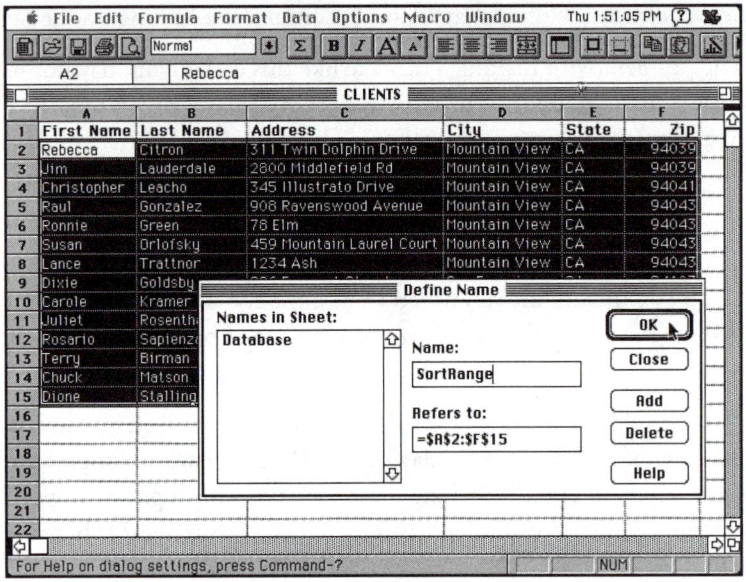


Figure 14.8
*Name defined.*

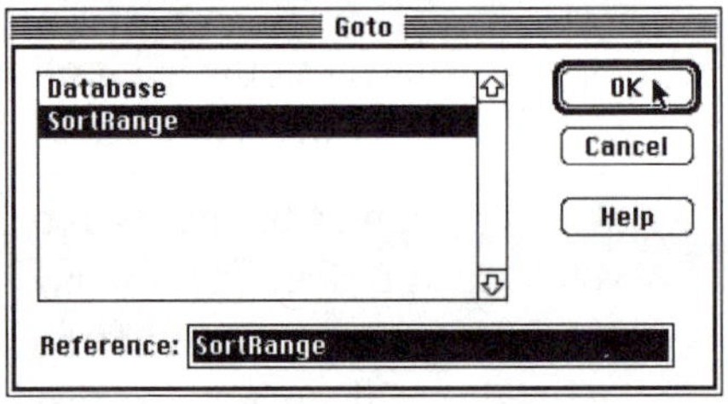


Figure 14.9
*The name in the Goto dialog box*

# Practice

In this session, you will build a database that looks like figure 14.10.

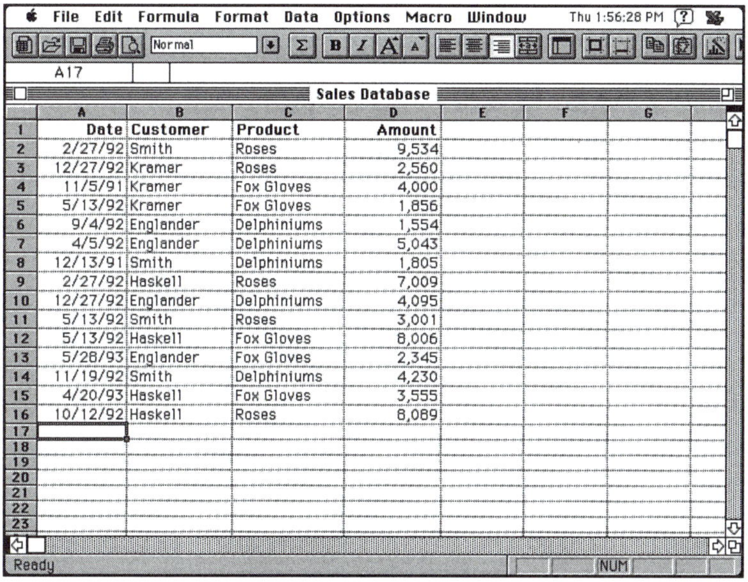

| | A | B | C | D |
|---|---|---|---|---|
| 1 | Date | Customer | Product | Amount |
| 2 | 2/27/92 | Smith | Roses | 9,534 |
| 3 | 12/27/92 | Kramer | Roses | 2,560 |
| 4 | 11/5/91 | Kramer | Fox Gloves | 4,000 |
| 5 | 5/13/92 | Kramer | Fox Gloves | 1,856 |
| 6 | 9/4/92 | Englander | Delphiniums | 1,554 |
| 7 | 4/5/92 | Englander | Delphiniums | 5,043 |
| 8 | 12/13/91 | Smith | Delphiniums | 1,805 |
| 9 | 2/27/92 | Haskell | Roses | 7,009 |
| 10 | 12/27/92 | Englander | Delphiniums | 4,095 |
| 11 | 5/13/92 | Smith | Roses | 3,001 |
| 12 | 5/13/92 | Haskell | Fox Gloves | 8,006 |
| 13 | 5/28/93 | Englander | Fox Gloves | 2,345 |
| 14 | 11/19/92 | Smith | Delphiniums | 4,230 |
| 15 | 4/20/93 | Haskell | Fox Gloves | 3,555 |
| 16 | 10/12/92 | Haskell | Roses | 8,089 |



Figure 14.10
*The Sales database.*

1. Before you go ahead and type it all, select the range first: Click on A1 and drag over to D16.
2. Type the word *Date* in A1 and press the Tab key. When you type the last field name *Amount* and press the Tab key, the cell pointer moves down to A2 so that you can continue typing.

Remember not to use the cursor arrow keys because using them loses the selection, although it's not a big deal if you do. Just reselect the necessary range and start typing again.

# Name That Range

1. You need to select only the rows you want to sort, row 2 to row 16.

2. Name this selection so that you can use the Goto command to select it the next time you want to sort. Choose Define Name from the Formula menu.
3. Type *SortRange* and click the OK button. Note the name in the formula bar.

## Sort by One Key

First sort so that the dates go from earliest to latest list.

1. Leaving the range selected, choose Sort from the Data menu.
2. Move the window if you can't see the top row of the selection.
3. Notice how $A$2 in the First Key text box corresponds to the first date in the Date column, which has the marching ants border (see fig. 14.11). Excel is asking, "Do you want to sort by Date?"
4. Say "Yes" by clicking OK. Wicked fast sort! Now your records are sorted by date.

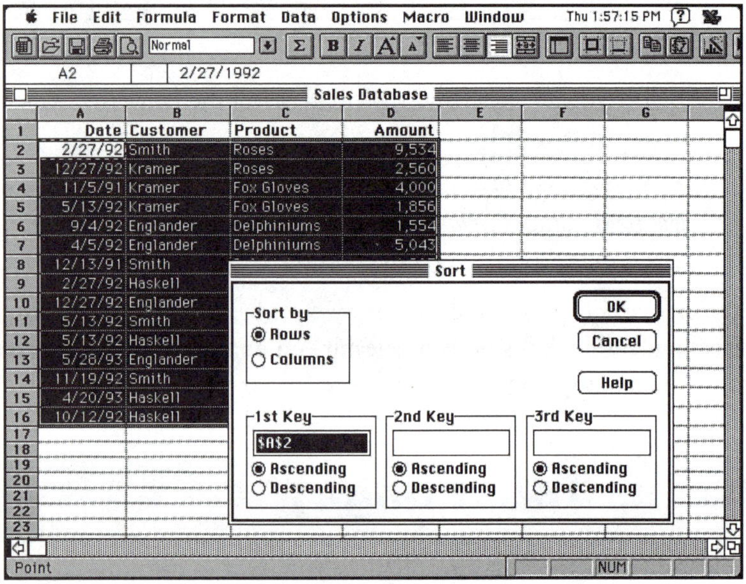


**Figure 14.11**
*Sorting by date.*

# Sorting by Two Keys

If you look at dates that appear more than once, you see that customers are not sorted within that date.

1. To select the records to be sorted, choose Goto from the Formula menu and double-click SortRange.
2. With your records selected, choose Sort from the Data menu. Again, $A$2 is in the First Key text box.
3. To sort by customer after sorting by date, click in the Second Key box.
4. Click on the top record, right under the Customer field heading to select B2 (see fig. 14.12).
5. Click OK.
6. Look at any records sharing the same date. The customers are now alphabetized within each date.

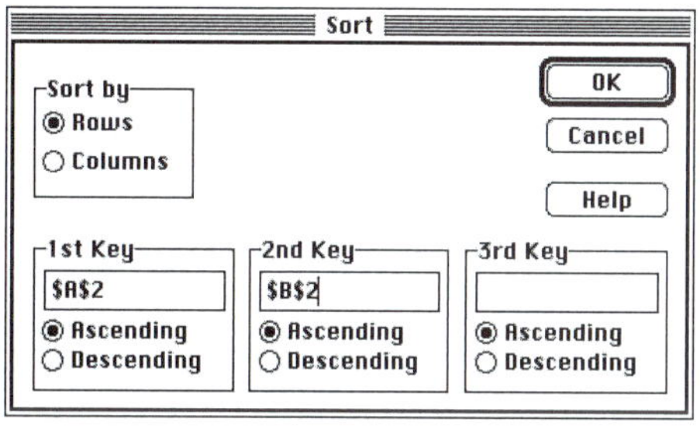


**Figure 14.12**
*Sort dialog box with two keys.*

# Descending the Ladder

Finally, sort by Amount, with the numbers descending from highest to lowest:

1. Choose Goto and double-click SortRange.
2. Choose Sort from Data. This time, click on the first record immediately under Amount to replace $A$2 with $D$2 and click the Descending button. This is how you tell Excel that you want the highest

number first. The other times you didn't tell Excel anything, so it used the default, which is always *Ascending*—unless you tell it otherwise.

3. Click OK.

## Set Database

To use the Data Form, tell Excel this area is a database:

1. Click and drag from A1 to D16. Note you *are* including the field headings.
2. Choose Set Database from the Data menu.
3. Click anywhere on the worksheet to deselect the range that was selected when we chose the Set Database command.

## Check It Out

1. Go to the Formula menu and choose Goto.
2. Double-click Database. Your database should be selected. Note the name in the formula bar.
3. Press an arrow key to deselect the database—you are just checking. The database doesn't have to be selected to use the Data Form, your next practice step.

## Data Form

1. Choose Form from the Data menu.
2. Scroll through the database, clicking the scroll bars.
3. Click the New button and type in a new record, pressing the Tab key to move from field to field.

4. After typing into the last field, press the Return key, and the new record will be added to the bottom of the database. Note you get another empty record in the Data Form.
5. You can continue typing new records at this point if you need to practice your typing.

## Criteria

Find all the records in which the Amount field is greater than $1,000.

1. Click the Criteria button. Note the blinking Insertion point in the first field. Either click in the Amount field or press the Tab key until the Insertion point appears in the field.
2. Type *>1000* in the Amount field.
3. Click the Find Next and Find Previous buttons. They'll jump you through the database, from record to record, only stopping at those fulfilling the criteria. When the last record is reached, you'll be alerted with a flash or a beep.
4. Click the Help button and scan the information.
5. Click the Close button.
6. Choose Quit from the File menu, unless you want to continue working and playing with Excel.
7. Save the database with the name Sales Database.

# Summary

You can use Excel to track information. Each row is a record; each column is a field. You can sort by selecting the rows you want sorted. Be sure to select *all* the columns and rows you need sorted.

To use the Data Form from the Data menu, select the field headings and records and choose Set Database from the Data menu. After choosing Form, click the Criteria button to tell Excel which records you want to work on. Click the Find Next and Find Previous buttons to go through the subset of records.

## Exorcises

1. Do you have to use the Set Database command before sorting?
2. Why don't you select the headings before a sort?
3. To sort from Z to A, do you click Ascending or Descending in the Sort box?
4. Which menu holds the Define Name command?
5. What's the first step in naming a range?
6. Spaces are allowed in a range name—True or False?
7. How can you get Database listed in the Goto box?

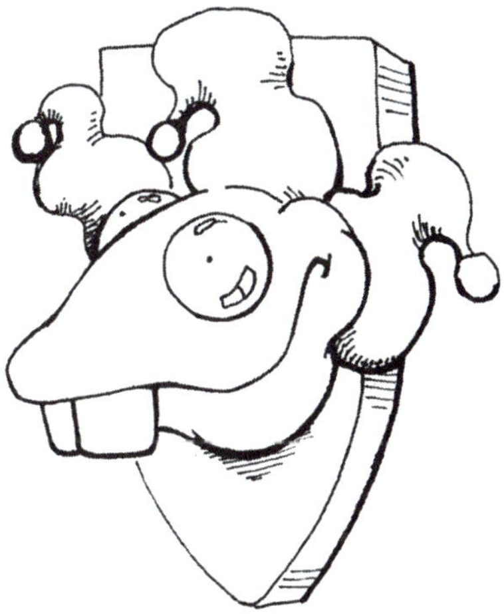

15th Encounter

# Creating Charts

## Goal

Master techniques of making pie, line, column, and bar charts, both regular and 3D.

## What You Will Need

Start with Excel running, with the Income and Expense worksheet visible.

## Terms of Enfearment

| | |
|---|---|
| Data series | Category axis |
| Gallery | Chart Wizard |
| Value axis | Legend |
| X and Y axis | Embedded |

# Briefing

Often, it's easier to understand and to analyze your numbers when they're used to create a chart (also called a graph). Charts turn numbers into pictures that instantly make sense. If you decide to explore and to change your numbers, the chart instantly changes. Talk about instant graphitication!

## Topping the Charts

There are many different kinds of charts—pie, line, column, and bar are the most popular. You can look at your numbers in these different formats and see which is the most effective.

Pie charts work when you're dealing with only one range of data and want to compare the pieces of the pie. Each piece represents a number in the worksheet. All the numbers *must* be higher than zero in a pie chart.

Line, column, and bar charts are all appropriate for showing trends over a number of time periods or for comparing different variables (like sales or expenses).

The first step in creating a chart is producing the worksheet that holds the numbers. If you have just one series of data, called a *data series*, it can be put in either a row or column; either orientation works fine (see fig. 15.1).

## Old Traditions Die Hard

When you need to chart more than one series of data, try to preserve the traditional worksheet design, in which the time periods are column headings and the different categories are row headings. This design will make the charting process much easier (see fig. 15.2). As does keeping the top left cell empty.

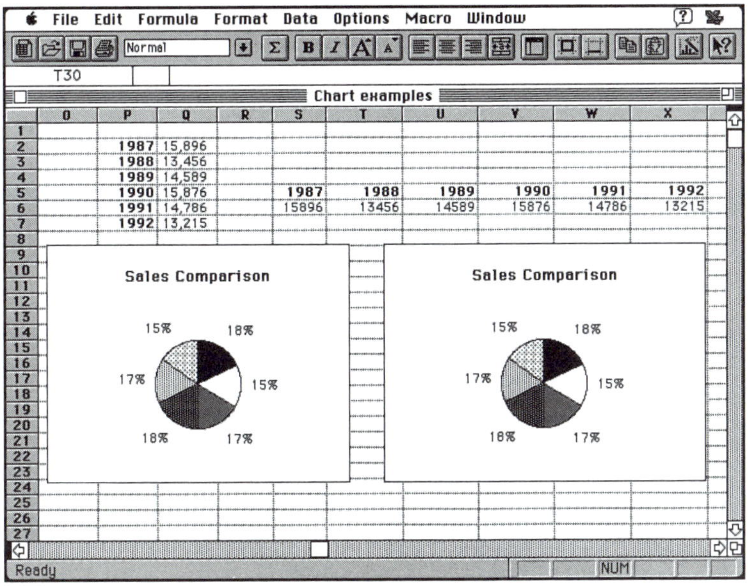


Figure 15.1
*Two different orientations.*

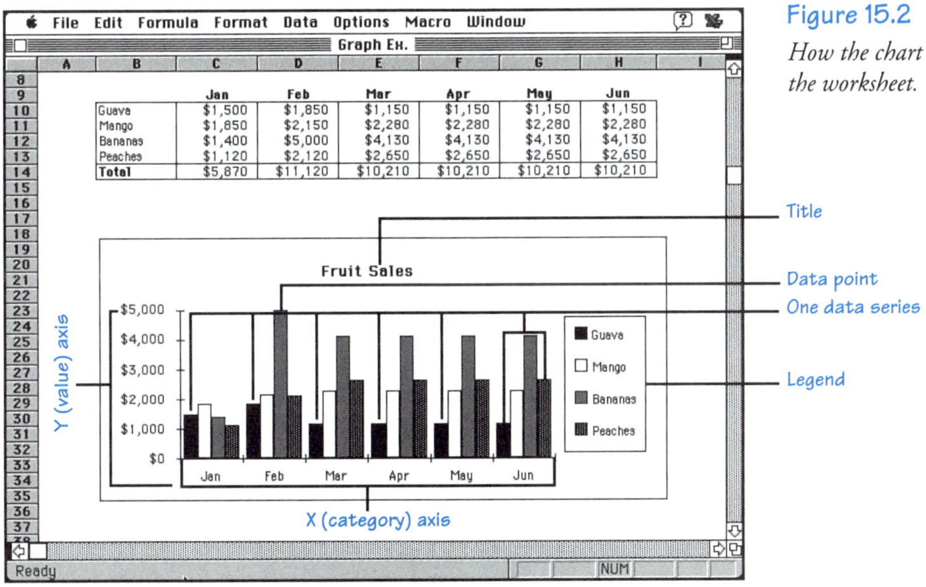


Figure 15.2
*How the chart uses the worksheet.*

## We're Off To See the WIZARD

The *Chart Wizard* tool walks you through the steps for creating a simple chart. (You don't even have to follow the yellow brick road.) As always, first select a range and then click the tool (see fig. 15.3) and drag through an empty range in the worksheet. This drag tells Excel where to put the chart.

The Chart Wizard window appears to handhold you through the next few decisions about your chart. Like a genie out of a bottle, the Wizard does most of the work for you.

**Figure 15.3**
*The Chart Wizard tool.*

## Good—Bedfellows

After going through the Chart Wizard windows, your chart appears, embedded in the worksheet. Now, you can print the worksheet and chart together and print more than one chart on a page.

You can change the embedded chart's size and shape and move it so that it's positioned well on the worksheet.

To move an embedded chart, make sure that the worksheet is active and click the embedded chart once. Position the mouse pointer inside the chart and then click and drag.

To change the size and shape of the chart on the worksheet, position the mouse on any of the selection handles around the chart and click-drag when the pointer changes shape (see fig. 15.4).

## The Right Tool for the Right Job

You can enhance the chart with formatting changes and with additional text, arrows, and borders using the Chart menu and the Chart toolbar.

After you create a chart, Excel automatically adds the time saving, user-friendly Chart toolbar to the bottom of the screen (see fig. 15.5).

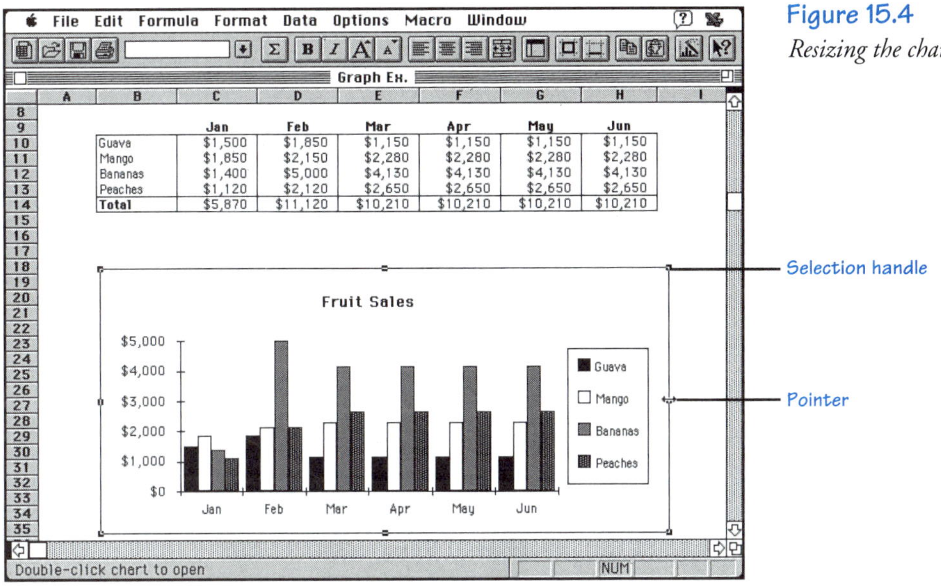


Figure 15.4

*Resizing the chart.*

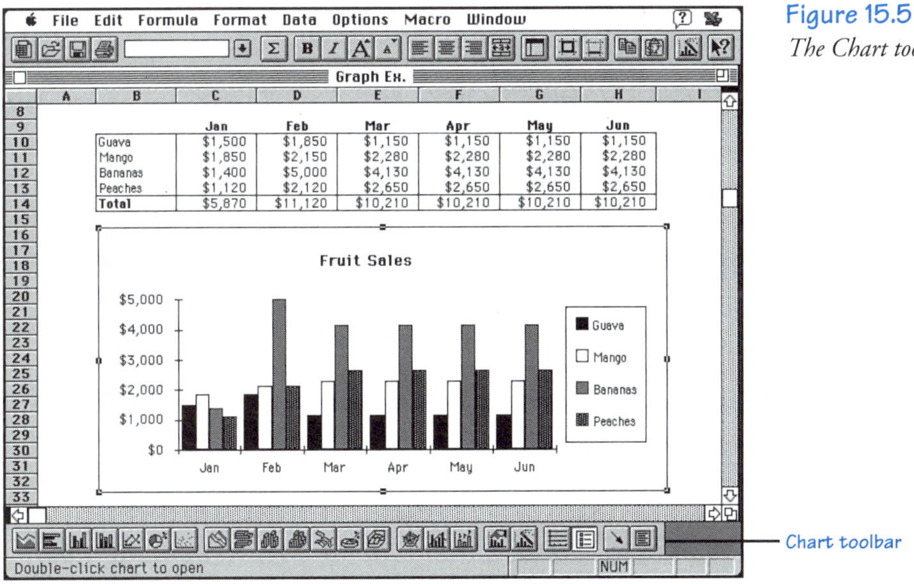


Figure 15.5

*The Chart toolbar.*

If you double-click a chart that's embedded in your worksheet, it becomes a separate window, and the menu bar changes to the Chart menu (see fig. 15.6).

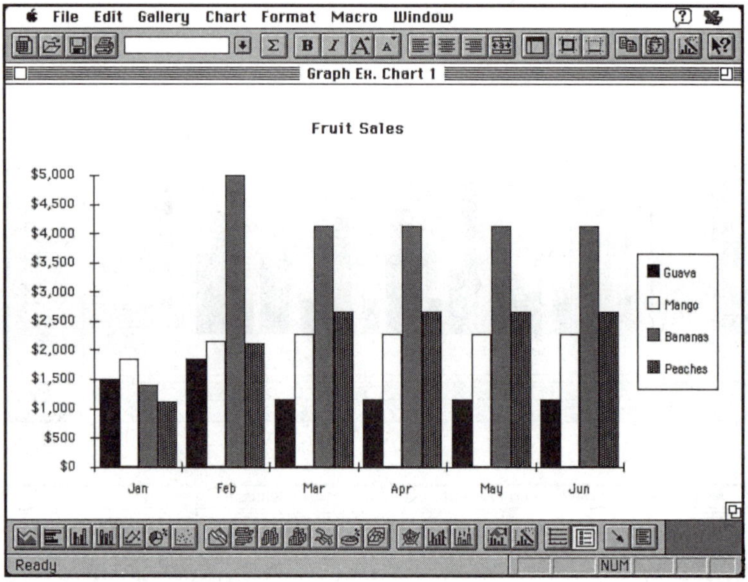


**Figure 15.6**
*A Chart window.*

Because the chart is now in its own window, you can see it listed in the Window menu along with the worksheet. You can choose one or the other from the window list. You can also use the Arrange command to fit them both on the screen.

The Chart menu automatically appears whenever the active window is a chart.

# Bars and Stripes

Remember! To activate one or the other window when they're both visible, click anywhere on the document. You can always tell which is active by seeing which title bar shows the stripes.

All the commands in the *Gallery*, Chart, and Format menus relate to charting issues.

# Gallery Hopping

The Gallery menu has a check by the current chart format. Choosing any of the formats, including the checked one, gives you another set of choices.

Many of the commands on the Chart menu, such as the Add Arrow and Add Legend commands, are handled in the Chart Wizard process and with the Chart toolbar.

You could spend half a lifetime exploring the ins and outs of the Format menu, but a grasp of the basics is enough for most of us. Go to the Format menu when you want to change the look of any part of the chart.

You're probably sick of hearing this by now—remember to select whatever you want to change. To make the title larger, you have to click it first. You can tell that the title (or any object) is selected by the selection handles surrounding it (see fig. 15.7). You can select the whole chart by clicking on the chart window, but not on any particular object in it.

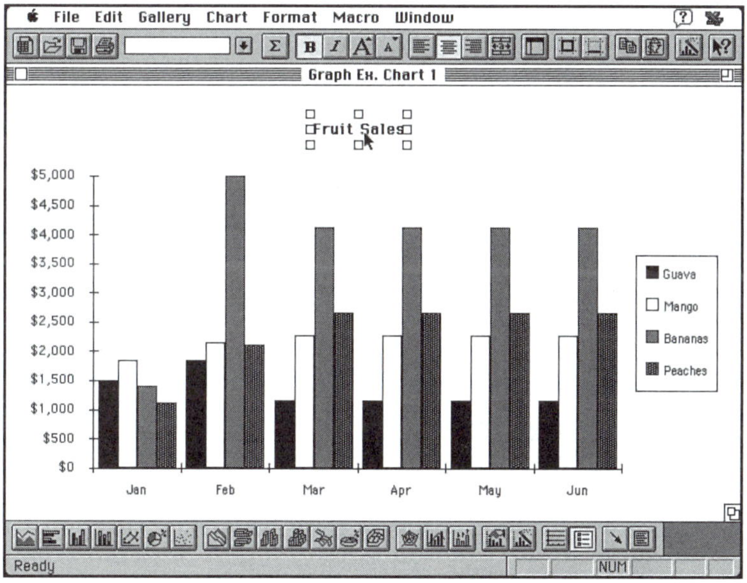


**Figure 15.7**
*The Chart title is selected.*

The Patterns command in the Format menu displays different windows depending on which part of the chart is chosen. Double-clicking on part of a chart will open the Patterns window, like choosing it from the menu (see fig. 15.8). The Patterns window changes depending on which object you choose (see fig. 15.9).

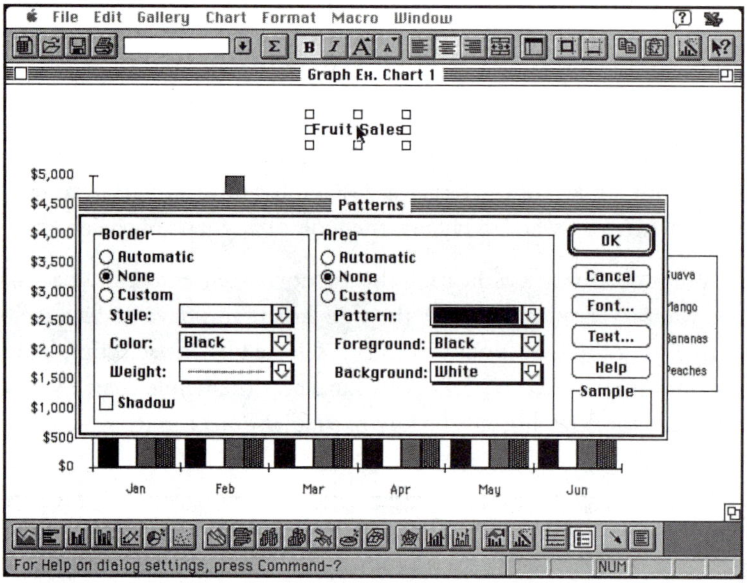


**Figure 15.8**
*The Patterns dialog box when the title is double-clicked.*

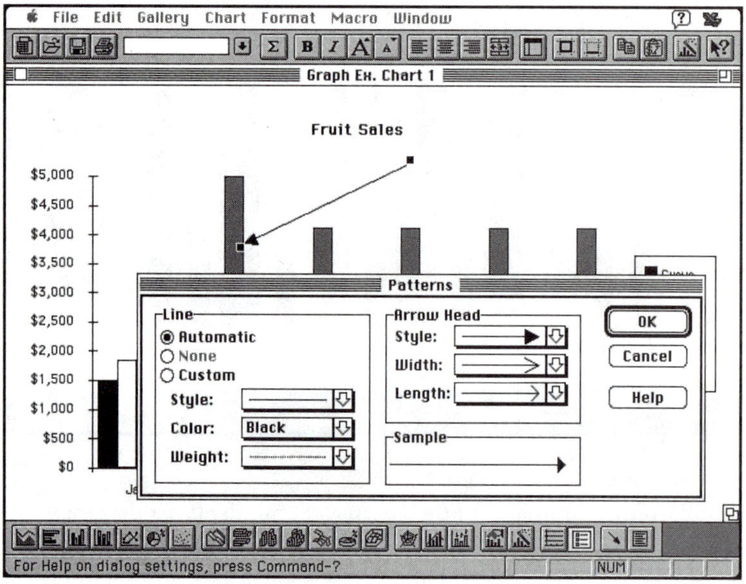


**Figure 15.9**
*The Patterns dialog box when an arrow is double-clicked.*

The Format menu is probably where you can spend most of your time when fine-tuning a chart.

Use the Font command for formatting selected text on the chart. You should start by selecting the whole chart to change the font throughout.You can select the whole chart by clicking on an outer edge. Continue with further enhancements to different parts, like making the title a larger font size and bold (see fig. 15.10).

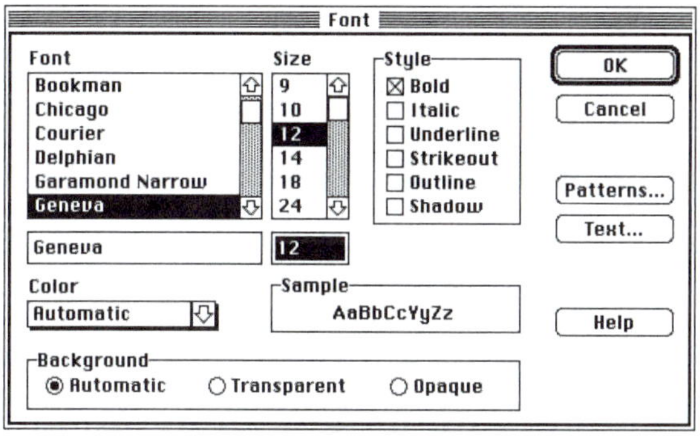


**Figure 15.10**
*The Font dialog box.*

With the Text command, you can change text orientation (see fig. 15.11). If you have text along the Y *axis* (which runs vertically), you can experiment with the different vertical orientations (see fig. 15.12).

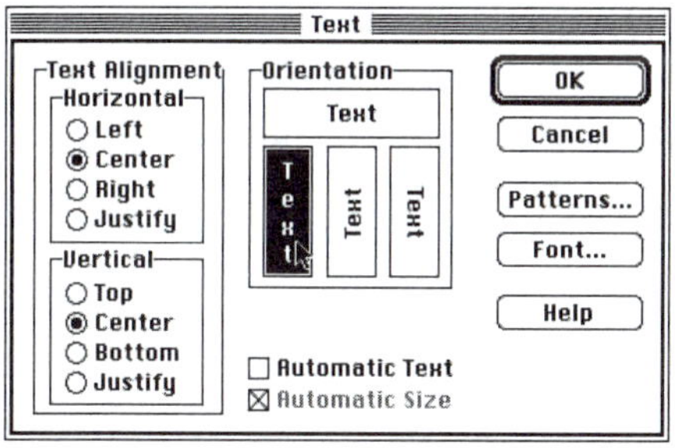


**Figure 15.11**
The Text window.

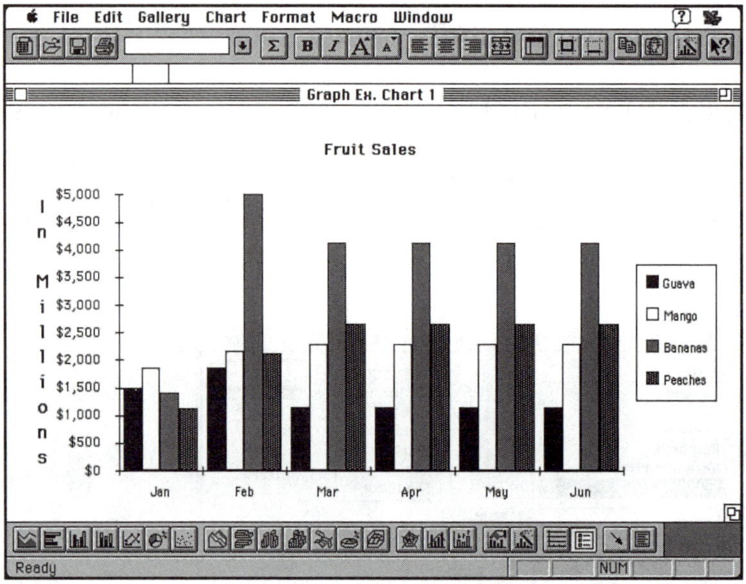


Figure 15.12
Text (In Millions) along the Y axis in vertical orientation.

With the Scale command, you can alter whatever axis is selected. Changing the highest (Maximum) and lowest (Minimum) numbers on the scale can really change the look of the chart. For example, if you select the Y axis, choose Scale from the Format menu, and change the Maximum number in the Axis Scale dialog box (see fig. 15.13), the result would look like figure 15.14.

The Pattern, Text, Font, and Scale dialog boxes all have buttons for going to the other three dialog boxes, so you can make all your changes to a selected object before clicking OK. This is a neat feature for saving time. Use it or lose it!

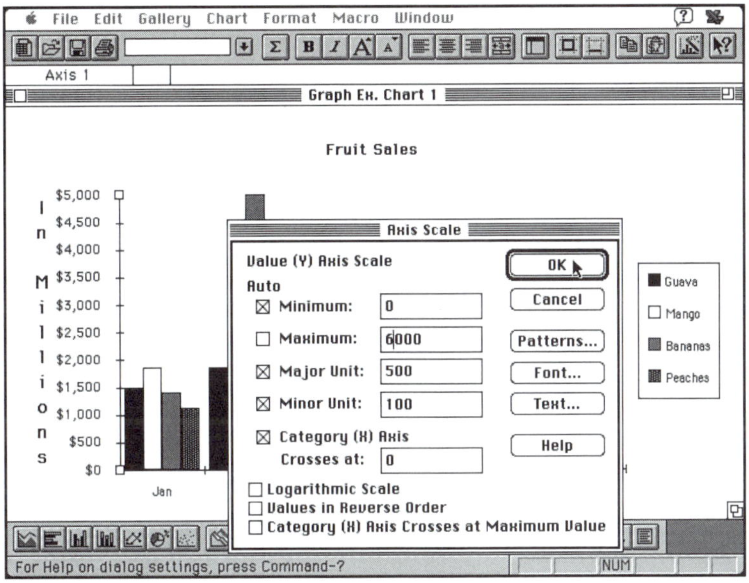


Figure 15.13
*Changing the Maximum number.*

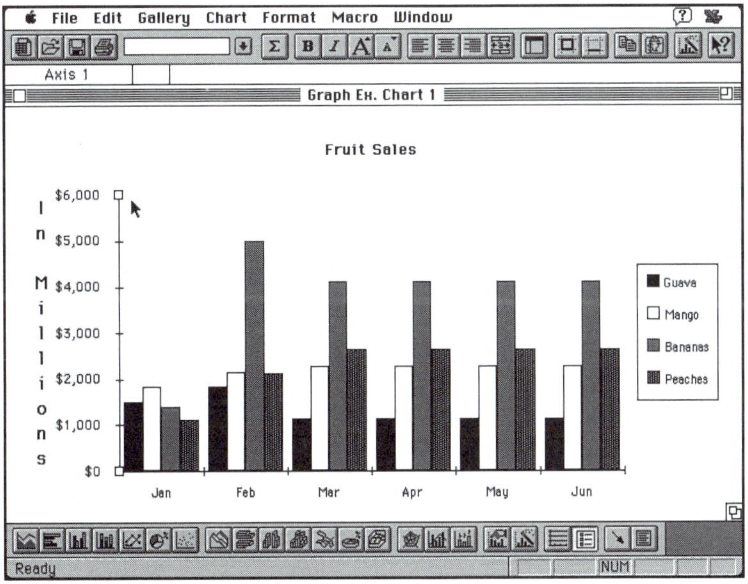


Figure 15.14
*The change in the chart.*

## Saving the Chart

As long as the chart is embedded, it's saved as part of the worksheet. This guarantees that the chart won't be separated from its numbers.

## Printing the Chart

You can print charts as part of their worksheet or separately. If the worksheet is active, Print Preview shows you how the page will look with your numbers and the embedded chart. You can move the chart and change its size to make it relate properly to the numbers.

To print a chart separately, double-click the chart so that it appears in its own window. Print Preview shows you the defaults (see fig. 15.15). Click the Page Setup button if you want to change the orientation, size, header, and footer (see fig. 15.16).

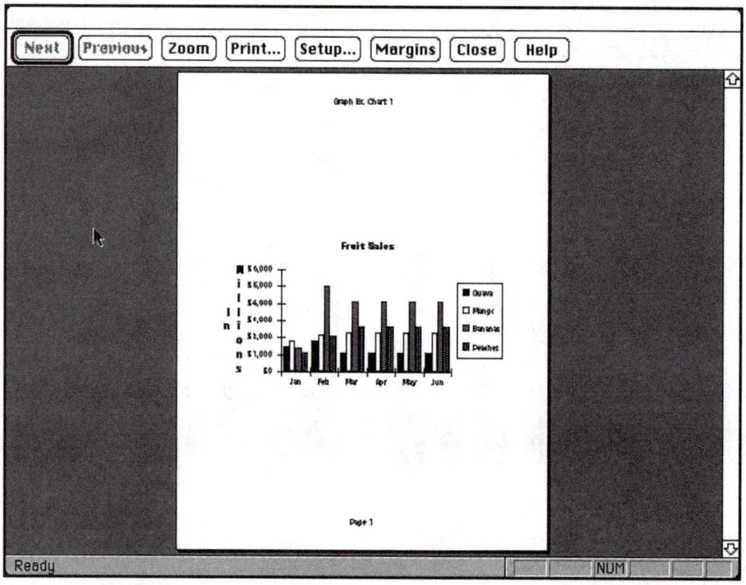


**Figure 15.15**
*Print Preview.*

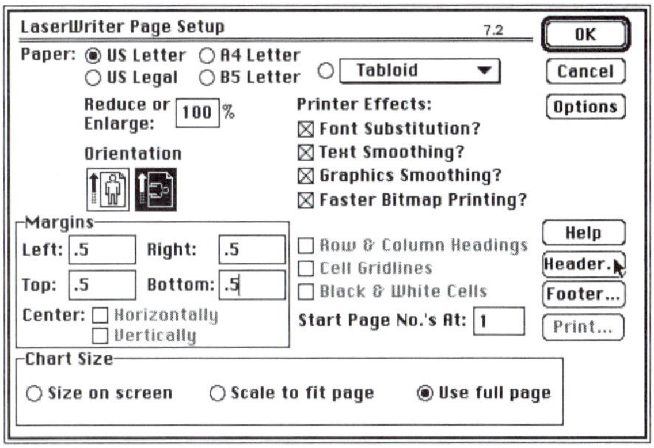


Figure 15.16
*Page setup for a chart.*

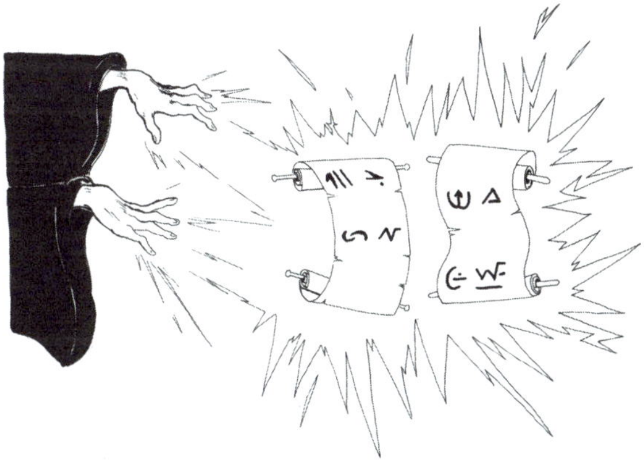

# They're Out To Get Us

To print your chart separately on its own sheet of paper, its appearance is frequently less than satisfactory when you check it in Print Preview. Usually, you want your charts to fill the page:

1. Make the margins as small as possible (.5 or .25).
2. Click the Setup button and change to wide orientation.
3. Click the Use Full Page button.
4. Delete the Header and Footer.

## Too Many Arrows Spoil the Chart

Sometimes, you add an arrow to a chart and then decide that you don't want it. You might think that pressing the Delete key when the arrow is selected will delete it, but it won't. You have to choose Delete Arrow from the Chart menu while the arrow is selected.

If you double-click the embedded chart so that it appears in its own window and then click the Save tool, the Chart becomes another distinct file, as well as remaining embedded in the worksheet. Normally, it's not necessary to do this; just save your charts as part of the worksheet.

# Practice

We will start this session with a pie chart.

1. Click the New Worksheet tool, type the information shown in figure 15.17, and save it as Clothing sales.

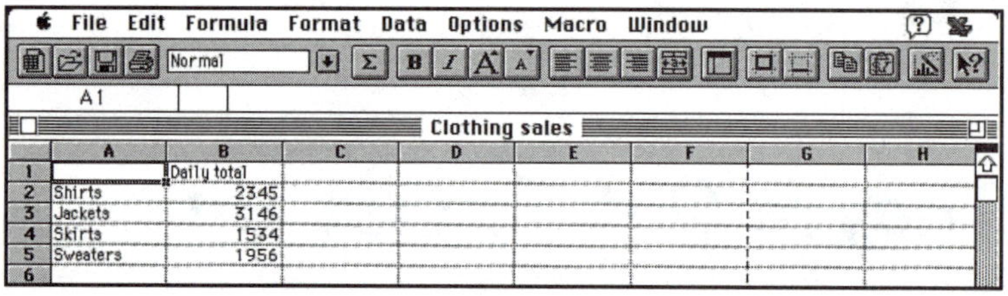


**Figure 15.17** *Dry goods.*

2. To select the table, click the empty cell to the left of the Daily total and drag down to the bottom number.

## The Wonderful Wizard of . . . Charts

1. Click the Chart Wizard tool and click-drag across an empty section of the worksheet to tell Excel where to embed the chart (see fig. 15.18). You'll move and change the chart size later, so don't worry about that now.

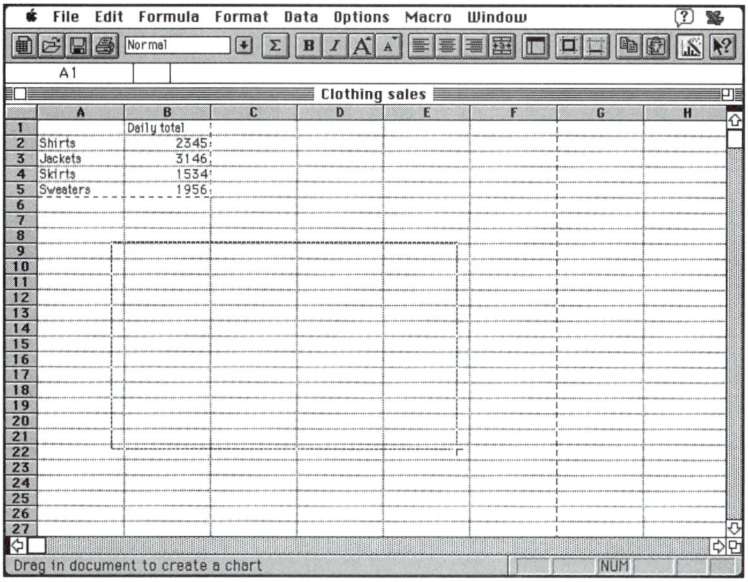


**Figure 15.18**
*Click-drag in the worksheet after clicking the Chart Wizard tool.*

2. When the Chart Wizard window appears, move it if it's hiding your data.
3. In the first Chart Wizard window, you see a text box showing the selected range (see fig. 15.19). Note the marching ants around the selected range in the worksheet.

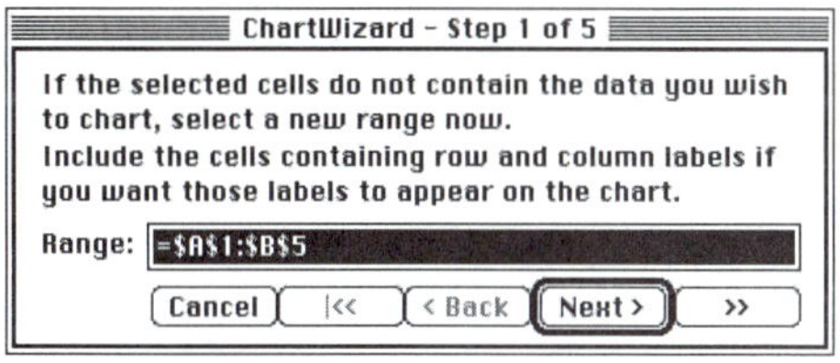


**Figure 15.19**
*The first Chart Wizard window.*

4. If the range is wrong, reselect the correct range in the worksheet. It's probably right, so just click the Next button.
5. In the second window, shown in figure 15.20, double-click the Pie chart (the same as clicking it once and then clicking the Next button).

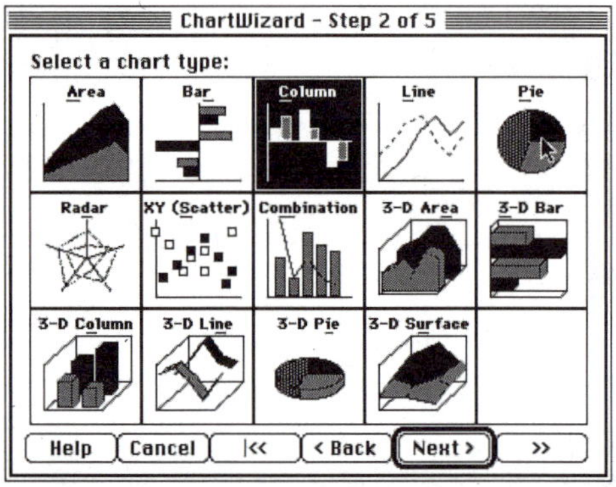


**Figure 15.20**
*The second Chart Wizard window.*

6. In the third window, choose the seventh pie type to see what the letters (A, B, C) and the percent signs mean (see fig. 15.21). Click the Next button.

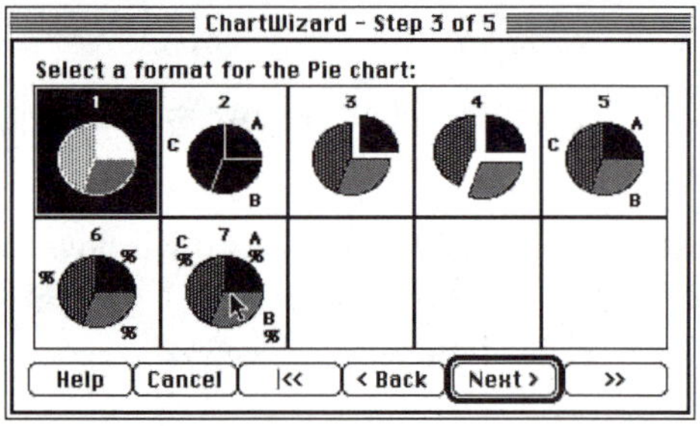


**Figure 15.21**
*The third Chart Wizard window.*

7. Lo and behold! The fourth window shines forth with a beautiful chart! (See fig. 15.22.)

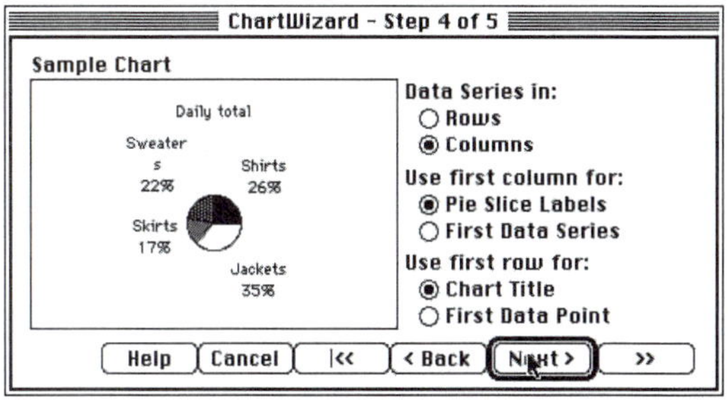


**Figure 15.22**
*The fourth Chart Wizard window.*

8. Experiment by clicking the unselected buttons and then change them again, so that the chart looks right.
9. Click the Next button.

# A Legend in Its Own Time

1. In the fifth window, shown in figure 15.23, click the Yes button for a *legend.*
2. Note that you don't need a legend with the kind of pie you have so click the No button.
3. No need to change the title. Just click OK.

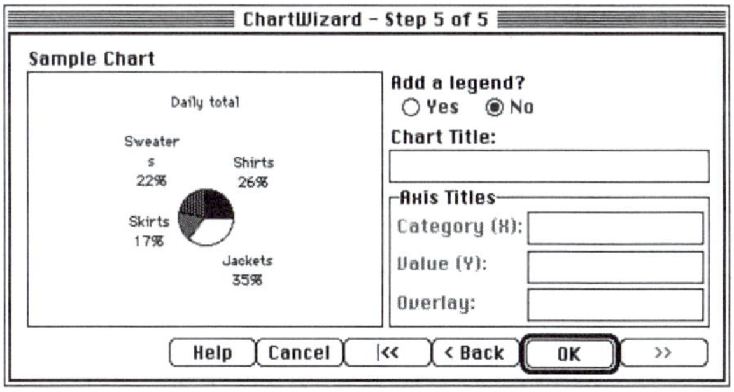


**Figure 15.23**
*The fifth Chart Wizard window.*

You're back in the worksheet, and there is the chart. It should be selected (see fig. 15.24).

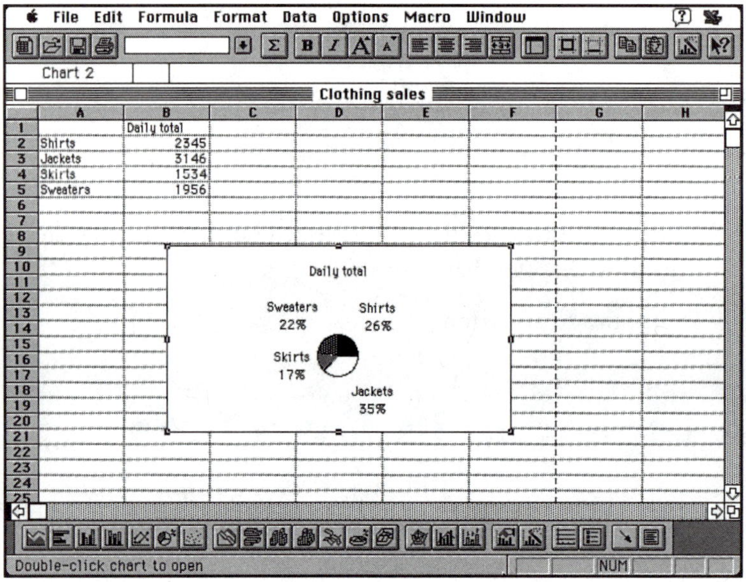


**Figure 15.24**
*The embedded chart, selected.*

# Movers and Shakers

1. Move the chart by positioning the pointer in the middle and then click-dragging.
2. Adjust its size by positioning the pointer on any of the selection handles and dragging.

# Chart Toolbar to the Rescue

1. If it's no longer selected, click again to reselect the chart. Note that a new toolbar has appeared at the bottom of the screen.
2. Click any of the first 13 tools to change the chart. Admit it, this is fun!

3. Click the 14 through 17th tools to see that they cannot be used with only one range of data.

## Switching to a Chart Window

1. Double-click the chart.
2. Note the changed menu bar.
3. Double- click the title. When the Patterns dialog box appears, click the Font button.
4. Make the title bigger and bold. Click OK.
5. Choose the worksheet from the Window menu. Note the changes to the chart.

## Print Preview

1. Choose Print Preview.
2. If the positioning doesn't look right, click the Close box and move the chart around on the worksheet until it looks good in Print Preview.
3. Click the Save tool and print.
4. Close the worksheet.

## Create a Column Chart

In this session, you type another table with four rows of numbers (4 data series).

1. Click the New Worksheet tool and type the information as shown in figure 15.25.

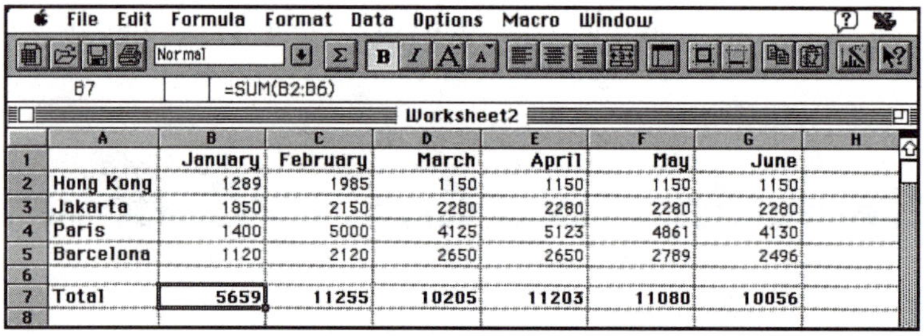

| | A | B | C | D | E | F | G | H |
|---|---|---|---|---|---|---|---|---|
| 1 | | January | February | March | April | May | June | |
| 2 | Hong Kong | 1289 | 1985 | 1150 | 1150 | 1150 | 1150 | |
| 3 | Jakarta | 1850 | 2150 | 2280 | 2280 | 2280 | 2280 | |
| 4 | Paris | 1400 | 5000 | 4125 | 5123 | 4861 | 4130 | |
| 5 | Barcelona | 1120 | 2120 | 2650 | 2650 | 2789 | 2496 | |
| 6 | | | | | | | | |
| 7 | Total | 5659 | 11255 | 10205 | 11203 | 11080 | 10056 | |
| 8 | | | | | | | | |

**Figure 15.25**
*Exotic cities.*

2. Select A1:G5. *Don't* include the row with the totals.
3. Click the Chart Wizard.
4. Click and drag across an empty section of the worksheet.
5. In the first window, double check your range (`=$A$1:$G$5`) and then click the Next button.
6. In the second window, leave the column chart chosen and click the Next button.
7. In the third window, leave the default again and just click Next.
8. In the fourth window, switch data series in rows to Data Series in columns. Do you want to compare the cities to each other during each month? Or do you want to see how each city did over the six month period? After you see how the two interpretations are different, return the choice to **Data Series in rows** and click Next (see fig. 15.26).

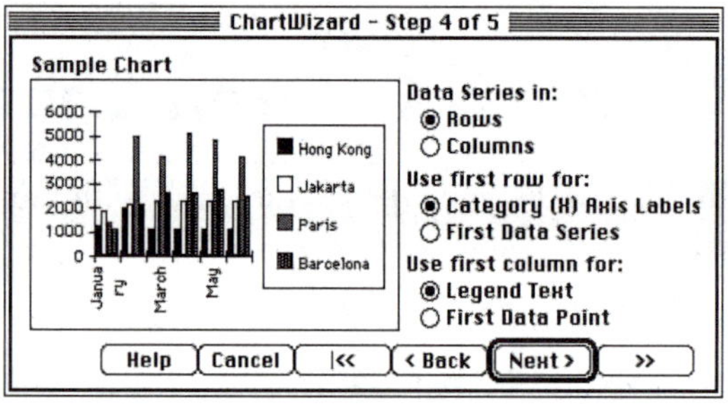


**Figure 15.26**
*Fourth Chart Wizard window.*

9. In the fifth window, you do want a legend, so leave "Yes" chosen. Type Sales in the Title box, *First 6 months of 94* in the Category (X) axis box, and *In Millions* in the Value (Y) axis box (see fig. 15.27).
10. Click OK.

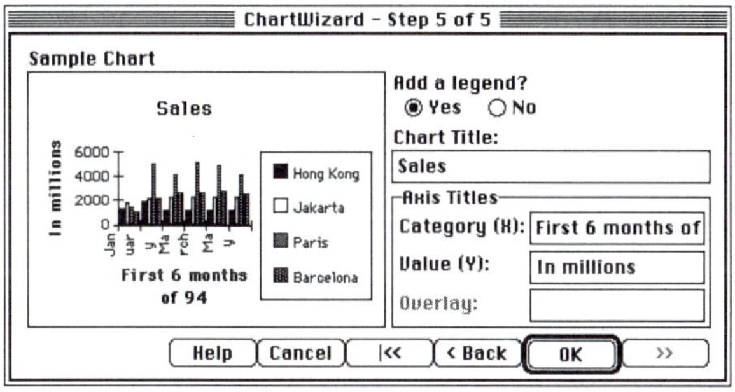


Figure 15.27
*Fifth Chart Wizard window.*

11. Reposition and resize the chart if you want. Even though it may look too scrunched, it doesn't matter because we are going to print it full size, on its own page.

# The Chart Window

1. Double-click the chart. Note that it has a title bar and that the menu bar has changed.
2. Experiment with choosing different chart types from the Chart toolbar
3. Experiment with the Gallery menu, which gives you more choices for each type of chart.

# Lurking in the Shadows

1. Double-click the title to open its Patterns dialog box.
2. Give it a shadowed border (see fig. 15.28).

3. Click the Font button to make the title larger.
4. Click OK.

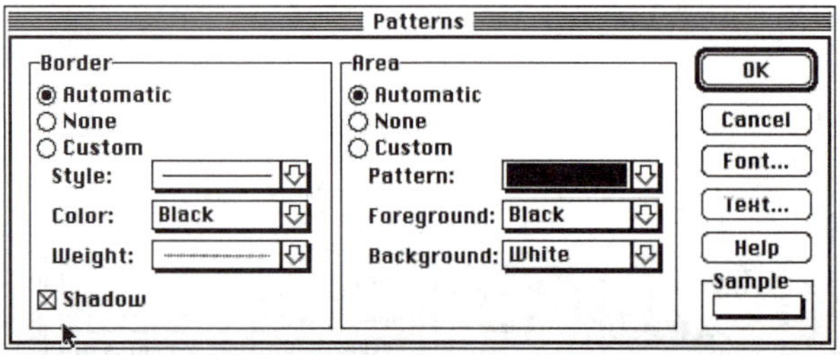


**Figure 15.28**
*The Chart title has been double-clicked to bring up the Patterns dialog box. The Shadow check box is clicked.*

# Straight as an Arrow

1. Click the arrow tool and watch it plop into your chart.
2. Click and drag the arrowhead end toward the top of the shortest Hong Kong column (see fig. 15.29). (Reposition the arrow by click-dragging on the shaft. Change its size by click-dragging on the selection handle at either end.)

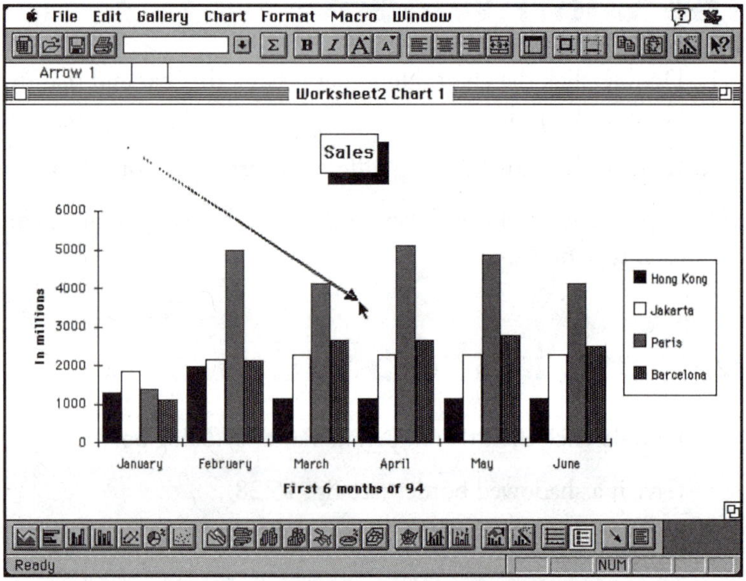


**Figure 15.29**
*Resizing the arrow.*

# Free-Floating Text Box

1. If any text is still selected, deselect it so that the formula bar is empty.
2. Click in the formula bar, type *Hong Kong Needs Work*, and enter it by pressing Return or clicking the Enter box (see fig. 15.30).

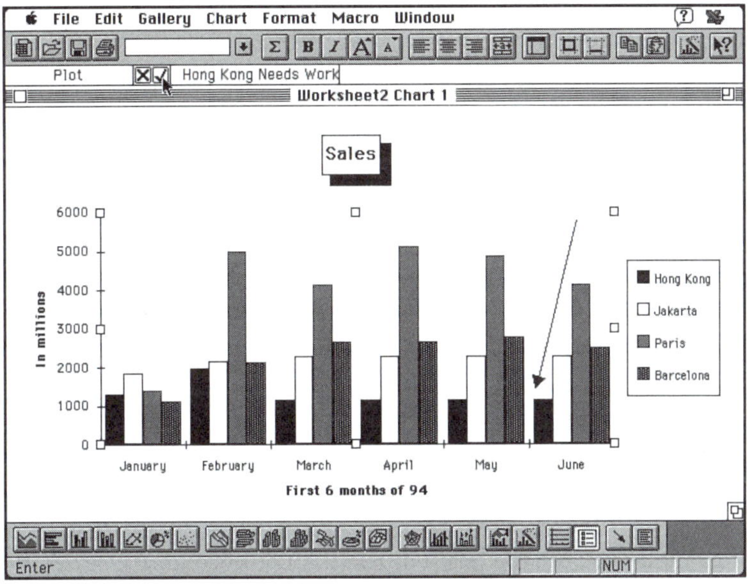


**Figure 15.30**
*Plopping free-floating text into the chart.*

3. Note that the text object has been plopped into your chart.
4. Reposition it next to the arrow.
5. Change the text orientation on the Y axis by double-clicking the axis, clicking the Text button, and choosing one of the vertical orientations.

# Play Time

1. Double-click one of the columns to change the border, pattern, or color of that data series.

2. Change the chart to a line and a bar chart.
3. Note the impact of the change on the different parts of the chart. As you can probably see, it's best to choose the type of chart first and then make your formatting changes.
4. Play for as long as you want. The more you play, the more experience you gain. When you're ready to stop, choose the worksheet from the Window menu list, save it as "Chart Practice," and quit.

# Summary

You can use the Chart Wizard tool to change numbers into pictures. The Chart toolbar lets you change charts quickly and easily. You can keep charts embedded in the worksheets and print them on the same page, or you can print charts on their own page.

# Exorcises

1. What menu do you use to choose different kinds of column charts?
2. What menu lets you choose from a list of open documents?
3. How do you change the color of your columns?
4. In figure 15.31, which is the X axis? Which is the Y axis?
5. How can you activate the chart menu?

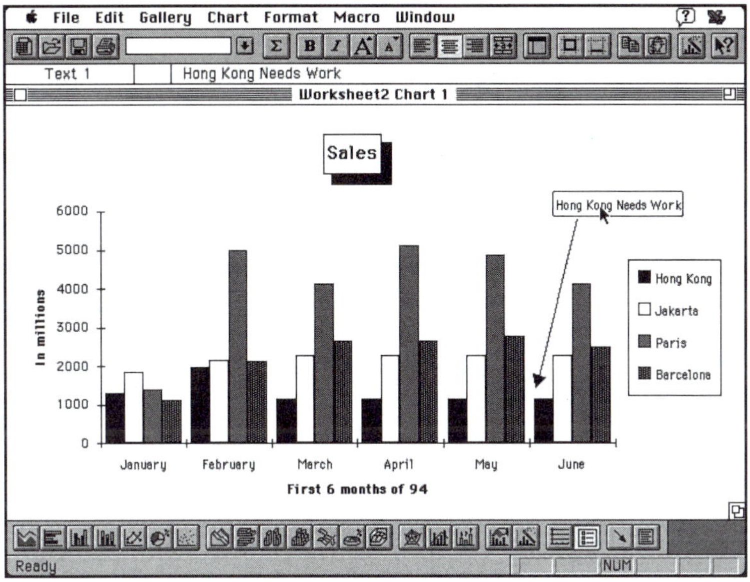


Figure 15.31
*A chart.*

6. What dialog box enables you to change the orientation of the printed page?

16th Encounter

# Taming the Toolbars

## Goal

Develop a working understanding of the toolbars—the Standard toolbar, which is the default, and the others.

## What You Will Need

Excel running with a fresh, new worksheet visible.

## Terms of Enfearment

Help tool
Docked toolbar
Customize
Autoformat
Utility

# Briefing

Throughout the previous encounters, you've been using tools on the Standard toolbar. In the last encounter, you had a great time with the Chart toolbar. Tools are so convenient, they can become habit forming. What a break, a healthy addiction for a change!

After using Excel for a while, you begin to get a sense of commands you frequently use that aren't available as tools on the Standard toolbar.

Wouldn't it be nice to click a tool to pop into Print Preview? How about having tools on screen for changing the font or font size?

If you were working with a large worksheet, wouldn't it be nice to have tools for zooming in and out? You can do this in Print Preview, but you can't make changes there. How about right in the worksheet?

# Capitalist Tools

All these *are* tools, available on other toolbars that can be on screen any time. In this encounter, you're going to explore the toolbars, including more tools on the Standard toolbar.

You're going to look at the range of tools available, learn how to open and close toolbars and how to position them on the screen, and add and delete tools from the Standard toolbar.

There are seven toolbars. To add one or more to the screen, choose Toolbars from the Options menu and double-click the desired toolbar.

You can see what a tool does by moving the mouse pointer on top of the tool, holding down the mouse button, and looking at the Status bar (lower left).

For a longer explanation and the official name of the tool, click the *Help* tool and click the tool you want to learn about (see fig. 16.1).

Figure 16.1
*The Help tool.*

This command asks Microsoft Help to show you a window that explains the tool. After reading the explanation, click the Help window's close box.

# What a Drag—NOT!

You can position a toolbar by dragging its title bar. If you drag a toolbar to the lower left corner of the screen, it becomes *docked* along the bottom (see fig. 16.2). Dragging it to the upper left of the screen will dock it as a vertical bar on the left.

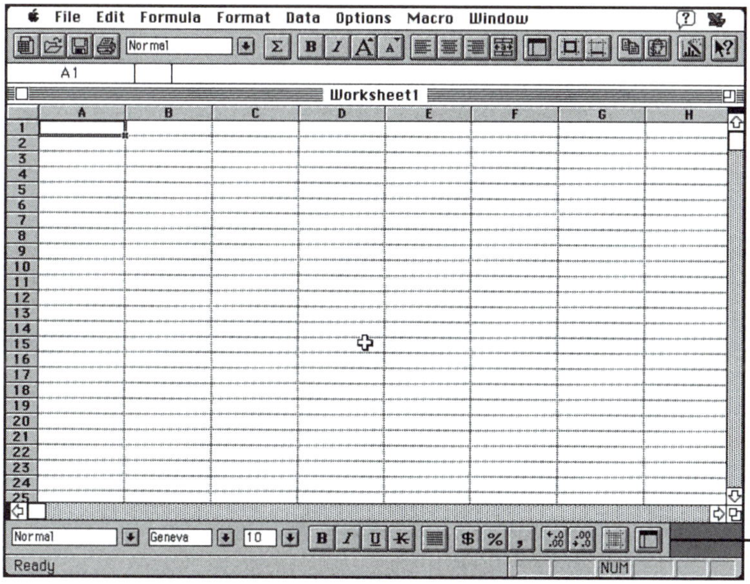


Figure 16.2
*A toolbar docked at the bottom.*

# Deepspace Nine

If a toolbar is docked so that you don't see the title bar and can't move it, double-click on the toolbar border (not directly on a tool). This undocks it.

Toolbars can be docked along any of the four sides or allowed to float anywhere on the screen. You can also stack toolbars under the Standard toolbar.

Toolbars with pop up menus, like Formatting, can't be docked as vertical toolbars along the left and right sides of the window, just horizontally along the top and bottom.

You can take a toolbar off the screen by choosing Toolbars from the Options menu and double-clicking the toolbar you want to hide.

# Customize

To add and delete tools from toolbars, the Customize window *must* be active. Choose Toolbars from the Options menu and then click the *Customize* button.

In the Customize window, tools are organized according to the kind of work they do, rather than which toolbar holds them. With the Customize window open, you can click a category on the left and then find out about the tools by holding down the mouse button while the pointer is positioned over a tool. Excel gives you an explanation in the lower left corner of the window.

To add a tool, drag it from the Customize window to any toolbar that's visible. You can also drag tools off any visible toolbar.

Don't be afraid to experiment. After you've added and deleted tools to different toolbars, you can always return to the default. Just choose Toolbars from Options and click the Reset button.

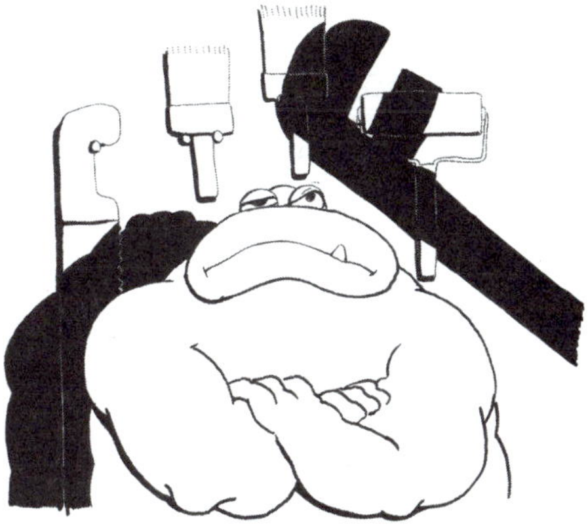

# They're Out To Get Us

If you try to dock a toolbar on the left or right side of your screen and it won't go, you're probably trying to dock one of the toolbars that has a pop up menu, like Formatting. Because the pop up menu can go only up or down, it's logical that the toolbar holding the pop up list won't dock on the side of the screen. You need to change strategies and move the toolbar to the top or bottom.

If you forget which toolbar holds your favorite tool, there's a listing of all the tools and their locations in the Excel manual called *User's Guide 2*. The list starts on page 166. If you can't find the tool there, you're imagining it!

# Practice

## The Whole Enchilada

1. Begin by using a wonderful tool on the Standard toolbar that you haven't used yet—the *Autoformat* tool. After you've typed a worksheet, you can tell Excel to format the whole thing by clicking this tool. First, type the little table shown in figure 16.3.

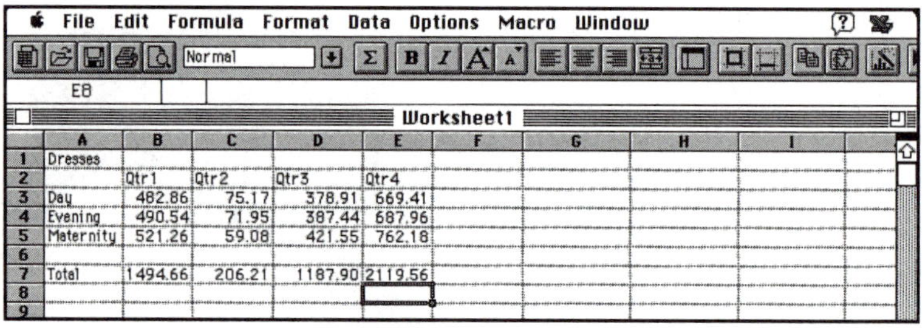


Figure 16.3
*Type this table.*

2. Select the table and click the Autoformat tool (see fig. 16.4). Amazing change, eh?

Figure 16.4
*Autoformat tool.*

3. Hold down the Shift key and continue clicking the Autoformat tool. With each click, the table is formatted differently.
4. Look at a list of all these choices, as well as samples of formatted tables, by choosing Autoformat from the Format menu (see fig. 16.5).

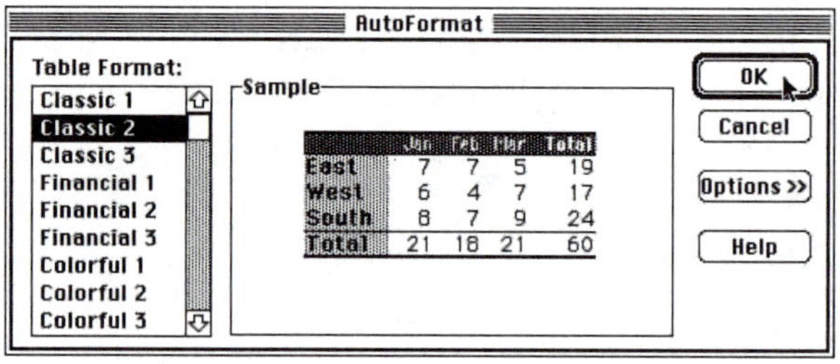


Figure 16.5
*The Autoformat command.*

# Lookin' Good

1. Show the Formatting toolbar by choosing Toolbars from the Options menu and then double-clicking Formatting.
2. Drag the Formatting toolbar to different parts of the screen by dragging it with the pointer on the title bar.

3. Move it under the Standard toolbar.
4. Double-click the Formatting toolbar to undock it. When double-clicking, have the pointer on an edge, not a tool.
5. Drag it down to the bottom of the screen.
6. Select the table on the worksheet again and change the font and font size using the pop-up lists on the Formatting toolbar.
7. Click the Help tool (far right) and click an interesting tool.
8. After reading the explanation, click the Help window close box.
9. Selecting the cells first, format the numbers with different number formats.
10. Select your totals and apply shading with the Light Shading tool (see fig. 16.6).

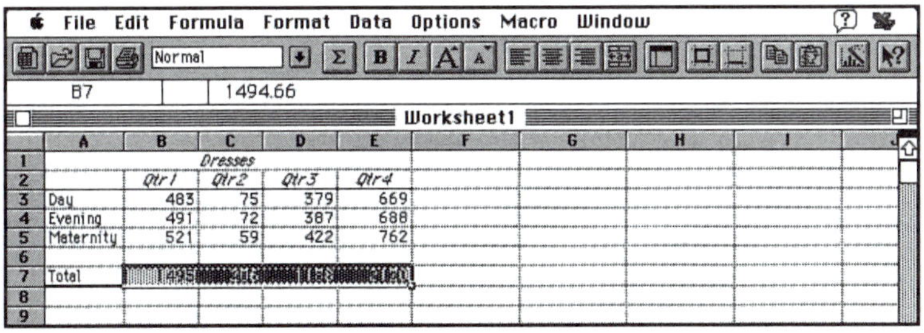


**Figure 16.6**
*Formatting with the Light Shading tool.*

11. Note which of the tools on the Formatting toolbar are already on the Standard toolbar.

# Utility Closet

1. Look at the *Utility* toolbar, by choosing Toolbars from the Options menu and double-clicking Utility in the list.
2. Click the Help tool and click the first tool.
3. After reading the explanation, close the Help window.

4. Using the Help tool, explore the first six or seven Utility tools.
5. To zoom in on a larger worksheet, open the file you created earlier called "Inc & Exp 2 Yr."
6. Save it with a new name: "Taming Toolbars."
7. Note that the Utility toolbar is still visible and in the same place.
8. Click the Zoom in and out tools to see more and less of the worksheet.

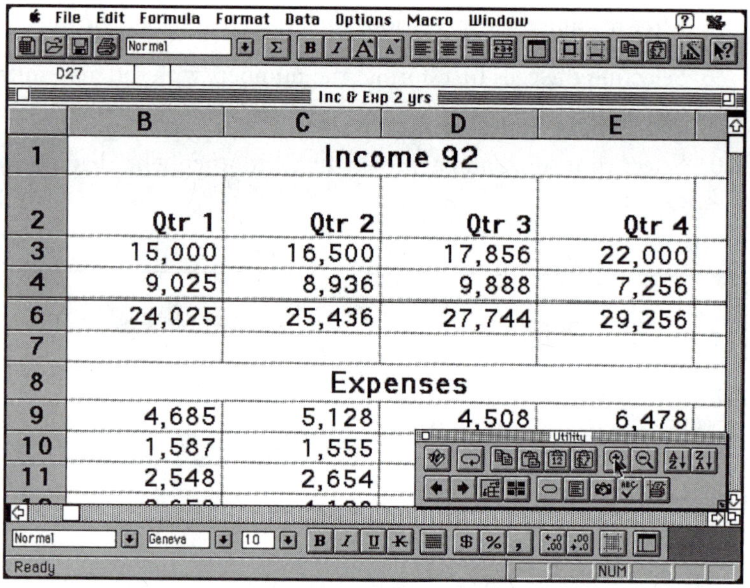


**Figure 16.7**
*Zooming in.*

# The Unmatched Undo

1. To use the Undo tool, select a cell, delete its contents, and then click the Undo tool—could be useful.
2. Close the Utility toolbar by choosing Toolbars from the Options menu and double-clicking Utility.

# Tweaking the Text Box

1. Show the Drawing toolbar next by using it from the Toolbar list (Options Toolbars).
2. Click the Text box tool and then click and drag a small area on the worksheet (see fig. 16.8). When you release the mouse button, an insertion point waits for you to start typing.

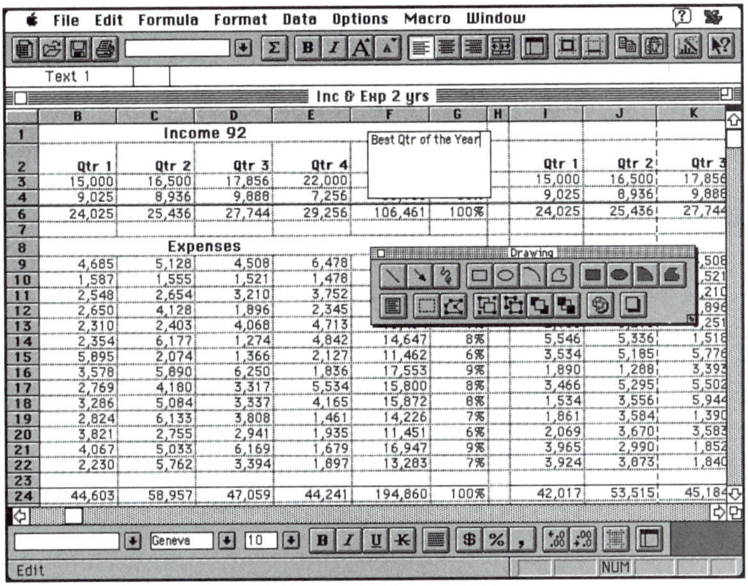


Figure 16.8
*Text box tool and text box.*

3. Type *Best Qtr of the Year.*
4. Click and drag across the text to select it.
5. Click the Bold, Center Alignment, and Increase Font Size tools on the Standard toolbar.
6. Use the Font and Font Size tools on the Formatting toolbar to change the font to Times 12.

7. Move the pointer to an edge of the text box.
8. Note how the pointer becomes an arrow pointer when on the edge of the text box, an I-beam when inside the box, and a crosshair pointer when over a cell. The I-beam tells you that you can type inside the text box. The arrow pointer lets you select the text box.
9. With the arrow pointer on the edge of the box, double-click. This should activate the Patterns dialog box for the text box.
10. Click the Shadow and Round Corners check boxes in the lower left corner.
11. For a light gray fill, go to the Foreground pop-up list and select the second to last choice (see fig. 16.9). If it's difficult to choose from the pop-up list, move the window higher on your screen.You can confirm your choices by looking at the sample in the lower right. Click OK when you are satisfied.

**Figure 16.9**
*Patterns dialog box.*

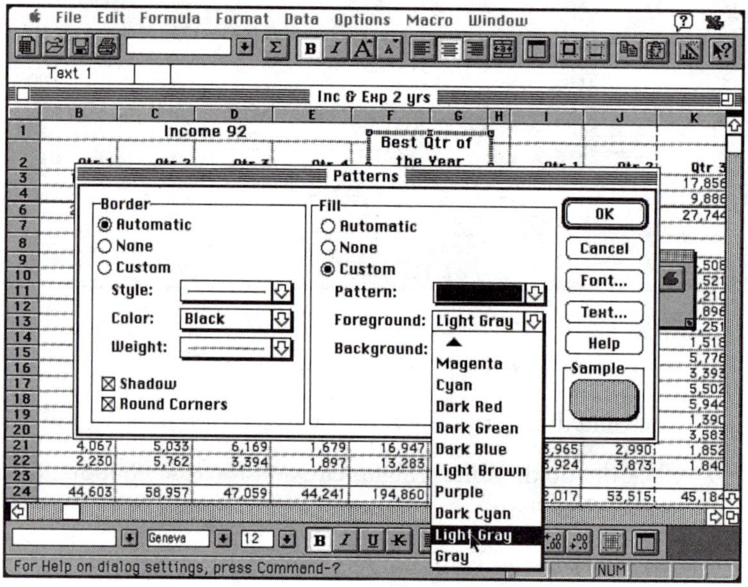


12. Change the size of the text box so that it fits tightly around the text. The text box should still be selected. If it isn't, move the pointer to the edge. When it becomes an arrow pointer, click once. Now position the

pointer over any of the little boxes (selection handles) so that the pointer changes. Click and drag to adjust the size and shape of the text box.

13. Move the text box near the cell that holds the highest Qtr total by moving the pointer to the edge and click-dragging.
14. If you have a color monitor, experiment with colors by clicking the Color tool. Each click changes the color of the selected text object.
15. Make an arrow by clicking the Arrow tool and click-dragging a small distance on the worksheet.
16. Note that the point of the arrow is on the end you drag towards.
17. Experiment with reorienting the arrow and moving it: Select it with a click, click-drag on the shaft to move it, click-drag on either end to reorient it.
18. Double-click anywhere on the arrow to change the color and type of arrow. Experiment with changes.

## Customizing the Standard Toolbar

1. Except for the Standard toolbar, close all the toolbars that are open.
2. Choose Toolbars from the Options menu.
3. Click the Customize button.
4. Note the categories on the left and explore by clicking a category, moving the mouse pointer over a tool on the right, and pressing down the mouse button.
5. Go up to the Standard toolbar and drag the Italics tool off the toolbar. Don't worry! You haven't deleted the tool, just removed it until you want to put it back.
6. Go back to the Customize window and click File on the left side.
7. Find the Print Preview tool (fourth in the top row). Drag it up to the menu bar, position it next to the Save tool, and release the mouse button (see fig. 16.10).

**Figure 16.10** *Adding the Print Preview tool to the Standard toolbar.*

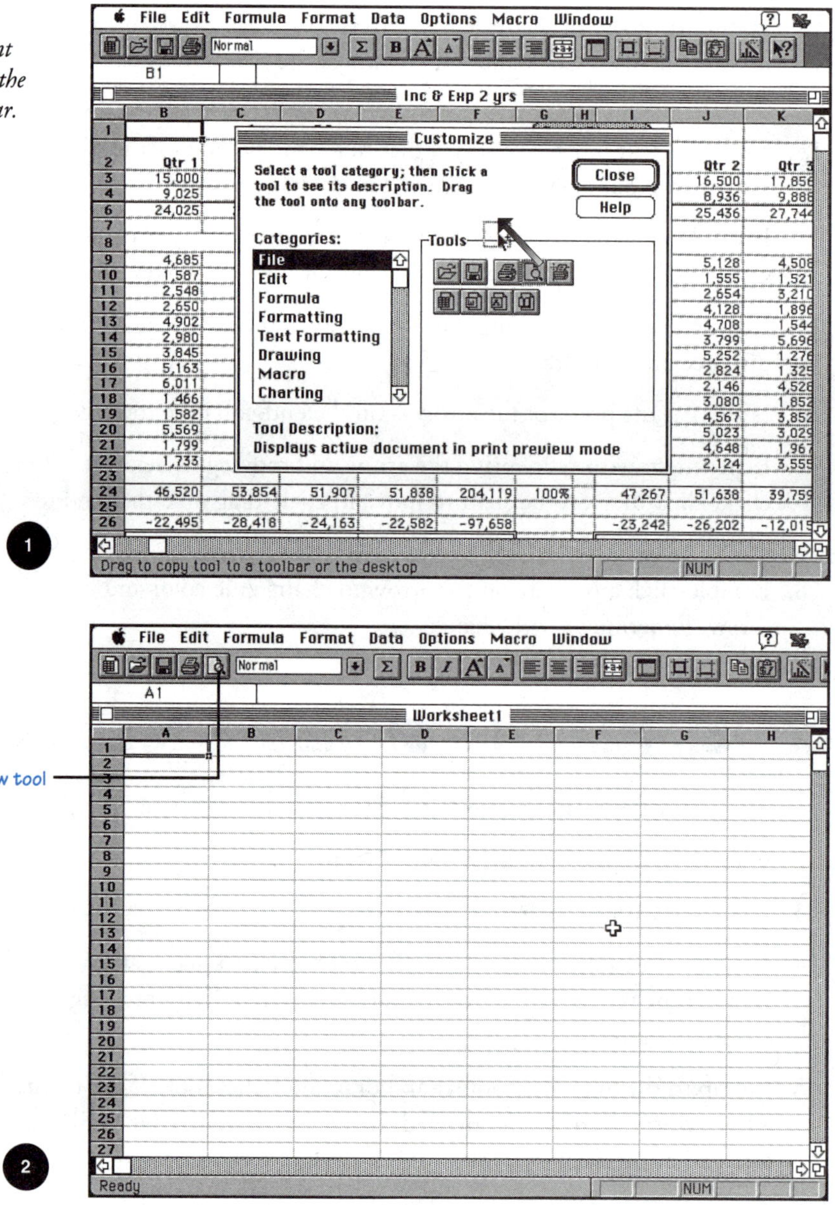


8. You can stop now if you want to leave the tool there.

   Or, you can click the Close button and again choose Toolbars from the Options menu.

9. Click the Reset button, and you are back to the default Standard toolbar.
10. Close Taming Toolbars, saving the changes if you wish.

# Summary

The toolbars make it easy to boss Excel around. You can learn about them by clicking them with the Help tool. The Toolbars command on the Options menu lets you show toolbars on the screen. You can leave them undocked in the middle of the screen or dock them on the edges of the screen. To move a toolbar, click-drag on its title bar. If you don't see the title bar, double-click the toolbar border.

To add or delete a button, choose Toolbars from the Options menu and click Customize. With the Customize window open, you can drag tools on and off visible toolbars.

# Exorcises

1. What menu holds the Toolbars command?
2. How do you dock a toolbar? How do you put it under the Standard toolbar?
3. What window must be active before you can add a tool to a toolbar? How do you get it on your screen?
4. How do you bring up a Help window describing a tool?

17th Encounter

# Making and Protecting Templates

## Goal

Learn techniques for creating and protecting templates that can be used over and over.

## What You Will Need

Excel running.

## Terms of Enfearment

Template
Data entry
File format
Cell Protection
Password Protection

# Briefing

Frequently, you design and complete a worksheet and fill it with particular numbers, saving it with a name like "1992 expenses." At the time, you think the worksheet is only answering a specific need, but later, you may realize that you could use the same worksheet again. If only it were empty of specific data, but with headings and formulas intact! Then, you could simply fill in the new numbers and save a lot of time.

# The Shell Game

In this encounter, you learn a technique that lets you use a particular worksheet design again and again, without having to clean up an earlier version filled with old information. The shell you are going to create is usually called a master or a *template.*

You can create a template by using one of the Options in the Save dialog box (see fig. 17.1). This option is the Template *file format.* After a document has been saved as a template, it opens as an untitled copy of the template, even though you choose the template from the file list. There's no chance of altering the template if you give the untitled document a new name.

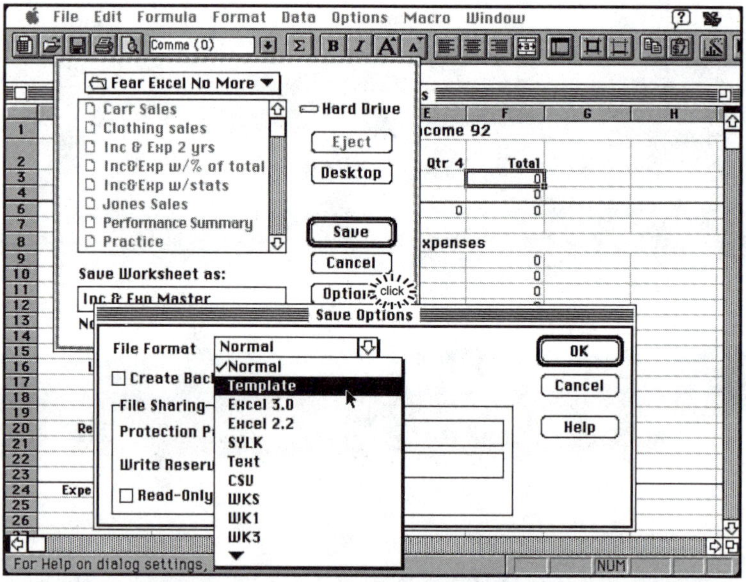


**Figure 17.1**
*The Options dialog box.*

## Worshipping at the Temple of Templates

When creating a template with a worksheet that's already completed, you must go through an initial clean-up period to clear the data-entry areas. The data-entry areas are the cells that hold your numbers, the raw data that your formulas look at.

During the clean up period, you must be careful to delete only data and not to delete formulas or headings.

Although you want to clear the numbers in these areas, you don't want to lose the formatting. Choosing Clear from the Edit menu and clicking OK does this. Although Excel uses the word `Formula` for the default button, it actually means that only the contents are cleared, not the formatting.

The Clear command has a keyboard shortcut you should learn right now: Command-B (for Blank out those cells), which deletes the contents of whatever cells are selected but doesn't remove the formatting.

After the data-entry areas are cleared, you can protect the worksheet so that anyone using a copy of the template (including yourself six months later) can't delete or change the formulas and headings.

## Jailhouse Lock

Whenever you start a new worksheet, every cell in that worksheet is locked. Obviously, this doesn't prevent you from entering data into any cell on the worksheet. Why not? The lock isn't activated until you invoke the Protect Document command (Options menu).

If you take a new worksheet and immediately choose Protect Document, you're locked out from every cell and can't do a thing to the document. However, if you select the data-entry areas and unlock them first with the *Cell Protection* command (Format menu), and then give the Protect Document command, it's a different story. Now, you can make changes in the unlocked cells and can't make changes to any other cell.

After a cell is selected in an area of unlocked cells, pressing the Tab key moves the cell pointer from unlocked to unlocked cell. This can make data entry an easier task.

## Security Alert

After giving the Protect Document command, you can click OK or add the protection of a password. If you just click OK, the locked areas can't be changed until the Unprotect Document command is chosen. Anyone can unprotect the document if no password is involved. This is still beneficial because it protects the document from unintended changes.

If, however, there's a need to secure the worksheet beyond protecting it from harm, the person choosing Protect Document can create a password. Anyone giving the command to unprotect the document would subsequently be asked for the password.

## Extreme Caution!

These passwords are case sensitive: if the password is "ABC," typing "abc" doesn't work. If you forget the password, you won't be able to unprotect the document. Even a duplicated file requires the password. To avoid aggravation, be sure that you need a password before using one. If you decide to use a password, keep a copy of it in a safe and secure place in case you forget it. The top drawer of your desk is not a secure place! Using your birthdate, social security number, phone number, or address is handing the password on a silver platter to whomever wants access.

*Password protection* has a number of levels of intensity. The least restrictive level forces the user to give the password when attempting to unprotect the document. It gets more restrictive from there.

For example, as the creator of a sensitive worksheet, you can make the window extremely small and then require a password for anyone wishing to zoom out.

# They're Out To Get Us

When a data-entry area is empty, formulas that refer to those empty cells may show an error message. To understand why you're getting an error message, click on one of the cells holding the message and look at the formula bar. Look at the example in figure 17.2.

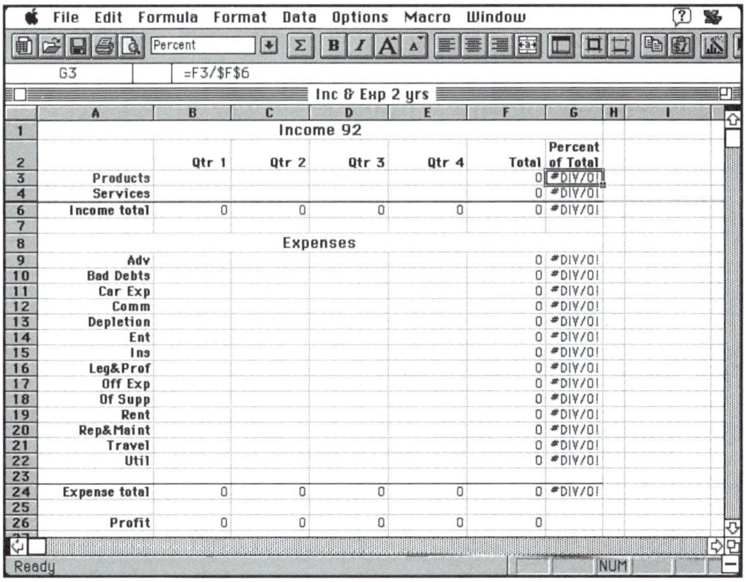


**Figure 17.2**
*Worksheet without data.*

This error message tells you that Excel is attempting to divide with an empty cell. This error message doesn't much matter, because it's replaced by results when new data is entered. However, seeing this message could disturb others who don't understand why it's there. To avoid the visual aggravation, you can replace the formula that returns the error value with one that shows zero instead.

The formula that eliminates the error message is `=IF(ISERROR(F3/$F$6),0,F3/$F$6)`. This formula uses two functions, one nested inside the other.

The formula says, "If it would cause an error message to do this formula, then put a zero here; otherwise put this formula here." Don't bother to practice creating this formula now. Just remember that you have an example if you ever need or want it. Your formula could be completely different than the formula in the example, but the syntax would be identical.

You would type the following formula, replacing the bold part with the formula causing the error value: `IF(ISERROR(`**`C4/$C$8`**`),0,`**`C4/$C$8`**`)`.

Remember to copy the new formula throughout the range showing the error message.

If a worksheet acts strangely or in an unexpected manner, it may be protected. Suppose that you try to change the width of a column, and the pointer doesn't change into a double-headed arrow. At times like these, remember to check the Options menu. If you see Unprotect Document, rather than Protect Document, you know why it's acting strangely.

# Practice

## Creating a Template

1. Open Inc&Exp w/% of total.
2. Choose Save As from the File menu. Name your play file Inc & Exp Master in the Name box.

3. Click the Options button, choose Template from the File Formats menu, and click OK. Then click the Save button.

4. Click any cell and choose Cell Protection from the Format menu just to see that all cells are locked when you start. Choose Cancel. (You will turn the lock on later, when you invoke the Protect Document command.)

## Natural Selection

1. Holding down the Command key so that you can select all areas at the same time, select the data-entry areas (see fig. 17.3). Be careful *not* to select formulas or headings. Select your data-entry areas from left to right and top to bottom, just like you do the typing. If you screw up, take a deep breath and start over from the beginning.

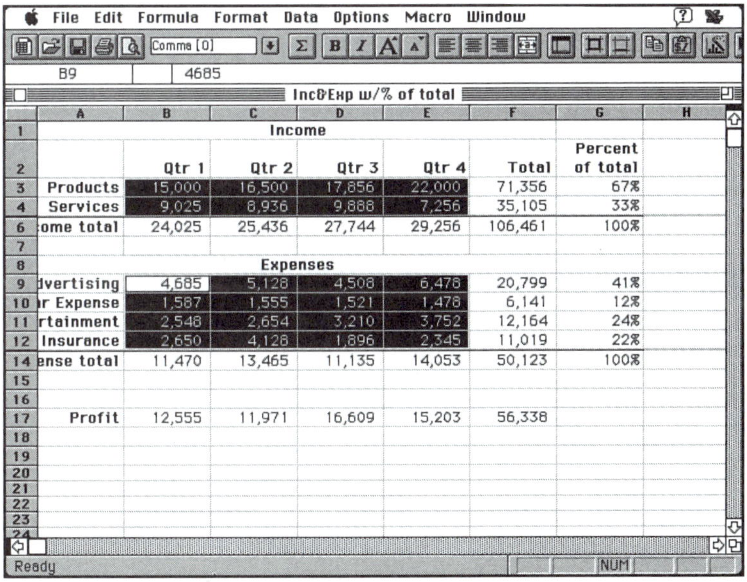


**Figure 17.3**
*Selected ranges.*

2. After all the data entry areas are selected, press Command-B to clear the cells.

## Cell Protection

1. Leave the data-entry areas selected and choose Cell Protection from the Format menu.
2. Clear the X from the Locked check box (see fig. 17.4).

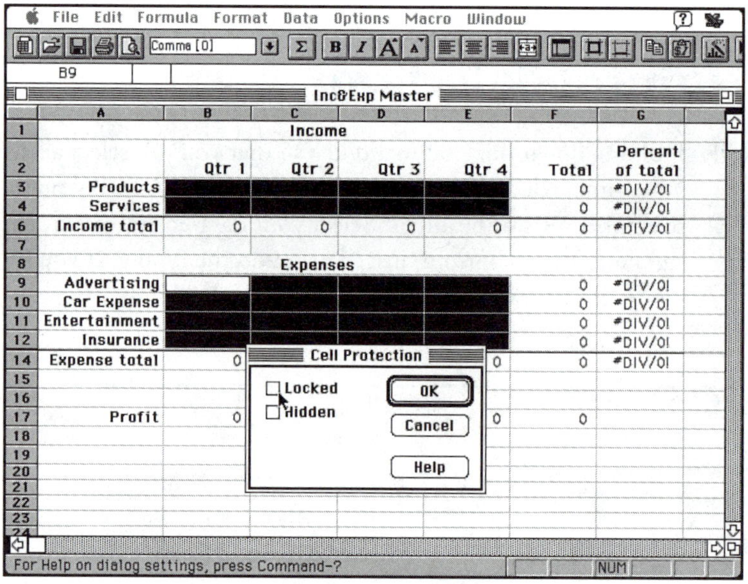


**Figure 17.4**
*Turning off Cell Protection (from the Format menu).*

## Drive Home the Deadbolt

1. Choose Protect Document from the Options menu and click OK.
2. Close the file, saving the changes.

## Open the Protected Document

1. Click the Open tool.
2. Note the different document icon to the left of the filename (see fig. 17.5). Excel is saying, "When you open this document, you will get a copy, not the original." Double-click the file name.

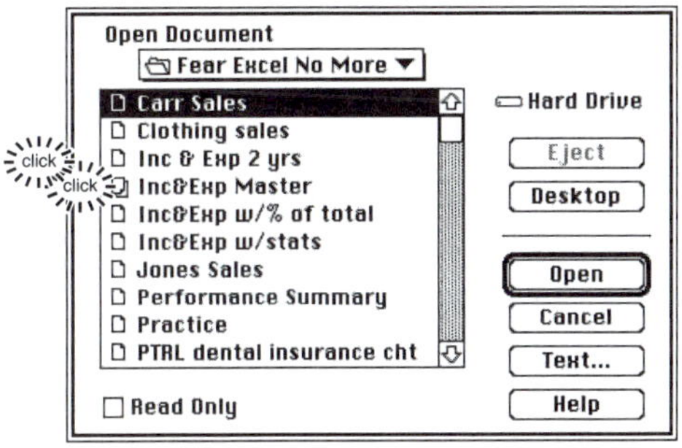


**Figure 17.5**
*The Template icon.*

3. When the document opens, note the number 1 has been added to the filename in the title bar.
4. Click the Save tool and the Save dialog box appears.

This is good. Normally, a document with a name would be saved again without the dialog box appearing. Let's call it "Inc and Exp 93." Now, it's not a template, just a normal document.

# Tabbing Through

1. Click the upper left cell in the data-entry area. Press the Tab key several times.
2. After you see how the Tab key keeps the cell pointer within the data-entry areas, click the upper left cell again.
3. Enter a few numbers, pressing the Tab key to move from cell to cell.
4. Click on a cell holding a formula. Try to type something. Note how Excel doesn't permit it.
5. Turn off the protection by choosing Unprotect Document from the Options menu.

# Password Protection

1. Try using a password this time. Choose Protect Document, type *abc* as a password, and click OK. Don't worry about the asterisks. Excel is

hiding your password from anyone watching your screen as you work (see fig. 17.6).

**Figure 17.6.** *The Password window.*

2. Type the password again when asked. This way, Excel makes certain that you agree on the password.
3. Test the protection by attempting to change a formula.
4. Choose Unprotect Document and type your password. The worksheet is again unprotected.

## For Your Eyes Only

To go to a higher level of protection, where even the size and position of the window can't be changed without the password, do the following:

1. Change the size of the document window by dragging the size box in the lower right corner.
2. Choose Protect Document and click an X into the Window check box.
3. Type a password of your own, click OK, type it once more when asked, and click OK.
4. Try to move that window or change its size.

# Summary

The template file format is chosen after clicking Options in the Save As dialog box. This saves the file so that it opens as a copy of the original. Your templates should include headings and formulas and should be formatted properly.

You may also want to protect your templates from inadvertent harm. Because the data-entry areas need to be adaptable, they must be unlocked before you give the Protect Document command (Options menu).

# Exorcises

1. What key do you hold down to select discontinuous areas?
2. What key do you press to keep the cell pointer inside the unlocked ranges?
3. What dialog box holds the Template file format choice? How do you get to it?
4. What menu holds the Cell Protection command?
5. Do all cells in a new worksheet start as locked or unlocked?
6. You can type your password in upper- or lowercase if you type the correct characters—True or False?

# Answers to Exorcises

## 1st Encounter

1. Software is a set of instructions to the computer, telling it what to do.
2. The most typical "what if?" scenario is a cash flow projection.
3. Hopefully, you plan to use Excel for financial analysis.
4. Any time period you need to get a grip on makes sense in a budget worksheet.
5. The line with the totals is the bottom line.

## 2nd Encounter

1. You hold down the Shift key to start the computer without loading extensions.
2. It is useful to register your software so that the software company can send you information and charge you less for upgrades.
3. You lock a disk by moving the black tab so that you can see through the disk.
4. About 9 megabytes of free space is needed for a complete installation of Microsoft Excel.
5. To find out how much space is available on a hard drive, open any window at the desktop and choose View by Icon from the View menu.

## 3rd Encounter

1. A click on a tool gives Excel a command.
2. The third tool allows you to save a worksheet.
3. The second tool gives the command to open a worksheet.
4. The status bar is at the bottom of the document window.
5. The cell pointer surrounds the active cell.
6. X34 is the proper way to refer to a cell.

## 4th Encounter

1. The cell pointer surrounds the active cell with a darker border.
2. The formula bar always tells you the active cell.
3. The cell pointer doesn't move when the Return key is pressed.

4. The right-arrow key and the Tab key are two keys that will move the cell pointer to the right.
5. The active cell can also be called your current cell address.
6. The fill handle is the name of the little box in the bottom right corner of the cell pointer.

## 5th Encounter

1. The cursor arrow keys are on the keyboard.
2. You click to the right of the scroll box on the horizontal scroll bar to see the columns and rows that are one screen over to the right.
3. Goto from the Formula menu allows you to move instantly to a specific cell reference.
4. You can press the right- and left-arrow keys to move the cell pointer to the right or left.
5. The area that holds your information is called the active area.
6. You hold the Shift key down to move past the active area when dragging a scroll box.

## 6th Encounter

1. Formulas always begin with an equal sign.
2. Autofill allows you to copy formulas.
3. When you click on a cell in order to enter a formula, the extra cell reference is included in the formula.
4. Relative reference describes the way Excel adjusts formulas that are copied.
5. The forward slash (/) for divide, the asterisk (*) for multiply, the minus, and the plus are probably on your keypad.

## 7th Encounter

1. A group of cells is called a range.
2. You have to select a cell before changing it.
3. Pressing the Command key allows you to select discontinuous ranges.
4. Click the juncture of the columns and rows just below the Close box to select the entire worksheet.
5. The Edit menu holds the Insert command.

## 8th Encounter

1. Times, Helvetica, and Palatino look good on a laser printer.
2. Choosing Font from the Format menu allows you to change the style of your text from plain to shadow.
3. Change your font size before adjusting column width.
4. Position the mouse pointer on the column divider between the column headings to change the width of a single column.
5. To achieve "Best Fit" for every column at once, select the whole worksheet and double-click any column divider.

## 9th Encounter

1. Print Preview is in the File menu.
2. Options-Display allows you to turn off the gridlines on the printed page.
3. Landscape orientation prints the page wide, rather than tall.
4. Headers and footers are in the margins.

# 10th Encounter

1. When you see a cell holding the message `DIV/0!`, click on the cell, look at the formula bar, and figure out the problem.
2. Relative referencing—When you copy a formula, Excel adjusts it, relative to its new position.
3. Absolute referencing—When dollar signs are added to a cell reference in a formula and the formula is copied, the cell reference does not adjust.
4. To put the dollar signs in a formula without typing them directly, choose Reference from the Formula menu with the insertion point next to the cell reference in the formula bar.

# 11th Encounter

1. The Formula menu holds the Paste Function command.
2. Press the first letter of the function to move swiftly down the Paste Function list.
3. There are nine function categories.
4. MIN is the function that tells us the lowest number of a group of numbers.
5. MAX is the function that you use to find the latest date in a column full of dates.

# 12th Encounter

1. Select the cell below and to the right of the headings before giving the Freeze Panes command.

2. The Window menu holds the Arrange command. The Options menu holds the Print Titles command.
3. The Windows menu holds the listing of all open windows.
4. To make more of your worksheet fit on a page, choose a smaller font and font size and a different format (without the dollar sign or decimals). Also, use Best Fit to narrow your columns.
5. The Scaling command (in Page Setup) allows you to tell Excel to fit your worksheet onto one page.
6. Unfreeze Panes is the opposite of Freeze Panes

## 13th Encounter

1. The dependent worksheet holds the linking formula: the source or the dependent worksheet.
2. The Window menu shows all open files.
3. If a window is not full size, clicking the Zoom box, in the top right corner of the window will zoom it up to full size.
4. Pressing the Shift key down allows you to select all the source documents in the Links dialog box.
5. The File menu holds the Links command.
6. The Window menu holds the Arrange command.
7. True. It is important to keep linked files in the same folder.

## 14th Encounter

1. You do not have to give the Set Database command before using the Sort command.
2. You don't select the headings before sorting because they would be sorted in amongst the records.

3. You click Descending in the Sort box to sort from Z to A.
4. The Formula menu holds the Define Name command.
5. Selecting the cells is the first step in naming a range.
6. False. Spaces are not allowed in a range name.
7. To get Database listed in the Goto box, select the cells making up the Database and choose Set Database from the Data menu.

## 15th Encounter

1. The Gallery menu allows you to use different kinds of column charts.
2. The Window menu allows you to choose from a list of open documents.
3. Double-click a column to change the color of all the columns in that data series.
4. The X axis runs horizontally across the bottom of the chart, and the Y axis runs vertically along the left edge of the chart.

## 16th Encounter

1. The Options menu holds the Toolbars command.
2. Click and drag its title bar to move a toolbar. To put a toolbar under the Standard toolbar, drag it under.
3. The Customize window must be active before you can add a tool to a toolbar. To get it on your screen, choose Toolbar from Options and click the Customize button.
4. To bring up a Help window describing a tool, click the Help tool (far right on the Standard tool bar) and then click the tool.

# 17th Encounter

1. Hold down the Command key to select discontinuous areas.
2. Press the Tab key to keep the cell pointer inside the unlocked ranges.
3. File Format from the Options menu holds the Template file format choices. Choose Save As from the File Menu to get to it.
4. The Format menu holds the Cell Protection command.
5. All cells in a new worksheet start as locked.
6. False. You must type your password using the original case as well as the original spelling.

# Afterword

I recommend that you go through this book again in the near future. You'll be surprised by how much more you'll learn the second (and even the third) time around.

## Disk

A 3.5-inch disk with all the worksheets, charts, etc., discussed in this book is available for $15. *Be sure to specify Macintosh or Windows version.* Send check or money order, please. **We do not accept credit cards for disk orders.**

Send your check and order to the following address:

> MacAcademy of the Bay Area
> 20 Sunnyside Avenue, Suite 186
> Mill Valley, CA  94941-1928

## Videotape

MacAcademy is a national organization devoted to Macintosh training and consulting. We produce an award-winning series of training videotapes on all the best-selling Macintosh programs, including Excel. Each tape is approximately two hours long. The tapes are an excellent way to build your budding Excel skills (and to learn every other program you need). The price is $49 each plus shipping and handling. Check, money order, or credit cards are acceptable. To order or to receive a catalog, call (415) 383-7801, fax (415) 383-0850, or write to us at the address already given.

# Index

## Symbols



## A

## D



## E



## F

## G



## H



## I



## K



## L

## U



## V



## W

## X-Z